DENIM AND LEATHER
SAXON'S FIRST TEN YEARS

MARTIN POPOFF

First published in 2021 by Wymer Publishing
Bedford, England www.wymerpublishing.co.uk Tel: 01234 326691
Wymer Publishing is a trading name of Wymer (UK) Ltd

Copyright © 2020 Martin Popoff / Wymer Publishing.
First published in Canada in 2020.
This edition published 2021.

ISBN: 978-1-912782-64-2

Edited by Jerry Bloom

The Author hereby asserts his rights to be identified
as the author of this work in accordance with sections
77 to 78 of the Copyright, Designs & Patents Act 1988.

All rights reserved. No part of this publication may be
reproduced or transmitted in any form or by any means,
electronic or mechanical, including photocopying, or any
information storage and retrieval system, without written
permission from the publisher.

This publication is sold subject to the condition that it shall not,
by way of trade or otherwise, be lent, re-sold, hired out or
otherwise circulated without the publisher's prior consent in any
form of binding or cover other than that in which it is published
and without a similar condition including this condition
being imposed on the subsequent purchaser.

Every effort has been made to trace the copyright holders of the
photographs in this book but some were unreachable. We would
be grateful if the photographers concerned would contact us.

Typeset by Eduardo Rodriguez
Printed and bound in Great Britain by
CMP, Poole, Dorset

A catalogue record for this book is available from the British Library.

Cover design by Eduardo Rodriguez
Front cover: © Martin Popoff
Back cover: © Wolfgang Gürster

Table Of Contents

Introduction	05
Chapter 1: The Early Years – "We connected with the punk feeling, but not the poor music."	09
Chapter 2: *Saxon* – "We were not pretending to be working class."	27
Chapter 3: *Wheels of Steel* – "Your feet didn't touch the ground."	43
Chapter 4: *Strong Arm of the Law* – "You got that one—now get the new one!"	69
Chapter 5: *Denim and Leather* – "A bit more experienced, a bit less poor"	89
Chapter 6: *The Eagles Has Landed* – "I'd bought tickets to see them!"	99
Chapter 7: *Power & the Glory* – "It grabs you by the throat and pulls you in."	111
Chapter 8: *Crusader* – "It covered pretty much the four corners of the musical square that they played in."	137
Chapter 9: *Innocence Is No Excuse* – "I think it's one of the greatest heavy metal LPs of all time."	165
Chapter 10: *Rock the Nations* – "We had a producer that was going deaf."	183
Chapter 11: *Destiny* – "It's a Marmite album for us."	195
Chapter 12: Epilogue – "We do bring the past back with us when we play live but we don't live there."	213
Discography	242
Interviews with the Author	247
Additional Citations	248
Personal Credits	250
About the Author	251
A Complete Martin Popoff Bibliography	252

Introduction

Welcome back to another Popoff excursion, a book that hopefully will warm the cockles of your New Wave of British Heavy Metal heart because it's time for a deep dive into the glory years (and a few not so glorious years) of the one and only Saxon.

My first and fondest memories of Saxon involved sidling up to what would be my own import copy of *Wheels of Steel* at one of the two righteously cool hippie head shop/record stores in Spokane, Washington, either Strawberry Jam or The Magic Mushroom. Yes, I know, I didn't jump on with the debut. Pretty sure, anyway. No, it was right in the thick of the excitement of the NWOBHM and the two leaders at the time were Motörhead and Saxon. Now *Wheels of Steel*... it's funny, but just like Tank later, Saxon felt to me like Motörhead with a little more musical sophistication. At 17, it hadn't exactly clicked in how great a lyricist Lemmy was, so I was pretty much unaware that the lyrical sophistication side of things went emphatically to Motörhead.

As well, soon, after getting a few more NWOBHM records, a sense that these guys were a bit older, or at least a bit more rooted in the '70s, began to emerge. As the following pages explain, this is a bit of a false narrative, but it's sensible given the picture of the band on the back of *Wheels of Steel*, with their moustaches and thinning hair (plus they were sitting). Also, there was a sense of history to the name, plus the suggestion that they already had a second vocation as bikers, and indeed, the simplicity of the album cover somehow suggested a conservatism associated with being an established act.

I joined the Motörheadbangers and Saxon Militia Guard fan clubs right around that time, but I don't remember how many goodies I got in the mail, and I'm really racking my brains to recall if anything was autographed. Anyway, me and my buddies, we loved our Saxon and then were thrilled with how fast the new records were coming... even if the two right after *Wheels* didn't exactly feel like marked improvements.

My next fond memory is getting to see Saxon live on the *Power & the Glory* sandwich band tour, Saxon being the meat and cheese between lower slice Fastway and upper slice Iron Maiden, who were storming the gates of hockey palaces with *Piece of Mind*. This was also in Spokane, Washington, and I do recall that Saxon were conquering heroes live, no weak links, again exuding experience.

But this brings up a head-scratcher of a mystery point to my personal propensities with Saxon. Through the making of this book, and hearing the opinions of the guys in the band plus various producers as well as talking with fans, it seems like everybody has forgotten how absolutely lethal the *Power & the Glory* album is. There's this lazy narrative that sets in periodically but all too often that the record is somehow Americanized. To be sure, Jeff Glixman produces and it was made in Atlanta blah blah blah, but to my mind, it's the rowdiest, dirtiest, most distorted and ear-yanking record from the band yet, not to mention the most violently and even drunkenly performed.

And also to my mind, it's far and away the greatest Saxon album, three-and-a-half times the record that *Wheels of Steel* is, and there's nothing else even close. Everything just comes together on that record, molten production values, and this new drummer in Nigel Glockler who just beats the hell out of every song... and then unfortunately goes on to demonstrate that it was an anomaly, because his decisions aren't all that particularly great across the rest of the albums of the '80s, although he does put something of a stamp on *Crusader*. That was another thing I learned from this book: as much as Nigel willed that album into the pantheon of the gods well outside the purview of what a drummer usually does, he wasn't a god himself.

So yeah, my love for that record is so awe-inducingly tall and apparently exaggerated to the point where it's one of the main reasons I wanted to do this book, namely to show that the much lauded golden period for the band doesn't end with *Denim and Leather*, but is in fact punctuated with many exclamation points by *Power & the Glory*.

Another reason is the fact that of any band I haven't addressed in book form yet, it's basically Saxon and Uriah Heep that I was getting asked for the most. And then enticing me forward, which has become somewhat of a pattern or fashion or methodology, this book was sorta already "started," because I had already written up the story of *Power & the Glory* as one of my Ye Olde Metal short document essays, although it was one that hadn't occurred in print, but only as an eBook, along with many others never in print yet, at zunior.com. But yes, as these things go, it sometimes helps me along to notice that, hey, I've kind of started this book, time to finish it now.

Something else to point out, as you can see, this book covers only the first ten years of the band's recorded history. And the reason for that is twofold: as planned—or forecasted, or telegraphed—covering this amount of years and this amount of albums worked out to exactly one book of average size. Second, Saxon is a band for which I did not want to write my usual complete, dedicated chapters for all of those records in the '90s and 2000s and 2010s. As good as they are—and as I argue in the pretty substantial epilogue, in this book—they tend to blend into each other. It's commendable, really, that Biff and the boys have put out so many records in the 2000s, and like I say, even if most or all of them are certainly better than the last couple of albums talked about in this very book, their historical importance doesn't really call upon me to write complete, full chapters for every one of those.

I mean, there's a wee chance that I might do it. If this book turns out to be some sort of crazy hit and I'm signing and packing them up all day daily for weeks on end, that might send me down that path. Because again, back to the first point, having taken care of the early years in one proper-sized book, covering all those records will likely work out once again to the exact length of one average book. And then I'd have a two-parter, the same way I've done it for a bunch of bands lately, including Sabbath, Priest and Maiden (of those, Maiden will certainly get a third instalment, barring death, and if I can pull myself away from drawing made-up record ads, which is slowly taking over my life!).

But yes, for now, please receive this book in the spirit of my Whitesnake and Riot books, namely a celebration of the early years, but with a long enough final chapter that gives a decent overview of what happened after.

Oh yeah, one extra happy thing that fell out of this process, I learned to appreciate just how good an album *Innocence Is No Excuse* is. I hope that folks go back and give that one another spin and come to the same conclusion. I've also learned that there's much love out there for *Crusader*, even though me an' my buds were pretty ticked off at it back in '84 and my disdain hasn't waned much since, other than the surprise at realizing that "Sailing to America" is my favourite song on the damn thing.

Martin Popoff
martinp@inforamp.net
martinpopoff.com

The Early Years

"We connected with the punk feeling, but not the poor music."

Like their main elbows-up competitors Iron Maiden, Saxon were saddled with a long history of trying hard to sell hard music when no one in England cared.

But Honley, West Yorkshire's Biff Byford and the boys soon found themselves at a further disadvantage, toiling away in the north, working class Barnsley, South Yorkshire to be precise, dreaming of the big time from afar, unaware like all of us that heavy metal would soon be on an astonishing ascent, and Saxon would find themselves in the thick of it, forging metal and espousing its benefits.

The heroes of our story would come together through a merger of two bands, who themselves had roots in the likes of Blue Condition, Pagan Chorus and The Iron Mad Wilkinson Band reaching back to 1970. Peter Rodney "Biff" Byford and Paul "Blute" Quinn—Paul had a beard like Bluto, from the Popeye cartoons—had most recently a band called Coast, which had started as a three-piece with Biff on bass, Chris Morris on guitar and a drummer called Dodd.

Incidentally, "I had this nickname in school," notes Byford, explaining his new name. "My brother was called Biff, so I kind of inherited it from him. You have to blame my brother, really. He's the bastard that got the name in the first place. In America it's a bit preppy to be called Biff. And in *Back to the Future* you've got that guy called Biff as well."

"I came from a working class background," continues Biff. "It wasn't easy, it was very poor, but it wasn't unhappy, if you know what I mean. I was quite happy in my childhood. I think I was, anyway. But we had a lot of problems and tribulations, like you do with a working class background. It was the industrial North, with all the factories and brick houses—that's basically where I was brought up."

Byford's mother died when he was 11, but not before she stoked an interest in music on the part of Biff through her playing of the piano and the organ at church—Biff sang there as well. A few years later his hard-drinking father lost his arm in an industrial accident. Biff had to help with keeping the family afloat immediately, working young—carpenter, steam engine-stoker—but avoiding work in the local coal mine because he was too tall to deal with the three-foot coal face. The family didn't even have a car.

Growing up happened quick in other ways as well. At 15, Biff had a 16-year-old girlfriend that suddenly found herself pregnant. A hasty marriage was put together which produced a total of three children before it dissolved. Biff has also had a second marriage with no kids, and now a third that has lasted 26 years, which has produced four children.

"Probably some time in the '60s, I would think. '65, '66," answers Biff, on when he heeded the call to rock. "I wanted something different, something to try to move out of that cycle of working in industry, the stuff that my friends worked in, the mines and the factories. Generally working class jobs, really—that was my future at the time. My friend's brother was in a band, and we used to go and watch them rehearse, and then I really got into it. We were buying singles in the '60s, from the Kinks and the Rolling Stones (the first song Biff learned on guitar was "Paint It Black"). We were rock fans, back in the day. We liked the rockier stuff. We weren't really into, too much, sort of soul music but the more rock-orientated stuff, although blues music was quite popular with us as well. But yeah, my friend's brother, you know, taught me some guitar and that was it."

Biff points to seeing Led Zeppelin at the Bath Festival in 1970 as a turning point, but he also fondly recalls Nazareth, Status Quo and The Sensational Alex Harvey Band.

After picking up the guitar but even before Coast, there was The John Verity Band, which establishes the connection with the man who would much later produce the first Saxon album. And even before that was the aforementioned Iron Mad Wilkinson Band, that Biff remembers for its drug use. Biff quickly became anti-drug after trying LSD and smoking a bit of pot—he didn't like what he was writing on pot, but more so it was unease with the feeling of being out of control.

Confirms Verity, "I knew Biff and Paul, because they were in the last version of The John Verity Band before I joined Argent. I had lived in America for a while, and I had an American lineup of my band, and then I came back to England in the early '70s. I was looking for new musicians and I met Biff and Paul. Biff was my bassist and Paul was the other guitarist, because I'm a guitar player as well. And in the new lineup of The John Verity Band, whilst we were rehearsing, I got the phone call asking me to join Argent. So the guys very kindly were really pleased for me, and of course they said I really should do it. So off I went and did Argent, and then they re-contacted me some time later and said, 'Well, we formed this new band that we really want you to hear.' And they knew I was producing different people and they asked me if I would come up and see the band. So I did do, I thought they were great and I invited some other music business people to come and see them. And it resulted in a management deal that put together their first album deal."

This was the all-important hook-up with Norman Sheffield and Trident. Famed for managing Queen, Trident had also managed Argent. Just after the brief collaboration with Verity, beginning at the end of '73 and playing through '74, Coast supported the likes of Cockney Rebel and Be-Bop

Deluxe. The band had been good enough to get fourth place at the Tetley Sound of the North battle of the bands, with Chris Morris winning £50 for best guitarist. They had also become the resident act at local venue Changes and begun playing at colleges and universities across the country.

In July of '74, Morris would quit, scuttling a proposed tour over to The Netherlands. It is at this point that Biff collars Paul Quinn to join Coast, plucking him from Pagan Chorus, a self-described "cabaret-style pop" group and not the mean proto-metal band a name like that would suggest. Despite recording some demos at a studio owned by Be Bop Deluxe's Bill Nelson, things go downhill from here, with a name change to Blenheim suggested, formed from a merger of Coast members and players from another local act called Trace.

Meanwhile, Graham "Oly" Oliver and Steve "Dobby" Dawson had a band going called SOB, working out of Mexborough, and like Coast, they became regulars at Changes, playing there 11 times in 1975. Much like another North England axeman called Tony Iommi, Graham was playing with a disability.

"Me and Steve Dawson have been together since 1969," explains Graham. "From school. SOB started about '72, '73. Before that we were just in a pop band called Blue Condition, which was the name of a Cream song sung by Ginger Baker. And then we went to see Free in 1970, and we named SOB after the album, *Tons of Sobs*."

"But yes, I had an accident in my hand. I got it trapped in a door and chopped my finger off to the first knuckle, on my index finger on my fingering hand. A massive inconvenience. So I have to play... I have to make one note sound like ten, you know, because I had an injury to my hand. So I do all the quite simple riffs. The worst thing is you can't do the one-finger vibrato like B.B. King or Randy Rhoads or Eric Clapton or any of the great players. Which, no matter what kind of music it is, you always use your first finger, your index finger, so I had to pick a finger. And first position chords are tough. So sometimes I'd have to work out different positions and fingering and inversions, but I always get there in the end. It's not easy; believe me. I actually tried

Tony Iommi's prosthetics when we toured with them, on the *Heaven and Hell* tour. We jumped off *Back in Black* to *Heaven and Hell* and we tried his fingertips, but because I'd lost so much, they wouldn't fit. We did try the idea, but I figured out how to do without."

Later in '75, Oliver and Dawson brought into the fold Byford and Quinn, along with drummer John Walker, forming a new version of the band. Graham specifies that it was Steve's suggestion to try get Biff in the band, after Coast had lost their drummer, and they themselves had lost their singer. The two of them listened to a tape of Biff singing, which then led to a jam. Biff said he would join on one condition, namely that Paul Quinn be brought into the fold as well. This turned out to be further synchronicity: SOB's departing singer had also been their second guitarist.

"Exactly," says Graham. "Steve had got a demo off him. I don't know how he got the demo. It was a reel-to-reel. It was a song called 'Lady.' And it was a Coast song, and Steve said, 'You know, this guy's a great singer.' And he just had the idea of… they had lost their drummer, we'd lost our singer, and we had a meeting in a motorway café, on the highway and decided to have a trial. Biff really didn't think he could sing full-time. But Biff's vocal career came solely out of Steve Dawson's vision that he could be a great vocalist. People should remember that without Steve Dawson, there would be no Biff Byford as we know him today."

John Verity says he had a hand in this as well. "Well, yeah, when the guys came back to me later to asked me to produce them, they had two bassists. Biff was still playing bass and Steve was playing bass. So they had two bassists playing at the same time (laughs). And it was me who talked Biff into being the front man. Partly because musically it was a bit messy—I mean, two bass lines. And also the image thing. I just thought they needed somebody out front."

Biff's alcoholic father at this point had ended up in a shelter, so Biff asked him if he could sell the family home to help finance the band, to which dad consented. Biff bought some equipment with the proceeds and moved in with a roadie. Getting to gigs happened via what Biff calls "the tripe van." "Sid Cummings, Tripe Dealer" was painted on it and an overcoat of black couldn't quite hide the mark of its previous owner.

Along the way, explains Oliver, SOB became Son of a Bitch. "When Biff and Paul joined SOB we still did gigs as SOB, and we were playing the Nashville rooms in London, and a guy called Alan Bown says, 'You should not call yourselves SOB. You should not use the initials; it sounds like Son of a Bitch to me.' Because it was right in the punk era. And that's when Son of a Bitch was born, by a guy, trumpet player, with a band called Alan Bown. It was Alan who named the band Son of a Bitch. He said we should go down that road."

All of them were now in their mid 20s, continuing business as Son of a Bitch for a couple of years until the guys figured out that the name of their band was limiting their career aspirations—around Barnsley they had still been referred to as SOB, allowing them notices in the paper and on gig posters. "The first gig we ever did together was at the Dickens Inn in Rotherham," recalls Oliver, placing the occasion as late January or early February of '76. The Centenary Rooms were after (February 6th at the Centenary Rooms is often cited as the debut). And yes, for a while we had John Walker on drums. Pete Gill joined in November '77 after John quit. So that show would've been John Walker. First gig we did with Pete Gill would've been January, February '78."

As Steve Dawson told Rhino about this debut show, "The first thing we did, we didn't actually rehearse. Graham and me had got a gig booked in a bar in Rotherham one Saturday dinnertime, so we used that as a rehearsal (laughs). We needed the money! So basically we got up and jammed. The place was full of people, and we went down really well. And we also had a show that evening as well, so basically we just got together without rehearsing or anything and just got it together straightaway."

Explained Pete Gill to Perun.hr, with respect to his joining the band, "I was working as a session musician in Germany and I came over to England for the weekend to watch the Zeppelin film, *The Song Remains the Same*. I bought a Melody Maker magazine from a street vendor and there was an advertisement in there for a seriously heavy rock drummer. I phoned immediately and the next Monday we all had a rehearsal at the local grammar school and the atmosphere was absolutely amazing, we just looked at each other and said, 'Fuckin' hell, let's do it."

"I was about 14 when I got my first drum kit," continues Pete. "Music that was popular when I was a young man was the Beatles, the Rolling Stones and the Mersey sound as it was called—I loved it then and I still love it now. Choosing this, I suppose it just comes naturally for a musician. You pick up your chosen instruments and take it from there. My first proper band, I would've been 16. When we were growing up, we were all crazy about music and the places for live music were the local youth clubs or music halls. Then of course we would sneak into pubs to watch bands; we'd only be 16. The legal age to go in a pub is 18 but we were so obsessed with music it became our lives. I think you can say that about every true musician. Of course living in a big city we had a city hall and all the major concerts of the time would stop off and play here. That was an amazing time."

Classic lineup in place, the development of these players would be exacerbated by the fact that Barnsley had a thriving music scene, helped by being situated between two thriving music towns, Leeds and Sheffield. There were venues of various sizes, and aforementioned regulars like The Sensational Alex Harvey Band and Nazareth rolled through and demonstrated what good rock 'n' roll looked and sounded like.

But as Paul explained, the guys were learning from the even earlier legends of the day, in a quest toward making their own mark. "You find this with a lot of metal bands," begins Paul, "that they like quite a broad spectrum of music. In my case it ranged from Chicago to Yes and Deep Purple and the obvious two originators of what became metal guitar, Hendrix and Clapton. Later, we were starting to hear about Judas Priest more by the amount of gigs they were playing. UFO were also in the similar circuit tours. The Scorpions were even coming and playing working man's clubs and I was talking to their original guitarist, Uli. There was Thin Lizzy, with their twin lead harmony playing."

And later on, there was even an influence from punk, Paul admits, something Steve Harris never would. "Sure, in terms of playing eighths, eighth notes. But Deep Purple was doing that and maybe even Led Zeppelin, because of things like 'Communication Breakdown.' I can't remember Hendrix doing much down-stroking; he was more of an alternate picker. But the punk attitude, 'We may be on social security but we've still got our pride,' that attitude carried over to us definitely (laughs). We obviously tried to find work, so we didn't annoy the government departments too much. But we got off it as soon as we got any gigs (laughs)."

"We were based around Yorkshire but we got around a lot," continues Paul, on what it was like plying his trade away from the centre of the universe. "We went to the Northeast of England, forayed into Wales and London. Basically, whatever we saw in the newspaper that was advertising rock music, we'd call up or send them demos. The gigs were in pubs which were working men's clubs, drinking clubs basically. Workers with cheap booze (laughs). A lot of them wouldn't accept bands that were playing new material so we didn't tell them (laughs.) We kind of went in and built up a following that used to ask us whose song we were playing and we'd say, 'Well, ours in this case.' But it got so that when the punk explosion happened, people were telling us to shove off because we were old hacks now. That didn't faze us. We upped the aggression levels and became more like musical competitors for them, but still as aggressive if not more so. You kind of have to compete when that happens."

A typical SOB set list of the day, circa mid to late 1976, would include the likes of "Freeway," "Lift Up Your Eyes," "Envy," "Taking in the Dollar" and a ballad called "Anne Marie." Demos were recorded and they were soon heralded as the most promising band on the local scene, showing well in various band battles, but often losing out on career advancement to punk acts.

"Actually it was a bit rough because the punk thing was really heavy then," agrees Byford, who, with Quinn would be part of Saxon from the beginning to this very day (it was Biff who was in the seven-man Iron Mad Wilkinson Band, beginning on guitar and then picking up his bass and vocal skills along the way).

"It was right in that London thing, and what you could call punk. And we found it quite pitiful, actually, being a long-haired band playing more rock-based stuff rather than frantic energy fashion music. Although we've had the influences quite a lot in our songwriting later on. I mean we quite liked a lot of the stuff like Sex Pistols and Clash because it was a bit rebellious. But they didn't really like us, if you know what I mean. They were all like short hair, green, blue hair with spikes and nose rings. It was definitely a bit of an against society-type movement, punk."

It's hard for the guys to forget punk, because in November of '77, there was a punk riot which almost cost local bands of all stripes their gigging privileges. It all added to the animosity between camps that would fester into brawls between punks and "longhairs" all up and down the country.

"In those respects we were definitely antiestablishment as well," continues Biff. "But in them days, '76, '77, we weren't really writing songs like that. We started writing songs like that a bit later on, 1979, '80, 'Backs Against the Wall' and 'Never Surrender' and all that type of sentiment. But yeah, it was quite difficult for us to get gigs, but we had strongholds of followers. Like, Wales was a great area for us—South Wales, there was a great stronghold of heavy rock. And the northeast of England, what we called Geordie-land, Newcastle area—that was a big stronghold where we could play. And obviously Yorkshire, where we were from, was good. So we had this area where we used to tour around the clubs playing our own songs, really, and we created a following."

"But before that, the band Paul and I were in together, I played bass at the time, and sang," continues Biff. "And we were more into prog rock, actually, Yes, Genesis, Jethro Tull. We were more... I wouldn't say jazz but it was in the more musical end of prog rock. It was like the more melodic passages and highly melodic choruses. And the band we joined, really, was a bit like Free. Just a riff going around and around endlessly, you know what I mean? Same riff, basically. So when we joined together, those two styles sort of clashed in a great way, really, and that created our sound, of course. And thrown in that mix was obviously the other influences we had."

"I think we got the sense of the end of an era, but yeah, we would go see them," answers Biff, asked about the heavy bands on their last legs in sort of 1976. "We were massive Sabbath fans and Purple fans, and Uriah Heep, Wishbone Ash, Thin Lizzy, American bands like Black Oak Arkansas—these were influences in our early songwriting. There was a sense that those bands were still big and they were still household names, but I just think that the members were moving on to different things. In that sense, yes, it was the end of that era. Wishbone Ash was really influential in my early years. I loved their melody, I loved their lyrics and things. 'Throw Down the Sword,' which I did on my solo album, is bit of a battle song and I suppose it inspired me to go down the road of writing quite historic songs. And they were the first band I heard doing the twin lead guitars, which was quite interesting. So yeah, they're really influential for me and many other people around about that time."

"The bands before that influenced us as well; obviously there's Cream and Jimi Hendrix in the mix," continues Byford. "We go as far back as the Kinks. But yeah, we got a feeling for playing heavy riffs from things like Sabbath and like I say, some of the big bands that were playing around. But Judas Priest and Rainbow and people like that, I think they were too new to influence us. I don't think they were as connected to the big bands as people think they are. I just think they were around and sort of filled the gap, really, between those years and our era."

"Like UFO—they were around," adds Biff on this tack. "UFO and Priest and bands like that, I think they were like the connection between the more long, drawn-out solos that used to happen in the '70s and being more song-orientated, as were Rainbow, But we were more into playing the song as powerful as we could, and still are obviously. For us, playing a song fast had to fit the lyric. So we were influenced by those bands but I think we had quite a unique approach to our music."

The narrative that is forming is that the band that would become Saxon was going to sound like a cross between classic hard rock and punk, with a little bit of extra "song orientation" from the second wave of metal bands, those big in '75 and '76 for the first time.

"Very basic, and very much like an extension of punk music," is how Steve Dawson describes Son of a Bitch, underscoring this idea. "A lot of the songs that we played were very fast, very uptempo, and we wanted to get as much energy across as possible. Like when you listen to a lot of the early metal stuff, it's just an extension of punk music, but played to a higher degree of musicianship and singing. And that's basically what we sounded like. Because when you're just starting out with anything, you're not very good at it. You get better the more you do it. The first Saxon album and the first Iron Maiden album don't really sound anything like the later ones because we were just naïve, really, in terms of how to make a record and how to write a song."

"We'd been through a period of punk in the '70s," explains guitarist Graham Oliver, "and throughout all that period, we continued to play the style of music that we played: heavy rock. And I'm talking about the late '70s, really. If it wasn't for me and Steve, there never would've been a Saxon. Because when we came together in '76, we did all the gigs like The Music Machine in London, all these early gigs that were punk strongholds, and played our style of music which was really unfashionable at the time. You had Deep Purple and Sabbath 'round about '70, coming out, and Zeppelin were on the peak from '68 to '72, and then punk started."

"So rock became unpopular, although we were like really heavy rock. We had the aggression of the punk people, but we didn't like the music, although we were the same age. And we ended up doing gigs like Manchester with The Clash. We even played with the Sex Pistols one time, when they were coming up. So we had all the energy and aggression. I don't know if aggression is the right word, but the fire of the punk feeling."

"We wanted to play music without the long drawn-out, self-indulgence of the bands of the early '70s," continues Oliver. "That we didn't really like, to be honest. When bands like Yes came out with those long and drawn-out songs, we just didn't connect with it. We connected with the punk feeling, but not the poor music. I think the good stuff like The Clash came through, but it was really difficult for us. We were playing gigs in London, for like £20, and it cost us £50 to get there and back."

"We did gigs where people were wanting to spit and jump about, and like I said, we had the energy of the punks but better musicianship. So you could play a gig in Barnsley if you were good. But if you were a punk band and you weren't very good, you couldn't get away on fashion and punk alone—you had to deliver. In London you could do that. You could play the Marquee, and everybody there is into the fashion statement regardless of the band. But once you got to Sheffield, Leeds or anywhere, Birmingham, you had to play the music and deliver. You couldn't make it on just fashion alone."

"But we just believed in the music that we all grew up with collectively," continues Oliver. "And that belief and dedication in the music probably comes through in the early Saxon stuff. It got into the grooves of the vinyl. It's hard to categorize something that you've done yourself, because obviously people who were not involved in it will perceive it in a different light. We're that close to it. But I believe the passion that we felt at the time does come out of the tracks, and probably that's why we wrote songs like 'Dallas 1 PM,' with lyrics about subjects rather than just booze and girls or whatever."

Noted Steve on the Clash gig, "All I can remember is me being covered in spit (laughs). I learned to keep your mouth shut while you're playing at that gig. The music that was popular at that time was punk music, and the rock fans wanted to hear a new rock band and there weren't any—that's how the New Wave of British Heavy Metal got started:

because it was an alternative take on punk. 'Cause, I mean, in the early albums, it was a mixture of heavy rock and punk, really. You can't be un-influenced by what you're hearing on the radio all the time. And let's face it: the Sex Pistols are quite a heavy band! So that sort of influenced us a bit."

This new Yorkshire-based conglomeration, with their punk-infused approach to the classics, would soon find themselves part of what we might call a third wave of British heavy metal, or maybe a "New Wave of British Heavy Metal."

And this wave was happening everywhere, if somewhat on the down low.

"Around Yorkshire you had quite a few bands," explains Tygers of Pan Tang vocalist Jess Cox, "but I mean there was no specific town. Saxon are from Barnsley, which is out of Yorkshire. You had Gaskin from Hull, which is sort of Humberside but it's still kind of east of main Yorkshire. There was nothing like London or Newcastle. I mean Newcastle, if you actually write them down, the amount of bands from Newcastle, you'd be shocked. Hellanbach, Raven, Satan, the Tygers, Venom, White Spirit, Saracen, Avenger, Tysondog, Warfare... you just go on and on."

"The working man, mostly," answers Paul, when asked why Newcastle was such a great NWOBHM town. "The shipbuilders would be into very loud noises (laughs). They probably needed the metal to get past their tinnitus. It's big in lots of industry areas—Birmingham, Wales."

Joining these new metal ambassadors would be Son of a Bitch, who in 1978, would record a three-song demo tape with now ex-Argent singer and guitarist John Verity at Tapestry Studios. French label Carrere Records' new A&R guy in the UK, Pete Hinton, saw some promise in the guys, and came up from London to catch a gig at the Civic Hall in Barnsley. Hinton would recommend the band to label head Claude Carrere, back in France, and Managing Director of the new UK office Freddie Cannon, who would take a listen to the band's tapes and sign them, mid-1978, to a five-figure deal.

"He discovered us at Bradford, at Talk of the Town," says Graham, referring to Pete Hinton. "I think we had about 16 people in. Again, without Pete Hinton, EMI and Freddie Cannon, because that's who they worked for at the time... and then they were just being headhunted by Carrere Records. So when Pete Hinton saw us and Freddie Cannon got to know about us, they were still actually with EMI Records—they were just about to move from EMI to Carrere. So Freddie took us in and Claude Carrere heard the demo and flew us to Paris. And Claude said that as he soon as he heard the solo on 'Frozen Rainbow' he decided to sign us. Which is fantastic, and an accolade for me. I swear to God that's the truth—that Claude Carrere himself told us while we were at the office in Paris, at HQ, that it was my solo. So I'm pretty proud of that."

"It's Talk of the North, actually," says Pete, when I ask him about the "Talk of the Town" summit—Garry Sharpe-Young has cited Talk of the Town as well, but I've found no other mentions of Talk of the North. "And it was in the northern city of Bradford. And what happened was... a convoluted story, really; it just shows you how much luck is involved, doesn't it? I worked for EMI Records, and because I was the new boy, I was given the job of doing the Melody Maker Rock/Folk contest. That was sponsored by the music paper, and they had a lot of venues all around the country, and I was representing EMI Records, and we had journalists on the panel and it would also be a local person as well. But mostly they were held at universities, actually. Oh, and to digress (laughs), I'd been to Queen Mary University in London, and the representative of Queen Mary University was a person called Bruce, who ended up in Iron Maiden (laughs)."

"Anyway, so I was up in Leeds, I think, and I got handed a cassette by a chap there. He said, 'I think this band is really good.' I listened to the cassette and then got in contact with the band and arranged to go see them up in Bradford, Talk of the North. That's what we did in those days: we went a long ways to see bands. And then on the night I went into the venue, I think there were 29 people there, and there was probably another six or seven on the guest list; there weren't many people there at all. And I can remember this: Biff had this knife, and during the act he threw this knife onto the stage, and I was frightened that it was going to hit a nail and bump off into the crowd and hit someone. There wasn't much health and safety in those days, I guess. And then Paul had his famous spinning guitar even then. But you know what? The music was so atmospheric; even then they did 'See the Light Shining,' which was so atmospheric. And yeah, that was the first time I saw them."

"Then we got the representatives down at EMI and we talked to them. And what happened was, was that EMI weren't too keen on taking the band. And at that time, I had joined Carrere Records, with my line manager from EMI, Freddie Cannon, who was fully behind Saxon. But EMI didn't want the band, and they made it quite clear. So we said, well, if we're gonna start up this new record company, let's make Saxon our first signing."

Pete could sense somehow that the future for heavy music looked promising. I did, yeah, because that was always my background. I can't remember when we first started calling it heavy metal. I think at that time we called it heavy rock. But because we were a French record company, we saw that heavy rock was still big in Europe. And so it kind of gave us the impetus to go through with the signing of the act. And the other thing about it was, it was so obvious that they were a live act, which meant that they could promote themselves on the road. And also at that time in the UK we'd gone through the punk thing—'76, '77—so what I believe what happened was that the youth was in. They talk about punk clearing the way of the dinosaur bands; I don't think it's necessarily to do with that. I think it was to do with the fact that youth was in, that there was this youth thing. And certainly Saxon filled that bill. Well, Son of a Bitch, as they were then called, of course."

"That bill," being, as it was soon to be called, the New Wave of British Heavy Metal. "Well, that's right. Punk had been around with Elvis Costello and The Damned and things like that, and then it got turned into the new wave. And I actually had said, 'It's actually a new wave of heavy metal.' And then somebody came up with the New Wave of British Heavy Metal, which I thought was much better, to be honest. But I do remember saying that, although of course it can never be corroborated for sure. But to be honest, a lot of people were probably thinking that at the same time. And then it got termed by Geoff Barton into NWOBHM, which is better."

John Verity corroborates that Pete and Freddie were right in the midst of changing companies. "Yes, I think that's the sequence of events. Pete and Freddie were already interested. We did a load of demos and I agreed to produce them. We did a load of demos in a small studio in London. And then I think they played those demos around and at that point Pete at Carrere got involved. I think first of all it was when he was at EMI. Then of course Carrere came onto the scene and I was asked to do the album. They were just perfect, really, I thought, for the time. But I mean, I hated the name Saxon. They were called Son of a Bitch and I thought the name was great, for the music. But the record company were worried about people being offended, I suppose."

"Our early years were totally by accident," explains Biff. "We came to the point where we existed really, by lucky accidents. One of our first demo tapes ended up at EMI. The guy left EMI and went to work for a French company and took the tape with him. So the deal we were offered was from that company, who were an independent company. But we could have easily signed to EMI and maybe Iron Maiden wouldn't have been signed to EMI? But that's how history goes, isn't it?"

Continued Biff, on Carrere, "They had their own office. They had a big office in Mayfair, actually. It was really un-rock 'n' roll. But yeah, they had a whole place, full-on. And don't forget, we were distributed through Warner Bros., which were absolutely massively powerful in that early rock era, the '70s and '80s. They had Van Halen and all those bands and they certainly knew the market."

Saxon would be the label's third UK act, following Clout and Incredible Kidda Band. Credit for the name change usually goes to Cannon, who figured he couldn't get far with a band called Son of a Bitch.

Explains Graham, "We had a meeting with Carrere Records, in Newcastle, in a Newcastle hotel, at the Railway Hotel at the railway station. The top guy, Freddie Cannon, came up to one of our gigs in Newcastle, one of our early gigs as Son of a Bitch, and we'd been signed to Carrere, obviously, but America wouldn't go for Son of a Bitch, obviously, and so we had a meeting. We did the gig and then we met Freddie at 12 o'clock in the hotel and we stayed there until three or four o'clock in the morning and we ended up with the name Saxon. It was a joint effort. I can't remember which one said Saxon to start off. Actually, I think Freddie Cannon said Anglo-Saxon, and it got shortened to Saxon."

Explains Pete, "Whereas Son of a Bitch is a mild sort of swear word in the UK, Freddie was American, and he was very, very aware that a lot of radio stations wouldn't actually say the name on air. Because it's not a mild swear word in America, or wasn't at the time. You know, things change now, don't they? So he was very aware. We spent ages and ages trying to find a bloody name for the band. We went through all sorts of names. Diesel, I can remember; Propaganda, that was another one. And then what happened was, that Freddie was walking down Bond Street in London, and he saw a shoe shop, which is actually called Saxone, Saxon with an 'e.' And he thought that it was Saxon. You know what I mean? He didn't realize that it was Saxone, that it was like a French word. So he came back and said, 'I've got the name! I've got the name! Saxone.' We went, yeah (laughs). And I think we had to tell him that there was no 'e' on the end, you know? But it did actually come from seeing that shoe shop."

Biff informed the locals of the name change from the stage at a Barnsley Civic Hall gig in December of '78, telling the local fans not to worry, they would always be Son of a Bitch back home.

But let's not forget: things had developed slowly, with the guys in Saxon grinding away for three years, each of them now pushing 30, playing support to bands like the Heavy Metal Kids and The Ian Gillan Band before getting the above modest deal. Notes NWOBHM expert John Tucker, "Yes, there were things happening, but the big problem is they weren't getting reported because no one was interested. But all those bands were slugging away somewhere. I'd hate to think how many gigs Saxon played before they actually got signed but that's how you honed it. You just keep going. You play for people like a dog, but you play your guts out and you learn the good bits and the bad bits."

And so Saxon enters the '80s… one year early, writing with open minds borne of prog training, writing earthy and traditional borne of classic rock and blues training, and writing with speed and aggression borne mostly of animosity—albeit with a wee bit of admiration—for the clear-cutting of rock convention that was punk. The boys from Barnsley were tempered steel, with dues paid, and for once in their lives, they'd have rock 'n' roll career timing on their sides.

Chapter 2

Saxon
"We were not pretending to be working class."

Record contract in hand, albeit not a glamourous one, Saxon set about recording what would be their debut album, working at Livingston Recording Studios, Barnet, London from January to March of 1979 with John Verity producing.

"It was great," recalls Verity. "I ended up getting involved with Livingston. That's how impressed I was with it. I bought shares and I stayed involved for a few years. It's in North London and so the guys, they were just in hotels locally. Livingston was a little bit out of the way. It's not in London as such so it wasn't a place that people would kind of hang out. We just worked and got on with it."

The *Saxon* record would be done and then issued within days of the birth of the New Wave of British Heavy Metal, making Saxon the first NWOBHM band with an album out, depending on what one thinks of Motörhead's place in this maelstrom of metal. Indeed, the album sees issue on May 21st, two months after Motörhead's *Overkill*, but two days after an issue of Sounds featuring Ted Nugent on the cover declares in a headline the existence of a "New Wave of British Heavy Metal," attached to a piece reviewing a live package of bands that were frankly, mostly, somewhat ahead of Saxon's game despite not having full-length records out.

There were hints across the album that the band was celebrating their hard rock roots against any trace of punk, as many bands would shortly do. But Judas Priest had already gotten the ball rolling, exhibiting this pronounced identification with and pride in heavy metal with recent *Killing Machine* songs like "Rock Forever," "Hell Bent for Leather" and "Take on the World."

"Well, there weren't a lot of bands that did it," agrees Biff. "We did it, obviously, with songs like 'Heavy Metal Thunder' and stuff like that, and obviously Judas Priest did. And to a certain extent so did Queen. So I think to sing about your audience and to sing about the music that you love, some bands can do it and have done it. And as the audience grew, then we could sing more about it, about the link between the audience and the band. It's denim and leather—that's what that's about. We're basically praising the audience; we're saying, 'You're a fantastic bunch of people and we're in this together,' that sort of thing. And Judas Priest did do that, obviously. But I don't know, that sort of passion from an audience affects me. And if it affects me in a profound way, then it will end up as a song. Some people would say that was a bit cheesy and would say love songs are what it's all about, but I'm not one of those people. I like to say it how it is, and from the streets, basically. That's what we felt like. We felt like we were one big fucking tribe of people all together."

But this much more focused message would come later, across the second album to some degree and most definitely sharpest on the third and fourth.

"On the first record, though, we could have gone one way or the other," opines Byford. "If you listen to the first album, *Saxon*, it's very mixed. There are some very heavy metal tracks on there and some very melodic tracks. But the producer was into doing all the backing vocals and things, so he did a big backing vocals job on all the ballads and stuff, and we sort of had our full reign on the heavy metal stuff. But probably the choice of producer wasn't great and so that first album was a very mixed bag. It wasn't until *Wheels of Steel* that we actually got our act together."

"When we did the debut album," figures Graham, "it was pretty much directed by John Verity; he was instrumental in getting us our album deal. And the people who signed us up... Norman Sheffield and Dave Thomas and Trident were the organization that had Queen at the time. And John didn't really have the vision. Great, talented guy, but he's very much like an early Mutt Lange, all glam and that kind of thing. A really good engineer and good producer, and a good singer in his own right. But we were like angry young men, and the tracks calmed us down on that."

"It didn't turn out the way I wanted it to turn out," says Verity, in his defence. "Often, when you're a producer of a project, you get stuck between different political things that are going on. So the album didn't end up the way that I saw it in the first place. Which is a shame, really. And I think some of the guys probably thought the same as well. Because there was a move to make it radio-friendly for America, it ended up being a little softer than I would've liked. I did a lot of vocal backgrounds on the album with that in mind. Things like 'Frozen Rainbow,' one of my favourite tracks on there, I did all the vocal harmonies on that, to try and make it a little bit more AOR, if you want. But I'm not sure it's really what the band wanted. I was kind of torn between what other people wanted, you know what I mean? It was a bit of a political, unpleasant social situation, really, a bit of a battle between the management and the band and the record company as to what they thought the direction should be—and I was stuck in the middle."

With respect to who wanted what, John chuckles and says, "You know what? I couldn't work it out in the end. There were so many mixed messages that I was getting that I really didn't know which way to turn. My main concern was not messing it up for the band. Because I cared about those guys. And I just didn't want it to go tits up. I just wanted it to work for them. They were managed by a company called Trident, who were managing Queen at the time, and they were really powerful and they could've really helped the band, so I didn't want to upset anybody, you know?"

Steve Dawson goes so far as to say that the end product was some sort of melange of new recordings and the band's demos with John, telling Rhino, "What happened was that we'd made a lot of demos with John Verity, who produced the first album, and we'd gotten signed up on the strength of those demos. So we went into a studio in north London and made a record, but when we made the record, we took the rawness out of the songs, if you know what I mean. We made it too good a record! So when we presented it to the record company, they didn't like it. They rejected it. They said, 'That's not what we signed up! We wanted something raw!'"

"So what we did was we went back into the studio with the original demos and added to them, so it made the sounds better, and put extra instruments on, replaced guitars or bass, stuff like that. So basically the first album is demos that've been worked on. I mean, we were mortified that we'd spent all this time in the studio making, like, a Boston record! (laughs). Harmonies, keyboards, you name it...and they told us it were crap! But looking back, it was good for us. It was a good learning curve."

Before we get into the music, there's the matter of the self-titled record's album cover. Before Iron Maiden would arrive with Eddie, Saxon was there, like Motörhead, bringing an image that made you think heavy metal over and above what we would get from other '70s bands, Priest included at this point. In both cases, as well as with Maiden, this would be accomplished with illustration, and in Saxon's case, a rough 'n' roll depiction of a Saxon fighter.

"The warrior... oddly enough, we got that from Frazetta and his style," explains Paul Quinn. "We had English artists who could do a nice job and they were the ones that came up with the logo as well. Frazetta had a book out of what he'd done with all his bands actually (laughs.) He had a really good compendium, omnibus book. Oddly enough, the fact that Britain was overrun... it was kind of an aggressive name, as long as it's not the Anglo-Saxon detrimental meaning. But fans were just manic. There was a working men's club concert secretary—the guy that booked us in the first place, in Wales—trying to hold this audience back. Y'know, half-heartedly 'cause how can one man hold back an audience from a stage? It was extremely funny and great times."

"For us, we were not pretending to be working class. We still are, in a way. We're still working in that it was kind of us against the world; it felt like that. It got marginally easier as we got more famous. We got signed in '78, but we didn't release until '79. The idea that we were harbingers of the metal scene was right for Britain because we were basically the first of that new wave to make any success. We did a tour after we changed our name from Son of a Bitch and played basically the same set with a few new songs that would end up on the first album, and with a new backdrop, which was the first album warrior instead of the Hulk, the Incredible Hulk, coming through the backdrop on the Son of a Bitch one."

As Steve Dawson told Marko Syrjala, "When we first got signed up with Carrere Records, we had to change our name, so when we agreed to be called Saxon, we wanted to have a logo like Queen, a really distinctive logo. This guy we worked with in the steelworks, Mick Scofield, was an amateur artist. He lived a mile from my house and I went up to him and asked if he could do us a logo. I said we wanted it to be medieval, English, like a Queen-type thing. Anyway, about three or four days later he rung me up and told me he'd done something. He had done the logo with the two axe heads and he had done an album cover as well for the first Saxon album, the warrior. It was on a big canvas and he never got paid for it. He just did it because he was a friend."

"The first album was actually key for the band on so many different levels," adds Pete Hinton. "The first thing was that out of that first album came the logo. Which has been used ever since. And that was designed by a friend of theirs up in Yorkshire. We wanted… I mean, he took his brief from us, probably me, actually, and we said we needed a double axe on the 'x.' I thought I was being very groovy. And he changed it to the double axe on the 'S,' which looks better (laughs). But the cover itself set the tone for the band.

I think it so quickly placed them in the market, i.e., they're not like pretty boys, you know what I mean? They're these rampaging Hells Angels-type people coming to your town, lock up your daughters, that kind of thing."

Into the music itself, if Saxon beat Maiden to the punch with an album, they also got there first with their own "The Ides of March"-styled intro. "Rainbow Theme" is a new heavy metal enough instrumental that sets up the album, advertising what's in the tin the same way the front cover did. Of course this story gets a little meta, because "The Ides of March" was a lift from Samson's own even closer version, "Thunderburst," from that band's second album, *Head On*, issued June 27th, 1980. While Steve and Thunderstick argue about who wrote it, here's Saxon doing something considerably similar over a year earlier.

"Rainbow Theme" transitions into "Frozen Rainbow" and at this point we're immersed in something conceptual and art rock. Except musically this is more so traditional meat-and-potatoes mellow bits mixed with bluesy jamming and uptempo chugging rock versus the complexity of prog. Lyrically, Saxon is also signalling heavy metal theming, with the brief and bizarre tale of a man deep beneath the snow who guards the secret of the frozen rainbow. In other words, Saxon is placing themselves next in line from Uriah Heep and Rainbow in terms of an aesthetic that would represent the literary side of something we will one day call power metal. The irony is that Saxon wouldn't do much of this— "Crusader" would be a famous, later example—nor would they sound particularly power metal… until the 2000s, when they would indeed embody a sort of very traditional, long-in-the-tooth power metal vibe on professional and polished record after record.

Biff loved the idea though, of a rainbow frozen in the ice, and for good reason—it's a pretty cool image. By song's end, the rainbow remains hidden, and along with it, the ability to hold "the power of life." The search continued, with the band recording an official video version of the song from their 2013 *Unplugged and Strung Up* album. In this version, longtime Saxon guitarists Paul Quinn and

Doug Scarratt play acoustically, joined by Biff who also plays guitar, his original instrument of choice from the early '70s. "I lived in France and we did these songs in the studio there," Byford told Jeb Wright, concerning the acoustic sessions. "We were just messing around. We transposed some songs into acoustic songs. 'Frozen Rainbow' I wrote way back when, on an acoustic. It is really like the original, only a little bit quieter. The lyrics become the most important thing when it's done this way and it really is an all-new concept for the song."

Noted Biff, speaking with MetalRules, "A lot of songs from the first album are written by Paul and I and they do have a sort of progressive rock feel. 'Frozen Rainbow' and 'Judgement Day' are written by me and Paul and the band Coast. The rest of the band… I mean, songs we wrote together were things like 'Stallions on the Highway,' which has a bit of the flavour of what was to come on *Wheels of Steel*."

Elaborating years later, Biff told me, "I was a huge prog fan. Yes and Genesis and all of the bands, really. Emerson, Lake & Palmer. There are elements of prog on that first album definitely. Me and Paul were huge prog fans and so there are a few proggy things on there that were obviously longer when me and Paul played them in our other band."

Next, "Big Teaser" is along the lines of Samson or Fist or Tygers of Pan Tang lite, hard melodic rock but with riff, much closer to various metal alloys at the verse than it is at the somewhat embarrassing chorus. Biff's lyric tells the typical deprecating heavy metal story of a woman who seems to have all the power, even if the guy thinks he's in charge. Little did the guys know—but as fans would point out—the term "big teaser" had shown up in a much more famous song from earlier in rock history, namely "Day Tripper" by the Beatles.

Says Graham, "Things like 'Big Teaser' were influenced by the Heavy Metal Kids, Gary Holton. That's why it's twangy like that, big Cockney-type. We had been touring with them. It was a bit of a strange period because punk was really big at the time and we were, as people, coming together, still finding our feet as writers together. I think there's some good moments on there, because when we did those songs live, they were a lot more in-your-face."

June '79, Carrere issued the song as a non-picture sleeve single, in 7" and 12" form, backed with the much heavier "Stallions of the Highway," also from the record. There's also a version that pairs the A-side with the down-wound rote NWOBHM balladry of "Rainbow Theme"/"Frozen Rainbow," as part of a single "series."

"Big Teaser" is a great place to immerse oneself in the drum tornado tendencies of Pete Gill. A maelstrom of energy, Gill hits everything in sight, driving the track with an inimitable style.

"It wasn't easy to record Pete's kit," laughs Verity. "I know Pete wanted a particular sound out of his kit, and it was the kind of sound that in that band format is quite difficult to record and fit into the overall thing, you know? So I think Pete was one of the ones that might've been a bit disappointed in the end. But everything can't be huge on an album. Something has to give, you know? Especially with a twin-guitar thing—there's a lot going on already."

But there were few problems in the performances, continues John. "No, exactly. And I didn't want to mess with the formula too much because I thought the band sounded great. They had it nailed, really, and the material was set in stone already. But yeah, I had to clean it up a bit because of this pressure of making it friendly for America. If you are aiming for a UK and even European market, it would've been a bit more raw, you know? The difficulty was to try and keep the rawness and sweeten it a bit without killing it. But again, they were really well-rehearsed. They had been gigging a lot. When they came into work with me, they were more or less straight off the road, and that's a good time to catch a lot of bands like that, with that type of band. In my opinion, you can't rehearse and routine that kind of material. It has to be fresh from being played live."

Next on *Saxon* is "Judgement Day," which splits the difference with what we've heard so far. It's uptempo and rocky like "Big Teaser" but it's also got the unexpected musical movements, suddenly becoming mellow for a long stretch in the middle before cranking up and adding more parts. The end effect is something akin to Budgie, aided and abetted by the obscure melodies, but more so just the oddity of the song structure.

Here Biff pens an anti-religion screed, prompted by his annoyance at having the Jehovah's Witnesses knocking on his door. The reference to judgement day comes from the fact that this renegade Christian cult tends to warn of various doomsdays, predicted then downplayed as they pass by without a peep.

"Stallions of the Highway" is the *Saxon* album's flagship track, beginning with the dramatic title on down. Blowin' free new format heavy metal all the way, it's an anthem, from a band who lives and dies on anthems whilst most songs below and behind fade into the woodwork. Bonus is that it's a biker anthem, with some pretty aggressive lines from Biff as well, some fatalistic, some violent. There's also a nice use of twin leads and a modulation of key. As mentioned, the band and label thought well enough of it to use it as a B-side but that status would be reprised, when a live version of the track is used as the B-side to "747 (Strangers in the Night)."

Explained Steve on his band's links to biker culture, "Well, in the first instance, both myself and Biff had motorcycles. And obviously that came through in songs like this one and 'Motorcycle Man.' But, really, the connection to the motorbiking world didn't come from us. Because the bikers in the Hells Angels and people like that, they picked up on it and sort of made it their anthem. And they approached us to play lots and lots of their shows, and we still do now. We played loads and loads of concerts for the motorcycle people."

"We've never ever had a problem with any Hells Angels or motorcycle shows—they've always been fantastic," continues Dawson. "They've always treated us with utmost respect. The only bit of trouble we ever had with anything to do with motorcycles, we did a motorcycle festival in the southern part of Italy and they insisted on taking us to the stage on five Harley-Davidsons. But trying to ride on the back of a Harley Davidson holding a bass, you can't do it. It's quite difficult, because you can't hold on. And a lot of those motorcycles are made for two people. And there was nowhere to put me leg—me right leg was on the exhaust pipe (laughs). So by the time we got to the stage, which was about a quarter mile ride, I had burned through my trousers and scorched my leg."

"Backs to the Wall" contributes to the building of the band's narrative and its suite of styles, sounding like a scrappy boogie rocker circa *Strong Arm of the Law*, briskly mid-paced, driven from the drums, a battle cry to independence. Utilitarian enough, the song was issued in November '79 as a single, backed with "Militia Guard." Indeed if it's arguably the third best song on the record, "Backs to the Wall" also contains a magic moment of band-and-fan solidarity in the half-time "Can't take my life away" refrain, Biff connecting with the punters potently for the first time.

"Still Fit to Boogie"… there's a title that is both self-deprecating and an embarrassment. A word like boogie would be passé once the NWOBHM would explode, and the idea of still being fit reveals a lack of self-confidence with respect to age. Thinning hairlines in the band would represent the physical manifestation that Saxon were entering the fray a little older than the rest. Finally, fit to boogie or not, no one wants boogie, or very few, as Vardis would soon find out. Plus at this point we were all watching Status Quo's fortunes wane, not to mention Foghat's, on the other side of the pond.

Saxon do indeed boogie on this track, but thankfully with some added punk and metal urgency, along with some nice twin lead appointments. Something we haven't addresses at this point is Biff's voice. It's a hard one to describe, isn't it? It's kind of high but not operatic, it's a bit nasal and yet there's power. And on the *Saxon* album, it's quite prominent in the mix, a mix that is gritty and midrangey, further hobbling the getting-over of the music.

Last track on the record is arguably the best, even though it's not exactly Saxon-esque biker madness. One would expect "Militia Guard" to be something of that ilk, but instead it's more like epic Thin Lizzy, like "Black Rose" or

"Vagabonds of the Western World." The mood is resolute, the tempo mid-paced and the stacked power chording sombre, and all this after a military snare introduction from Pete Gill, accompanied by traditional-sounding war music rendered through twin lead licks. What's more, Biff sings sad and low, as the song builds tension and develops toward prog breaks and respites and surprisingly plush background vocals. Biff's historical battle lyric also sounds like something Phil Lynott might do—think "King's Vengeance" and a couple others on the *Fighting* album, at least in terms of psychological dynamic. Biff has said that he admired the word militia and had wanted to write a song around it, coming up with this vignette that he says could apply to either the French or the Russian revolutions equally.

All told, "Militia Guard" is a hopeful and promising way to end the band's first album, furthermore neatly in symmetry with how it began, ambitious and striving for something of greater importance than post-British blues boom buffoonery.

Graham is all too cognizant of the *Saxon* album's disjointedness. "When we first joined together, we all had our ideas. I had ideas for the intro for 'Big Teaser' and 'Still Fit to Boogie,' whereas Paul had ideas for 'Militia Guard'—lots of Paul on there. But at that time we were pooling ideas, what we had before. We weren't having ideas together as much as we did on *Wheels of Steel*. The writing team was very embryonic at that point and we weren't sure what direction we were following. In the end we just ended up being ourselves. Myself and Steve were more into Free and Cream and Black Sabbath. Paul was more into Stevie Wonder and Deep Purple and Biff was into Trapeze, Glenn Hughes, melodic singing. So all these things came together in a big melting pot. And that's what made it so good, I think, really, starting with the next record."

"The first album, if I was honest, I thought that it lacked energy," reflects Hinton. "But this was a very normal thing that happened to record companies. If the record company saw a band live, and they loved them so much, they signed them, they put them in the studio and then proceeded to knock all the energy out of them. That happened to quite a few bands. Whereas we wanted to have the live energy of the band and put that on vinyl. That album was just their live set, and so therefore all that stuff was played live, and very energetic it was too, and really quite punky when I think about it now. I remixed a couple of things to give it a bit more oomph but I don't know how successful that was."

Fortunately, the Saxon catalogue has been the subject of a swell reissue program, with the 2009 re-do of the debut possibly offering the richest bounty compared to that of subsequent albums. Included are fully five album tracks in Son of a Bitch demo form from 1978, covering two different sessions. These are all album tracks and, alas, are not particularly different from the final product. Also on tap are five BBC session tracks recorded with Tommy Vance, played on the Friday Rock Show, February 15th 1980. Two of these jump the gun as *Wheels of Steel* songs but three are debut album tracks. There's also the live version of "Judgement Day" used as the B-side to "Suzie Hold On" from the next record. Finally there are three selections from the band's Donington stand, August 16th 1980—thoughtfully on the part of the compilers, these are all tracks from the debut.

Reflective of the lack of interest in this kind of music circa mid '79, the NME's Paul Du Noyer came away unimpressed, writing in his review of the record, "Fire and brimstone, blood and iron, stallions, swords and Saxons—'Saxon's impressive first LP captures the aggression of Yorkshire life.' Far for me to argue with a WEA press release, but the thing reminds me more of cheese-and-onion crisps. The Saxon saga began—no, not in Valhalla—'in the Rotherham/Sheffield area' where the lads 'first met when they used to heckle their rivals at gigs.' Since then, the band have organized a following for themselves around the North of England, and they should, with this album, consolidate it safely. The production is good, and their musicianship rarely falters. To me, the songs are mediocre and the lyrical luggage is absolutely dreadful, but Saxon probably operate in a world—the small venue heavy metal circuit—where volume, attitudes and loon pants are enough to ensure acceptability.

They've combined a serviceable Deep Purple thrust, plus suitably Ted Nugent-esque machismo, with the occasional Yes-like clarity and prefabricated profundity. The nicest thing about headbanging is it's so pleasant when you stop and go listen to something else."

Saxon would go on to sell 15,000 copies in the UK, a promising start, but as Biff tells us, the dam was about to break. Indeed, the band's belief in themselves as a live act would help set the stage for bigger and better things to come.

As Biff told MetalRules, *Saxon* was "really a do-it-yourself album. The back cover picture is taken from the workingmans club in the Northeast of England around Newcastle. I made this logo; me and my guitar technician made this half cut out of wood, the Saxon thing. Actually it was made just before we wrote *Wheels of Steel*. We had a very small backline at that time—just one Marshall (laughs)."

"We hit straight away," Biff told me, years earlier. "The fans were into it and they wanted us to play great and write great songs and they were with us. That's how it felt. It never felt to me like, 'Look at me, I'm a fucking smart-ass rock star in front of all these people.' It always felt to me as if we were very, very lucky and privileged to be popular and people come to see us, you know? For us it was more than people coming to see us. It was a fucking event. It was an absolute physical fucking transformation that took place for us, and still is. When we hit the stage it's not just about running around like prats looking good. It's all about connecting with the audience and putting that passion across. That's what it's always been about."

But as with the wooden logo and single Marshall, the beginnings of the band as a live unit found the guys challenged for stage attire. "We used to shop from Oxfam shops and things," continues Biff. "I mean we used to dress ourselves in things we found in shops for three quid. We weren't really aware of any sort of image. I went into a shop in London in '79, '80, and Bob Dylan was in there buying a leather jacket, like a black and white one. Actually bought three. The guy had got one left so I bought it, so that's the jacket I wore through all them early years, really. It was just a jacket. That's the one jacket that people associate with those early looks. It wasn't... we never had anything planned. It was just a random thing. We used to wear tight fucking clothes because we liked it, basically."

Asked about bands they shared stages with, Biff recalls, "Our first tour, actually, was with Slade. We did half the tour and Def Leppard did the other half of the tour. That was the first sort of support tour we did, really. Gigs after gigs. After that we supported Nazareth, and that was right on the verge of releasing *Wheels of Steel*, yeah? And then we toured with Motörhead on their *Bomber* tour, which obviously changed everything. That was when it really exploded, at that point there. We were just a support band and about to release *Wheels of Steel* but we weren't playing those tracks. We were playing tracks off the first album, but we never toured with anybody on the first album. In-between that we played a few shows with Rainbow, the 'All Night Long' period with Graham Bonnet. Yeah, we went down a storm and they kicked us off. So we liked that—it's all part of the rebellion, you know?"

Recalls Pete Hinton, "I had no fear in those days. I just phoned up Doug Smith, who managed Motörhead, and I said, 'I've got a good band, here, Mr. Smith,' you know (laughs). I didn't know him. I said, 'You've got lots of tours going on; have you got any chance for the band being on tour?' And what happened, well, he phoned me back, actually, a week later, and I remember so clearly, he says, 'I was sitting in bed last night with my wife listening to your album, and we think it's brilliant' (laughs). And he said, 'You've got a tour with Motörhead coming on.' Yeah, so from that first album came quite a few things that actually still stand the test of time."

"Saxon were great," recalls Lemmy. "We took them out on the *Bomber* tour with us. I feel a kinship with every band, whoever they are, even jazz bands. Because we're all doing the same shit; we're all overcoming the same bullshit to do what we do."

Indeed, as Biff says, Saxon had played two gigs with Rainbow and then showed up at the next, a Wembley gig, only to be told by a runner that Ritchie didn't want them around and that he'd gotten another band to open the show. Biff says that the band wound up touring with Rainbow again later, but relations with Blackmore were no better the second time around.

Also, as Biff explains, even by Slade and Nazareth, "We had all our own fans then. It was like two lots of fans. We were like young, young. Not all that young, really, but you could definitely tell the difference, you know? There were definitely badges on jackets with our audience, that sort of thing. Don't forget, we were probably a cult band, a band that people were discovering. Like a generation change, really."

Which paints an interesting picture, because in reality, the album the band was supporting sounded like a mix of three things: Nazareth, Slade and something zestier. I mean, there's no deep meaning one needs to ascribe to the pairings, but there's no question Saxon fit the style of the headliners, basically as a younger, faster version, a little fancier given the twin leads, with something to prove, more from the streets. It's interesting as well that all three bands were from the North.

And Saxon was a cult band not because of the NWOBHM, but because of a few years operating as Son of a Bitch. Finally, as Biff frames it, Saxon were "a band people were discovering" because as they went further afield, especially given the new name, their reputation as Son of a Bitch meant less and less.

And then Biff's comments on Rainbow, well, we see there his competitive nature, hitting the stage with a chip on his shoulder just like Paul Di'Anno. As well, there's the idea that Rainbow were joining pretty much ever other old guard band at that point with some sort of drama compromising the ranks, if not blowing the band to bits.

Similar to the Slade and Nazareth dynamic, October 13th 1979, a study in the evolution of the NWOBHM takes place when Nutz, Saxon and Iron Maiden play the University of Manchester, with Saxon being a cross between the old school hard boogie of Nutz and… the future.

"There was an explosion," relates Paul Quinn, "in audience participation, in enthusiasm. The audience were kind of swamping us by then because we'd been on the charts. But that's the '80s. Back to the '70s again, there were times when the headliners were thinking, 'I can't deal with this. Why is this band so fucking aggressive and why aren't we?' Sometimes I heard them say that to us. Occasionally people would say, 'You're amazing. Where do you find it?' I don't really know. The audiences, for example on the Rainbow tour… we were removed surgically from that tour because we were doing so well. It's got nothing to do, really, with any one person or any style of songwriting. It's just that the energy levels were so different."

Addressing their main competition in the beginning, Paul says that, "We would occasionally gig with Maiden. They were great live as well. Still are (laughs). Par for the course, I think." He admits that Maiden could be quite competitive with bands they shared stages with. "Yeah. They're sports fans, their bag, really. We backed them up later in America, with Fastway as well. But they're no more competitive actually on the stage than we are."

Last word on the *Saxon* album goes to producer John Verity, who would not be called back for a second go-'round.

"You know, we were kind of breaking new ground, but breaking old ground, if you know what I mean. Nobody said anything to me—there were no fall-outs at all. But towards the end of it there was a little bit of an uncomfortable feeling. I never discussed it with the guys, to be honest, but I did get it that this lack of rawness towards the end probably disappointed them a bit. The producer is always going to get blamed at the end of the day—I mean, I get that (laughs). So I'm a little bit sad about it, honestly, for the reasons we talked about."

"But it got the guys going. See, first albums are strange things, anyway. First albums are very often ways of kind of finding out where you're going to go next, you know? So they're never as complete as they might be. Because you're still trying things out. Maybe as they look back on it, they might hopefully recognize that we did a good job on it, and at least it was a way to start the whole thing."

Chapter 3

Wheels of Steel
"Your feet didn't touch the ground."

"It was a fantastic time and there were a lot of bands around. We would get reviews in the newspapers, we played a lot in the early days with Iron Maiden and we both would open for some of the bigger bands of the time. I think it grew out of the colleges. In the '80s our audiences were younger. People would latch onto the bands that were coming out and we were latched onto. I suppose us and Maiden were the favourite bands of that generation. Def Leppard was involved in that as well, although they won't tell you that, but they were. The whole heavy metal movement followed the whole punk explosion and heavy metal really exploded in the '80s. We were one of the bands that had the songs and were able to take it further."

So said Biff, speaking with Jeb Wright, setting the scene for Saxon's perfect timing with their second album *Wheels of Steel*. Fortunately the band would deliver what was a huge and heroic and yet still gritty statement, full of humanity and personality, set to distinguish Saxon from the fray as something oddly more experienced-sounding.

"We were trying to create our own sound," continues Biff. "We had a style of writing and a sound that people really bought into. Maiden, Leppard and a few other bands did as well. We had an album out that was very mixed between softer music and heavy metal. *Wheels of Steel* was really our last ditch effort to keep our record deal. We tried to relax and just write some music that we liked with our influences in there.

The first song we wrote was '747 (Strangers in the Night)' and it just exploded."

But the groundswell had already started, says Graham.

"Yes, well, the Motörhead tour in '79—wow, that's 40 years ago—we travelled with Motörhead on the bus, and when we got off the bus, with Motörhead, it was like the Beatles. People were like… I mean, Lemmy, the original Motörhead, the one with Phil and Eddie, was something to behold at that point in time. And when we were the guest band, it weren't like we were a support band and Motörhead. Even though Motörhead were headlining, it was full house. Everybody was into our set and going crazy. So you knew something was happening. Because now, normally, nobody wants to see support bands. They're not taking too much interest. This was different. So from December '79 to August 1980, it was like an explosion. Your feet didn't touch the ground. I mean, *Wheels of Steel* went straight into the charts at No.5, for example, which is fantastic. We were on Top of the Pops three times."

Further on this idea of Saxon's supposed experience relative to the other bands, according to Graham, that sentiment would be in error.

"No, because these bands, like Iron Maiden and Samson, when we did gigs, they all started at the same time as us basically. Going, you know, about the same time. So we had a lot in common. I know Dave Murray was a big Jimi Hendrix fan. So we'd spend hours talking about Hendrix. In fact, the last time he phoned me up, it was years ago, he wanted Al Hendrix's number, while Al Hendrix was still alive. He was in Seattle and I just had my Sunday dinner.

That was a surreal moment. I re-met Dave again, on the tour in Manchester last year."

Nonetheless it felt and looked that way to the outsiders going on the strength of Sounds magazine/newspaper and the pictures of the band on the records—as mentioned, the author had joined the Saxon Militia Guard in 1980 along with Motörheadbangers, so there was some additional print materials. But yes, Saxon looked sort of older, with the large foreheads, facial hair and the style of dress, not to mention Biff's height and square jaw—they just did not look like kids.

Biff remembers the *Bomber* tour as well as a sort of jumping-off point. "We went from playing to a hundred people a night to playing in front of 3000 in the space of two weeks. It really went crazy. We did Motörhead and then we did 60 shows in England."

UK journalist Garry Bushell, however, on the ground floor as both a punk and NWOBHM expert, seems to indicate that there was something to the sentiment that fans were sensing from abroad.

"Saxon were lumped into the New Wave of British Heavy Metal, weren't they?" reflects Bushell. "By Sounds. I wasn't on the road with Saxon; I only really ever saw them play up North so it was slightly different than the bands I'd seen down south in England because the fashions were very different. The kids who turned up at the gigs for Saxon... they had these huge, huge flares. Flares you could park a boy scout in (laughs). Saxon were less hip whereas Maiden was seen as 'happening.' Saxon was seen as a little bit past, even when they were happening (laughs) in that they weren't quite as up-to-date; they were a bit more mock-able. Biff was drinking tea, for God's sake. He didn't drink like the band. But Saxon had some great songs and maybe those metropolitan attitudes didn't translate across the whole fan base."

Ramp-up to *Wheels of Steel*, January 23rd, 1980, Saxon record a BBC session that is broadcast three weeks later on The Friday Rock Show. Three selections from the debut are joined with the much more risible "Motorcycle Man" and the aforementioned "747 (Strangers in the Night)."

Recalls noted metal producer Chris Tsangarides, on board shockingly early with Priest as engineer on *Sad Wings of Destiny* but now producing Tygers of Pan Tang, "Surprisingly, they wrote great pop tunes, and I mean, I fell off my perch when I saw them and Iron Maiden on Top of the Pops. It was always a hip hooray when you saw a rock band playing on that show—it was great to see. And they had quite a few hits back in those days, which goes to show how many people were buying their music. Although the name and the image, if you never saw them, but just saw it, you would think it would be some doom-ridden metal stuff, but it was far from it. It was very, very tuneful, great melodic pop songs, with heavy backing."

"They knew what the fan—people like themselves—liked," continues Chris, sadly since deceased, in 2018. "And the way I see it, you have to be a fan of the music that you were doing, because when you are working with this stuff, you think, would I buy it? If not, then something is wrong. 'We better sort something out here, boys.' But that's kind of how you approach things. Anyway, that's the way I do. You're a fan of it—do I like it as a fan? If I don't like it as a fan, why? That really is the root behind it all. They all are the same as their fans, and it's with the same people, except one lot plays it and one lot listens to it, that knows just as much about listening to it as they know about playing it (laughs). When the New Wave of British Heavy Metal bands came out, at the time, most of them looked like the fans. They wore the same cut-off denim over their leather. They looked the same—there you go."

The recording of *Wheels of Steel* took place February 1980 at The Who's Ramport Studios, Battersea, London, studio of choice also for Supertramp's *Crime of the Century* and Judas Priest's *Sin After Sin*. This was after writing sessions at Mountain Studios, a small facility in Wales, which, as Biff says, "was owned by vegans who lived in teepees."

"Joan Jett, John Entwistle, yeah, lots of people," recalls Graham, asked if any luminaries dropped by the Ramport sessions. "It was like a busy working studio. But it had loads of history. All The Who's equipment was in there as well. If you went up into the attic, it was full of Keith Moon's drums and smashed guitars, stuff that would be worth a fortune now. But I think it all got thrown in a skip at some point. Which is a tragedy. I think this was when… was it Island? I think Island bought the studios."

Explains Pete Hinton, now adding producer of the band to his list of job titles, "*Wheels of Steel* was done in 28 days, actually in two sections of 14 days each. The first 14 days, we recorded all the stuff they'd been on the road with. And the second 14 days was new material that they'd just written that I think they tested out on the road, but not very much. So to me, *Wheels of Steel* is actually an album of two halves."

"I wanted to get the energy of the live set onto tape," continues Hinton. "Because I felt that's what we didn't have on the first album. So I was always pushing them to play more aggressively, more energetically—faster, in some cases—so that it came over. Plus I was a great believer in lots of guitars—I love guitars. I mean, *Highway to Hell* was big at the time, and AC/DC had two guitars on the record and I wanted *more* guitars on our record (laughs). Which is why you've got a left and a right, which are probably doubled, then you've got a centre guitar as well, or maybe even two centred guitars, to give it that stereo spread. In terms of what else I did, there were a few bits and bobs lyrically that were made to fit a bit better. And I do remember working in the middle of the night with Biff on the vocals, and I think together we got something that was really special. It cost me a lot in chocolate. He said, 'If you want me to sing that, I need more chocolate.'"

Notes Biff on the sonic results the band were getting at Ramport, "It's a very large sound, *Wheels of Steel*. If you listen to it, it's all about performance, really, and the guitar sound is very, very British. I think we created a British guitar sound on that album, definitely. And it's the one album that everybody had to beat, actually. Don't ask me why. I mean, I don't know why magical things happen in studios. They just fucking do, yeah?"

"And you know, sometimes they don't and sometimes they do, and if the performance captures it, then it doesn't really matter how good or bad it sounds. If you've got a great song, it's a great song, regardless. I just think a lot of it's in the songwriting, the magic of the songwriting. So we just went into the Who studio, in London, which was quite good; I quite liked that. It's got a good vibe, and we just played everything at full volume, recorded it at full volume, listened back at full volume, and put it out. And it just went nuts, really."

"Right place, right time," adds Paul Quinn, "I think, is a lot of that. It wasn't particularly focused; it's still as diverse as we are now. It had really fast songs on it, and songs about driving fast or 'Don't let the bastards grind you down' type lyrics. A lot of our stuff is really either anti-war or something historical."

"As far as production goes, Pete Hinton was a very positive ideas man in that he'd give us a kind of insight into what was more economic and he did a lot of edits for singles. Like the 'Wheels of Steel' chorus became half of what the original version was. Sound-wise, he occasionally helped with EQ-ing the amps, although his engineer was good. He'd worked with Lizzy anyway, Will Reid Dick. Our soon-to-become manager at that point was Nigel Thomas and he tried anything that we put forward to him. We recorded guitars in a shower room for the brightness, and had a PA running as well so that we didn't wear our headphones in the studio. That was wild (laughs). Imagine trying to keep the sound of the PA away from the microphones that the guitar was using."

Officially produced by Pete Hinton and Saxon, *Wheels of Steel* was essentially a collaboration between the band, Will Reid Dick, and Hinton, who, remember, was an A&R man by trade, not a producer. There's a whiff of the "executive producer" credit to having Pete there, but as Paul confirms, he was in there getting his hands dirty as well. But let's not forget, at times, across interviews, the guys have summarized the situation as a form of self-production.

Explains Graham, "By the time we got to *Wheels of Steel*, what happened is, we finished with Norman Sheffield as management—he didn't really work out. We were put in the old studio in Battersea and when we were in that studio, we were pretty much left to our own devices. And what we did is we just hammered those songs down more or less live, and we didn't do the kind of recording where you put the drums down and then you put the guitar down and then you layer this and that—pretty much that's what happened with the first album. What you got with the second album, it was just us being us, and being allowed to do it with no direction. In fact Pete Hinton was just there to sit in the control room and say, 'That was a good take,' 'That works' or 'Do it again.' But that's all he did; he wasn't like a producer that kind of stamps his own ideas on how he thought we should be."

"When we wrote *Wheels of Steel*, we were angry young men, because we've just been dropped by our management," confirms Steve Dawson, on the business side. "We were managed by Norman Sheffield and Dave Thomas, who were Queen's managers, and we were signed to Trident for management. And they just spent all our money from the first album, and when it ran out, they just told us to get lost. So we had nothing. And so we were really disillusioned with music from before we got started, really. We just thought right, fuck you, we're going to make you wish you hadn't done that. And we went into this rehearsal studio in Wales, in the middle of nowhere, in the snow, with no heating, and it just made us write those songs—and it worked."

All the while, Saxon kept active building a buzz through their live presentation, even whilst recording this all-important second album. February 1st, the *Metal for Muthas* tour kicks off, headlined variously by Samson, Saxon and Motörhead. The none too specific tour featured, at various times, 22 different NWOBHM bands, including Iron Maiden. This was normal, indicative of a scene suddenly coalescing: February 2nd, Saxon headline London's Electric Ballroom, supported by Angel Witch and Sledgehammer. In March, Sounds issues its 1979 reader's poll results and metal dominates. Def Leppard wins best new band with Iron Maiden, Samson and Saxon making a showing. Rush, a major NWOBHM influence, wins best band. Geoff Barton, however, elsewhere in the issue, slags Def Leppard at length, for a second time in as many months. On March 2nd, the last of the *Metal for Muthas* tour dates takes place, a total of 30 of them in one month.

Wheels of Steel arrived on April 3rd, 1980, wrapped in an authoritative and simple jacket that again reinforced this idea of history and tradition and indeed all things military and of biker culture simultaneously. Once inside the record, biker culture is underscored through the storming first track, "Motorcycle Man."

Wide vistas of open chords stretch across quick, aggressive rhythms as Biff belts out what is a plain, unadorned testament to the joys of motorbiking, in not so many words. "I was a biker, so I mean, 'Motorcycle Man' was my theme song. I was in a club as well, actually originally. I did used to ride bikes up to my daughter being born. And then I decided to pack it in because I seriously risked being killed every day, as you do on a motorcycle. My wife used to do show-jumping on horses and I used to ride bikes, and we made a pact to stop doing it basically, so we did. But I was heavily into bikes and I still am heavily into bikes. And we do actually play a lot of biker festivals."

"But yeah, right through the '80s I had a bike. I used to go to all the concerts on a bike and I used a bike on stage in the early days. But I love bikes and I love the freedom of biking. It's not quite the same now, these days, with all the traffic. But in the '80s, late '70s, it was a rebellious thing to do. I suppose same thing goes to owning a scooter, you know, the Mods and the Rockers. It was still quite relevant back then—you had to choose one or the other."

Comparing his association with bikes to Motörhead's, Biff figures, "They don't ride, but I suppose it's the drug connection and the rebel connection with the biker. Lemmy is a legendary rebel. But people can relate to it. And in some respects, with bike gangs, the bike is not the important part—the gang is. There are quite a lot of bike clubs where people have got cars. They just like being in the bike club because they love it. I'm not particularly talking about the Hells Angels, who are genuinely a bike club, but I think people just like talking about bikes, being around bikes, and that has its own sort of thrill, doesn't it?"

Remarks Hinton on "Motorcycle Man," "I can remember that I went down... They had Dave Poxon and

Ron Bleckner, their managers, and they were about to go on tour, in between the two recording sessions. And I went down to a rehearsal room and they said, 'We're gonna play through the new material for you.' I went 'Great.' And they played me 'Motorcycle Man' and I just thought that was the best track I'd heard in my whole fucking life. And so much so that I said to them, 'You've got to play me that again.' And they went, 'No, fuck off.' I went, 'Please, please, play that for me again' (laughs). And I actually made them play it twice, so I could get the full effect of it; that's how powerful that bloody track is."

When I asked Pete about the way the song's chords stride weirdly independently over what was roiling beneath them, he agrees that, "Yes, they had that syncopated feel. But of course that was another strength of Saxon, is that Pete Gill and Steve, they laid down a beat that was so solid, you could do anything to it. And that, in a sense, was the difference. I don't think Iron Maiden do that. I don't think Iron Maiden do. I think they've got a groove and they stick to it and everybody plays the same groove. But Saxon could do that. Paul, particularly, was brilliant, and experimenting. But we didn't sit there with musical scores and say, 'Right, you've got one bar of 5/4, then a boogie beat.' With *Wheels of Steel*, it was very organic."

Further on Paul, in contrast with Graham, Pete figures that, "Sound-wise, Graham was very fluid in his playing whereas Paul was always more clipped. Does that make sense? Also, they didn't particularly choose who did the solos. I just said, 'You can do a solo' and it all worked out, you know what I mean? But all of the song arrangements, apart from one, were all set before we went into the studio. So in that sense, I didn't rearrange it. I just got the best out of what they had. Although we did put an ending on '747.' There was a difference there; they wanted it to just end and I said I wanted a fade on it. They wanted it just to end. But when it came to solos, Graham always had his solos all worked out in his head whereas Paul was very much more spontaneous."

"Stand Up and Be Counted" begins with time-honoured "Tush" chords (Motörhead went there as well), before the band transition to another structure featuring big, hanging chords. Biff places upon the song's near shuffle an inspirational lyric about fighting for one's place in the world. It's a straight optimistic sentiment, but given the context, it's easy to fold into the band's themes around being ambassadors for metal.

"There's the audience, true," explains Biff, "but there's also this idea that maybe Saxon and Priest, to some extent, were the first bands that are not apologizing for being heavy metal or side-stepping the issue or denying it. In fact in the '80s most bands were queuing up to say they weren't, actually. It was a thing: 'We're not heavy metal, we're heavy rock, we're rock 'n' roll, we're this.' But actually that doesn't matter at all. It's what the audience thinks you are, actually. You can tell journalists you're not heavy metal as much as you want, but actually at the end of the day people will make their own mind up. I mean it's the fine line between heavy rock and heavy metal, isn't it? There isn't a fine line from say Judas Priest to sort of Nine Inch Nails. Obviously that's quite a big change. But generally the line is quite dim, where it ends and where it starts. I just think it's more of an attitude than the music, sometimes."

Next, Saxon bestow upon us one of their classics, the dramatic and suspenseful "747 (Strangers in the Night)," on which big and simple stacked chords represent the hook, rather than representing servile support to what Biff is shouting about. Explains Graham, "I had that simple backing, just root and fifth on guitar, and then Paul came up with all the great guitar licks over the top of it. I would never have thought of that. But as a team and with our different styles... you know, that's one of the things. They say the band Biff's got now has two Paul Quinns. I don't know if that's true or not, but with us back then, our styles were different."

"Strangers in the Night" was of course the title of an old crooner classic, but it was also the name of the well-regarded double live album by UFO issued in 1979. They were essentially making fun of the old Sinatra standard while in Biff's case, it's more of a respectful extension, a thoughtful new interpretation of the phrase.

"'747' is like two songs really, running together," says Biff. "It's a song about a power cut in New York that happened in the '60s or '70s, and there was a plane coming in to land and obviously couldn't land. The lights went off and there was a big panic. It didn't crash; it just went off somewhere else. And there were a lot of people trapped in lifts and there were actually a lot of relationships that happened due to that power outage. I've got two songs really. I've got one about strangers meeting in the dark and one about a plane coming down to land and it's all going on at the same time basically."

The real life event was the so-called Great Northeast Blackout of 1965, with the flight in question being Scandinavian 911, not 101, as Biff calls it in the song. It was also a bit less than a jumbo jet (likely a Douglas DC-8), given that the 747 came into service in 1969, four years after the blackout. The documentary Biff saw was called *The Trigger Effect*, which had aired in October of '78. The event caused an overhaul of safety procedures promulgated partly because Flight 911 almost ran out of fuel during its eventual touchdown at Kennedy. Late June of 1980, Carrere issued "747 (Strangers in the Night)"/"See the Light Shining" as the album's second single and the song became a Saxon staple, played on every tour the band ever did moving forward.

Back in 1980 in Sounds, Steve cited "747" as the album highlight, remarking that, "If we had to pick one, we'd probably choose '747 (Strangers in the Night).' That was written about the time all the lights went out in New York, and that plane was stuck at the airport. We were sitting at home having our tea and we saw that on James Burke's Connections show and it inspired us."

Closing the 17-minute first side of the album's original vinyl was the record's title track, as anthemic as the song before it, "Wheels of Steel"/"Stand Up and Be Counted" issued as the album's first single, in fact in advance of the full record.

Graham lays some of the influence for this one upon Ted Nugent's smash 1977 hit "Cat Scratch Fever," although it's also been pointed out that there's a similarity to the concluding jam of Black Sabbath's "Rock 'n' Roll Doctor" from one year earlier.

But there's also an undeniable AC/DC influence. "That came from me," cops Biff, "because I really got into that *Dirty Deeds Done Dirt Cheap* period. And I actually took the band to a little pub in Sheffield to see AC/DC with Bon Scott in '70-something. And all that playing the same riff with the chorus appealed to me. It had a certain power, you know what I mean? Obviously, without AC/DC there wouldn't have been a 'Wheels of Steel.' Much the same as if there wasn't a Motörhead there wouldn't have been a 'Heavy Metal Thunder.'"

"You can't pin down your influences on one thing," continues Byford. "It just all fucking goes in there through your ear and bounces around your brain for a few years and then it comes out in different ways. That's the thing. So it's never a rip-off. It's a slight influence or it's the same sort of arrangements but different approach. I don't think they had an influence on the guitar riffs, because they were really into other things. But after I took them to see them, that changed us a little bit."

"I think England was one of their biggest major markets in the early days," adds Biff, again addressing AC/DC. "They had a massive following here. I went to see them a few times on the *Highway to Hell* tour thing, because we had the same promoter. I wouldn't be totally sure, but I think AC/DC broke in England first before anywhere else."

Paul agrees that the guys share a love of AC/DC. "Yeah, we saw their first tour of the UK, in the universities. I loved the fact that they kept their Celtic sound mixed in with their rock, you know that kind of Irish Chuck Berry meets Led Zeppelin thing. It's an amazing mixture."

On the lyric to this Saxon classic, muses Steve Dawson, "Somebody might come up with a title like, 'Oh, "Wheels of Steel;" what's that going to be about?' Originally it was going to be about steam engines, because I'm a fanatic on those things. Then you go, well, that's not really heavy metal enough (laughs). So we transposed it to a car."

"We had an American car at the time," continues Biff, "an Oldsmobile Town Car (Town Sedan—Town Car was a Lincoln) and I just fancied writing a song about it, that's all. I mean, originally my ideas for 'Wheels of Steel' was the 'Princess of the Night' song, but I switched mid-stream and went with a song about a car. The idea of 'Princess of the Night'... I mean, all of my lyrics are pretty much from my childhood or based on experiences or history, which again, is usually from my childhood, Dallas and things."

"But 'Wheels of Steel' was specifically about the car. It was basically about people's competition between each other with their cars, the hot rod type thing. That's the type of song it is. If you listen to it, it's basically a song about street rods and beating each other. Whereas 'Princess of the Night' is about a steam train. When I was a boy, I used to watch the steam trains come over the viaduct near where I lived. At night, they used to light up all the sky with all the fire and everything. And that was going to be 'Wheels of Steel' but actually 'Princess of the Night' was better. The train was called Princess Elizabeth, basically. Millions of people think that song is about a girl but it's actually not. But you know, people can think what they want to. It's up to them."

"So yes, the 'Wheels of Steel' riff is very AC/DC-ish. I was heavily into early AC/DC when I was getting the band together. I suppose that riff is influenced by them although it's not really their style because it's just continuous. But it's in sort of the same register. I mean, they're more likely to go up, where we just played it continuous, more like an English riff. But the original inspiration is from AC/DC."

Biff has also called the riff "more rugged" than AC/DC and has also said that the song fits the recurring Saxon theme of songs about going fast, which is mirrored in the band's approach to music.

"Wheels of Steel" marked the band's first appearance on Top of the Pops, Steve telling Rhino, "That show—it aired on a Thursday—was seen by millions of people, and it just transformed us overnight. We just started on that next rung of the ladder to success. When you're a kid, you know, that was the only show that you could watch music on in the UK. So I'd been watching the Beatles, the Stones, Cream, Jimi Hendrix, Deep Purple, The Who, all those massive bands. And then somebody tells you that you're going on?! I think I was drunk for a week before I went on, I were that nervous. And that was when my mum finally stopped telling me to get a proper job: when it came to 7:30 on that Thursday evening and I was on the TV! (laughs). It was a life-changing experience."

Side two of the original vinyl opens with another song that fits both of these ideas, namely transportation and Australia's finest. "Freeway Mad" features a boogie rock 'n' roll riff that is more rugged than AC/DC's forays into this field, with songs like "The Rocker." It's also about going fast. Musically, with the song's boogie structure, it hearkens back to the debut album, which in turn contains traces of post-British blues boom hard rock. With the addition of a few purely heavy metal guitar licks, a tentative modernization takes place, the same way Kiss, Ted Nugent, Aerosmith and even Montrose and Derringer marked an advancement upon the likes of Mountain and Cactus (with ZZ Top and Foghat somewhere in the middle). When Lemmy calls Motörhead "a rock 'n' roll band" it is because of songs of his similar to "Freeway Mad."

So it's no surprise that Graham says that, "'Freeway Mad' is an old SOB song that predates Biff and Paul Quinn."

This one comes from Dobby, who says, "I mean, I'm a bass player. I've learned myself to play guitar, in order to write songs. I only ever wrote one song on the bass and that was 'Freeway Mad,' and you can tell, really, because it's just a basic riff. But in learning to play the guitar, because I wasn't very good at it, you develop your own way of doing things. And a lot of the times when I wrote a riff, I would play it to Graham and Paul, and they would transpose it to proper chords, if you know what I mean. And it didn't work. The sound wasn't the same, so they had to play my invention of chords to get it to sound the same. I mean, on one song in particular, 'Back on the Streets,' on *Crusader*, they couldn't get the idea of how to play the opening riff. But in answer to your question, you never lose sight of what you start with. It's always with you."

As for the "Freeway Mad" lyric, well, on "Wheels of Steel," Biff is "cruisin' down the freeway" and "cruisin' 140," while here he's "burning down the freeway doing 90 miles and hour"—top to bottom, it's practically the same lyric.

The consistency of musical style continues with "See the Light Shining," where again Saxon are like a sped-up AC/DC or Rose Tattoo, tight, even punky, but definitely in boogie mode. Instead of augmenting with metal licks however, here the boogie lets up for a melodic chorus over which Biff croons a yearning "Show me the way." The lyrical message is again one of inspiration and ambition, striving to get to the top, led by a shining light.

"With 'See the Light Shining,'" remembers Graham, "Pete Gill was in the rehearsal room and he was listening to 'Highway Star,' *Made in Japan*, the intro, where there's drumming and then Blackmore started in with those chords—that's what inspired the intro to that. And then again, that's all my riff, the intro, then Paul put all the musical bits in—he did all that. Like I said, you can usually tell my stuff because it's the easy stuff. And Paul is like the MD, the musical director. In fact, Paul Quinn, nearly on every album, was the MD."

"Street Fighting Gang" is something more purely metallic, although its simplicity is in the rock 'n' roll spirit, again of something like "Tush." There's a brief flash of actual boogie woogie in the song's very brief chorus, but then we are quickly back to the frantic yet traditional verse riff. Lyrically, Biff spits nails about being a street tough reaching back to school days. By the end of the song, the school bully seems to have become a serious gang member, more than willing to "show you the blade."

"Suzie Hold On" is the closest thing to an AOR track or pop song on *Wheels of Steel*, an album, incidentally, with nothing approaching a ballad. No surprise it was issued as a single, the record's third, backed with "Judgement Day" from the debut, albeit in live rendition. Like many NWOBHM singles, this one was issued in a picture sleeve, and as befitting Saxon's buzz band status, it was available in both 7" and 12" formats.

Says Graham, "'Suzie Hold On' is my guitar riff because it's simple (sings it). You can't get much simpler than that. And Paul did all the middle eights, and the harmony guitar. That's when it was everybody did what they were good at. And then Pete Gill, he had a vision. He swore he had a vision of Keith Moon, and he played the drum break. Yeah, the church pulpit was still in there (Ramport was in a converted church). And when he was waiting to do his drums, the drum backing track, when he got to that bit, he swore he saw the ghost of Keith Moon. And that's when he did that fill. If you listen to it, that big fill, the drum part... it's more than a fill. It's a drum feature more than anything else."

This percussive maelstrom is followed by a classy instrumental passage elevated by some nice Scorpions-like twin lead work and modulation of key before the band gets together again at the end for some more of the song's warm and unadorned verse riffing.

Biff has said that the lyric is about a girlfriend who died from a brain tumour, which makes the sentiment, as well as the triumphant melody of the chorus, all the more poignant.

Wheels of Steel ends with "Machine Gun," the only song on the album that rivals the opening track for sheer heaviness. Beginning with a surprise guitar solo, the song coalesces into an aggressive and fast-paced riff that gives way to novel chords come verse time. When the chorus hits, we find out that the opening riff had a purpose, and that is to accompany Biff's simple repetition of the song's title.

It's unspecified, but Biff's lyric seems to depict Word War I rather than World War II. In any event, Byford is establishing a tendency to write about history and in many cases, the history of warfare and memorable battles, somewhat addressed on the debut but with many more songs along this line to come.

"I love sound effects on records," notes Hinton, asked about the massive explosion, sampled from Hiroshima, utilized at the end of "Machine Gun." "I don't know how keen they were, actually, but they let me have rope to hang myself (laughs). You know, I said, 'Let me try it; if you hate it, you hate it, if you love it, you love it.' And I just got a hold of the sound effects library from the BBC. You just phone them up and you pay the fee and they make you a tape. And so we did that with three things on the album, isn't it? Because it was the motorcycles for 'Motorcycle Man.' It was the 747, from '747 (Strangers in the Night)' and it was the big Hiroshima boom at the end—three things on there."

"'Machine Gun' is nearly all Quinny," relates Graham, singing the riff. "All that fast stuff, you know, that's nearly always Paul Quinn. And with 'Machine Gun,' I know Gary Moore came up to Biff at the Marquee and said the tremolo arm effects at the end, that was really cool. And that was all done on a Strat. It's a Strat and 100 watt Marshall. It's mainly noise, you know, doing all this tremolo arm stuff, and then I finished and then Paul picks up with that fantastic, big, roaring solo."

Summing up, Oliver figures that the magic of *Wheels of Steel* in totality was, "Because we were left to our own devices. We produced it, how we sounded. With Pete Hinton helping. There was no producer. The first one, we had John Verity producing it and he had been in Argent and Phoenix and he wanted backing vocals and the soft approach to it. And so it was a learning curve. Because we had never been in the studio, apart from getting our demos, to make a full record. And these people were famous people. So when the guy who manages you and puts you in the studio was managing Queen, Trident, Norman Sheffield and all that... Queen were so big, so you felt you had to believe these guys, you have to think they know what they're doing. You have to trust somebody."

In other words, as Graham says, they essentially self-produced, but one might add, with Pete Hinton as part of the "band," and Will Reid Dick as part of the studio. And to reiterate what Graham said earlier, *Wheels of Steel* had the band writing more as a team, versus each of the two camps bringing forward what they had from the past. The group writing credit on the album—often the kiss of death for band relations—really represented how Saxon did it, meaning that they all pitched in.

"There are no fillers on it at all," remarked Biff, speaking with Sounds back in April of 1980. "Everyone hammers away and we're pleased with them all, but everyone's got their own favourite, one which they played or did a bit more on. We haven't changed our music at all. If there hadn't been a heavy metal boom, we'd still come up with the same LP. We've always thought that our music was the next big thing anyway. Otherwise we wouldn't bother. Like, when we were down, and I mean, fooking *down*, people would come up to us and say that they thought that we'd become really big. We're not really bothered about the industry, because even if we got trodden on, as we have done in the past, we'll still be here."

But even as Graham and Biff are in agreement about all this team effort business, perhaps they've over-stated somewhat this idea that the record was self-produced, or even co-produced by the band. In fact, sure, the band contributed, but Pete Hinton was squarely producing, with Hinton quick to give substantial credit to engineer William Reid Dick as well.

"With Will, it was really funny, because basically when you choose the studio, an engineer sort of comes with it. And I wasn't an experienced producer in that sense. I hadn't made millions of albums. I was just finding my way the same way that the band was finding their way. And maybe that was the strength of that album, actually, that we were discovering things together as to what was possible. But me and Will, we just got on really, really well. His strength was definitely that he knew what we wanted without actually saying anything to him. Because when there was just me and Biff, for example, doing the vocals, I'd be talking to Biff and I'd be saying, 'Right, let's go do that line again.' And I didn't have to tell Will. He knew, he was listening, and he knew exactly what we wanted."

"His other strength is that he's really good at sound," continues Hinton. "If we described the sounds that we wanted, he kind of knew how to get them. And ultimately, as well, he is the best balance engineer that I've ever, ever worked with. And as a footnote, we met on that day in November 1979, was it? We started *Wheels of Steel*, and he's my good buddy to this day. We go to football every other week together. We meet every two weeks and we go watch football together. He's been my good buddy since the very first day."

Further on the working methodology of the team, Pete explains that, "We were lucky in the sense that the studio that we chose, Ramport, was a large room. We could section it off and put stuff around the drums. Essentially what we did was… this was the recording technique: we got all of the band in the studio and we went through it until we were happy with a take. And by take, it meant, really, we were happy with the tempo, the energy and most importantly the drums. Once we had that, we then started stripping everything away and replacing it. And this is because if the band are in the studio and they're playing all together, it means that the guitar mics have the drums coming through and the vocals have the whole band coming through. So there's a real loss of quality. So once we had the drums, we stripped everything else back."

"The way I like to do it was to do the guitars next. And then this meant that the bass could then… we put the bass on after, because then it meant that the bass could pump to the rhythm of the guitars. The guitars were obviously the accents, and then rather the bass didn't just go boom, boom, boom; it could do, boom, *boom*, boom, boom, *boom*, which kind of made it tighter. Then also, Biff always said that he liked to sing to the whole backing track when he put his vocals on. So then we do that; we put the vocals on and if there were any doubles or any harmonies, we would do that as we go. And that's basically it; there was no big secret about recording *Wheels of Steel* or the one after that, *Strong Arm of the Law*."

The 2009 reissue of *Wheels of Steel*, like the reissue of *Saxon*, included songs recorded live at Donington, in this case, "Motorcycle Man," "Freeway Mad," "Wheels of Steel," "747 (Strangers in the Night)" and "Machine Gun," all *Wheels of Steels* songs, plus "Stallions of the Highway" from the debut. Biff says fans have told him that at Donington, a plane could be seen flying overhead just as Saxon began playing "747." Also on the classy hardback digipak reissue of the album were demo versions of "Suzie Hold On" and "Wheels of Steel."

Reflecting back on the *Wheels of Steels* experience as a whole, Biff says that, "I think musically and lyrically—because obviously you have to split them in two—I think musically it was a great coming together of our influences, altogether, the five of us. I think more predominantly, the four of us really. The two guitarists, Dawson on bass, and me, fiddling around on the guitar and things. Although Pete Gill was there sometimes, I think the majority of the ideas came from the four of us. It was just a great combination of styles. Myself and Paul were more into the musical-oriented stuff and I think Oliver and Dawson were more into Free. In fact SOB, Son of a Bitch, *Tons of Sobs* was the name of a Free album, so they were heavily into that, which was quite old-fashioned. And I think myself and Paul jazzed that up a little bit."

"And lyrically, I just got my shit together at that particular point in time. I think up to that point, on the first album, two or three songs were mine and Paul's, like 'Judgement Day,' 'Militia Guard,' 'Frozen Rainbow,' and the co-written songs were like 'Stallions of the Highway' and 'Backs to the Wall' and the SOB-influenced song was probably 'Freeway Mad.' So it was a mixed album and I really wasn't getting my talents as a lyricist together yet. It was all a bit weird. 'Stand Up and Fight,' 'Frozen Rainbow,' you know? So on *Wheels of Steel*, I actually got it together and started writing quite memorable lyrics and really good titles for songs as well. Because the two things really go together. The riff has to fit the title with me. I'll keep a title for years if I don't hear a riff. Really, I will."

The now eminent Malcolm Dome, writing for Record Mirror at the time, wrote that, "Saxon, to be candid worry me. On the one hand, they seem quite at home when it comes to recording, yet put them on stage and their studio confidence just disappears! So I'm afraid *Wheels of Steel* is a two-edged weapon, which in its own right stands a fierce testament to Saxon's metallic charms, but has me wondering whether they can inject the hard-hitting material here with the sort of kamikaze megawattage it so patently merits live. However, this is Saxon and nagging doubts about their abilities to deliver on the line when it comes to playing in the flesh (where it matters most of all) are an unfortunate obstacle to my fully enjoying this album. Taken at face value, *Wheels of Steel* is a fine, brain-scrambling release of which any band could feel justifiably proud. The standard of musicianship is beyond reproach, and what's more, every number has been given a chunky, yet thoughtful arrangement and production job, which means they come across in the best possible framework. So just settle back and enjoy this and leave me to come to terms with my hang-ups about the band's lack of live charisma."

"*Wheels of Steel* got to me in no uncertain terms," wrote Geoff Barton in Sounds, the music weekly now clearly on Saxon's side. "The album's nothing less than a powerful, Kong-type, chest-beating, throat-bursting high-pitched, hollering triumph and the initial ringing in my ears caused me to succumb to the call of the wild. Badly.

It's quite simply the best heavy metal album of the year so far. Unlike another recent rock release, *Wheels of Steel* isn't streamlined and sterilized for stateside consumption; rather, it's loud, proud, as British as bangers and mash and a towering testimony to the revitalization of UK raunch 'n' roll. Let me just say that if you like your singers to have more vocal power than the whole Kop Choir, if you like your guitar playing more raw than a sabre slash across the stomach, if you like your rhythm section to pound like the Incredible Hulk's footsteps… in other words, if you like your music more than a little on the heavy side, then *Wheels of Steel* is for you."

Steve was all too cognizant of the press, and how things were now getting better with respect to the amount of praise being cast Saxon's way.

"The turning point for us was a guy came to see us from the NME, and he wrote a review. We played in London, and he wrote this review that really slagged us off. Said that we were rubbish, that we were dinosaurs and we sounded like Deep Purple, Black Sabbath and umpteen other bands all rolled up into one. But what he didn't realize was that he alerted a lot of people to our music, and from that day that he wrote that review, our shows were getting more and more people in. And it just went word-of-mouth."

"Because we were just a band on the road. We played every day. We didn't have any days off. We just played all the time, and so you would play a small show in England where there was nobody in, to being full. And the next time we would go back there were 200 people outside who can't get in. And then people in the press, like Sounds or Melody Maker or NME, would send somebody to do a review, and it just went from there and snowballed overnight."

"And then we made records and Radio One started playing them, because in England, as you know, we have national radio. Not like back in America where every town has a radio station, and you can be big in one town and not in another. In England, if you get airplay, everybody hears you. So after the first single, which was 'Big Teaser,' which got on the Radio One playlist, they were playing it five times a day or eight times a day. And it just started the ball rolling. And from there we released *Wheels of Steel*, and then that just really took off. And that worked for Iron Maiden and a lot of other bands at the same time."

"But I can remember that the rock journalists who didn't like our sort of music did everything they possibly could to give us a bad write-up (laughs). But obviously there were great journalists like Geoff Barton who was one of the main factors in helping us become very successful. He liked our music, and he gave *Wheels of Steel* a great review and it just went from there."

And then there were the fans, who were showing up to the shows practically in uniform. "Yeah, it was a bit like colours," muses Biff. "You wear your favourite band's patch on your back and you make a statement. You still do, actually. You still get guys who are wearing T-shirts and patches and you have no idea what band it is, and then suddenly like three months later they're big. So you do get that advertising your favourite band thing, still, actually. And the new generation of fans even today, they're coming to see us and they have sort of adopted that denim and leather patches and badges thing as well. You get young guys who are like 15, 16, and they're wearing denim jackets with all the Maiden, Motörhead, Saxon and Priest patches and they're really into it. I don't think it's particularly a retro thing. I just think that they like it—they like connecting with the band."

"I mean back in the '80s we were actually carved into more school desks than any other band (laughs). That's how it was. And kids would write our logo with like felt tip on their school bags and on their lunch boxes. We were really happening, actually. We were really one of those bands that had a sort of rebel image, against like parents, school, anything, really. Not that we pushed that, but that's just how it goes."

A live review for Record Mirror captured the mania, even if the writer himself could not headbang along.

"Seven o'clock and the steps of the City Hall are swarming with thousands of the denimed faithful," wrote Jack Bower. "In the streets the spivs hawk cheap and nasty Saxon T- shirts at £3 a throw that will shrink alter the first wash. But the kids are happy. Inside the hall it's the interval and they have a chance to talk about music and to make absolutely sure that all their mates know they are there at the Saxon gig and in with the crowd. The atmosphere is one of tense nervous anticipation. At the front of the stage the suicide commandos are in position and determined to 'get their rocks off.' The tension mounts and as the mob scream 'Saxon! Saxon! Saxon!,' the lights go down and the band's eagle logo is picked out by a single spot. Out of the PA comes a deafening barrage of noise. It is the sound of one thousand motorcycles roaring into hell. In a second the band are onstage and blasting into 'Motorcycle Man.'"

"The sound is muggy, distorted and unbearably loud, but the crowd is ecstatic, the hall one mass of flailing hair and sweaty heaving bodies. Onstage Biff, the lead singer, tells the kids that they are the best in the world and proudly leads them in a charming chorus of 'We hate the Mods.' The song that follows is 'Backs Against the Wall.' Everybody is happy. Everyone that is, except the boring old music critic at the back of the hall. To him Saxon's music is about as enjoyable as a night at a factory listening to the industrial lathes, All sense of dynamics and rhythm seem lost in a headlong rush to play forthcoming single '747.' The critic feels sure that Saxon would get the same ecstatic response if they just played a tape of a Concorde taking off. Play it loud, play it fast and give the punters what they want. It's the noise they need. By the time Saxon start on the encores, the critic's ears are ringing and he is feeling sick and dizzy. Wisely he heads for home."

Steve looks back on this time as Saxon's peak. "Yeah, it's got to be *Wheels of Steel*, for a number of reasons: 1) it was utterly and totally enjoyable to make; 2) it was successful, and that's what we wanted as a band; and 3), it pays my mortgage (laughs). Don't get me wrong, I'm proud of all the others, but if I've got to pick one, it's got to be *Wheels of Steel*. And if you asked all the members of the band, I'd be very surprised if they said any different. Because the band was a true band then. Everyone was having a laugh. If somebody came into the studio and knocked one guy down, they'd have to knock all the other four as well. We used to have a motto: 'You kick us down, we get up again and kick you back.' We were like the Musketeers: all for one and one for all!"

The tour in support of *Wheels of Steel*, says Biff, was just a continuation but a step-up. "We did the Judas Priest tour of Europe, we were playing everywhere, it was an endless tour. We did a lot of TV as well, which really helped."

In April the band was busy supporting Nazareth. Chris Collingwood from Sounds was there, remarking, "Here is the Wolverhampton Civic on a wet and windy

Wednesday. Once on stage, Saxon open with 'Motorcycle Man,' a slab of concrete from their new LP *Wheels of Steel*. Live, the motorbike sound at the beginning is transferred from menacingly loud to something that almost has your correspondence throwing up. God, it's so powerful that it makes Montrose's 'Bad Motor Scooter' sound like a Lambretta. While this cacophonic racket is going on, the band walk on. Graham Oliver first (a guitarist whose grimace makes Carlos Santana's look like Tony Iommi's) playing the main riff, nonchalant like, with the others coming on after him, and finally singer Biff (he's dropped the Byford) bouncing on straight into the 'two arms in the air' stage manoeuvre."

As Steve Dawson promised Chris afterward, "Next year we want to be the loudest band in the world. We've already had throwing up at gigs, so it won't be long before we achieve that ambition. We're already the loudest band to record at Ramport."

Saxon played every single night from June 1st through June 14th up and down the UK, culminating at the Rainbow in London on the last date. Another NWOBHM festival of sorts took place July 25th, when at the Hackney Rock Concert, Saxon co-headlined with Motörhead, and were joined by Spider, Angel Witch, T34, Sleek and Lightning Raiders.

September 11th to October 1st, 1980 represented a milestone for the band, namely their first dates in the US, supporting Rush on an intensive 16 dates up and down the East Coast. This was after the band's third album was recorded but just before it was sent to the shops. Unfortunately, the dates had limited effect on record sales for Saxon because of label politics. Warner Bros, who had *Wheels of Steel* in the US, had been ticked off by their dealings with Claude Carrere, and had only printed up the 25,000 copies of the album for which they'd been contracted. Those sold out quickly and from then, if a given newly minted NWOBHM enthusiast in the US wanted the record, they'd have to search out and pay dearly for an import copy.

"It wasn't easy, that first tour with Rush," recalls Paul. "We did almost the whole east coast, plus a little bit of

Louisiana. We had an RV, a van with the captain's seats in it and it got a bit hairy 'cause we brought an English bus driver with us and he had to navigate us around America and he'd never been before either. We tended to get drunk a lot in there, so that anaesthetized us to the amount of mileage we were doing. But the band and crew used to give us plenty of compliments. Matter of fact, the crew applauded us offstage every night. Not ours, Rush's. What a rush it was, to coin a phrase, to hear that sound of an American audience firing up when the lights go off. Whoa. Like the first time you see a steam train."

Chapter 4

Strong Arm of the Law
"You got that one—now get the new one!"

It's a rare thing when it happens but it almost always occurs when a band is firing on all cylinders and can do no wrong: in 1980, Saxon put two studio albums in the shop, and this while continuing to deliver the goods live, including their first dates in America.

"We were prolific," Biff told Darren Cowan. "We had a lot of ideas bouncing around. We were really into songwriting, and so when we finished the *Wheels of Steel* tour, we started writing the *Strong Arm of the Law* album. We wrote it very quick and recorded it in three weeks. The band banged it out; that's how it went. I don't think we thought much about it at the time, but looking back I think we could have slowed down a bit. We were moving faster than the audience. The audience had just gotten *Wheels of Steel*. They bought it and were processing it, picking their songs and we were touring a little bit on it. We came out and said, 'You got that one—now get the new one!' We probably toured more on *Wheels of Steel*, especially in America. It did really, really well in America. I think we cut the head off the monster a little bit, but it came together. I think we were moving faster than the industry; the industry wasn't ready for two albums a year. It was a bit of a one-off. People don't usually do it; it's a bit of a special thing. It's good to have something in common with Zeppelin, isn't it? There is no rock band on the planet that is not influenced by Led Zeppelin."

"It was only rushed in that it was put out too quickly," adds Graham, somewhat contracting Biff in terms of the timing of the writing. "But if you remember, in those days, you only had 20 minutes a side and we had lots of songs; we had songs spilling out of us. And most of the album was written, *Strong Arm*, so it wasn't such a rushed writing. The writing session that produced *Wheels of Steel* also produced most of *Strong Arm of the Law*. Some of the songs were finished and some were just embryonic. But we only had two... I remember playing the Bingley Barn Dance with Motörhead and Girlschool (Heavy Metal Barn Dance, Bingley Hall, July 26th; also on the bill: Angel Witch, Mythra, Vardis and White Spirit), and that was right slap bang in the middle of finishing off *Strong Arm of the Law*. So I can't remember which tunes were in which order, but I know that most of them were nearly finished anyway. And then we knocked it into shape. And Biff always had vocal melody ideas as well, so yeah, those things came about fairly easily."

Whilst recording, "We lived in Pimlico," continues Graham (writing sessions were "a big barn in the country," says Biff), "because it was cheaper to rent an apartment for six months than put us in hotels. So we did two studio albums in the studio in Ramport, which was just over the bridge from Pimlico. So that's what happened. We had five band and two road crew living there. Princess Di—Lady Di, as she was then—we used to see her every day, because she was living there before she married Prince Charles."

"We would have liked to tour *Wheels of Steel* more than we did, especially in America," says Biff, speaking with Jeb Wright. "We did the Rush tour and a few small headline shows. We did the famous one at the Whisky a Go Go where Metallica opened the show. We wanted to go out and do more touring with Judas Priest, or the Scorpions. Iron Maiden did just that; they did a lot more touring. Our record company and our management were scared of us being a one-hit wonder so they wanted us to write another album straight away, which we did."

"But we were on a huge roll. We were under a state of grace. The point I am making is that because we were doing the album, we were missing out on the opportunity to tour the world. We were too busy recording. It would have been much better for us to tour more on less albums. We could have written the albums, but we could have held them back for a while. The first major tour we did in America was the *Power & the Glory* tour with Iron Maiden, which was our most successful tour. It just goes to show you that getting in front of the right audience is the key."

But as Pete Hinton explains it, the recording triggered the touring. "Yes, but I agree that it was all kind of rushed. We finished *Wheels of Steel*, I think, in January, and it was out in April or May or something like that. By a month later, we were in the bloody studio again, and *Strong Arm of the Law* was released in November. So what happened was, the conversation kind of went like this: 'We've got to go and do an album.' 'Yeah, but why are we doing it now?' 'Because if we don't do it now, it can't be released. And if it can't be released, then you can't do your European tour. If you can't do your European tour, you can't do your American tour.' So the band were under incredible pressure, I think. But, boy, did they come up with the goods, didn't they? And if you think, over in Europe, *Wheels of Steel* is seen as like *the* album. In America, *Strong Arm* is seen as the album. I think it's much more cultured. I think it's much more cohesive."

"For *Wheels of Steel*, we wrote some great tunes, and then, more or less, our management wanted us to do another album straightaway," says Steve Dawson, giving his take on the timeline. "Which was unheard of. And looking back on it, it was probably a mistake (laughs). We should have kept touring on *Wheels of Steel* a bit longer. So *Strong Arm of the Law* was written quick. But we were on a songwriting roll, so we wrote all those songs together, and so obviously then there's more money coming in, and then you've got more time to write your next record."

"But it's amazing, really, when you think about it: we made two records in one year. That was through greedy management (laughs). I mean, if we'd made *Wheels of Steel* today and it'd had the same success, we would still be on tour in five years' time! It's done different now. But then, because it was new to us to make records, we were like eager beavers. We'd have made ten in one year if we could've done. We just loved doing it! If you've waited ten years for something and it finally happens, you just want to keep doing it. We were, like, 'We're doing it! We're in the studio and making records!' It's only later in your career when you sort of put barriers up about working this way or that way. What I'm trying to say is that in those times, it was really a laugh and enjoyable."

Late May through August of 1980, Saxon work at Ramport Studios on tracks slated for the band's third album. "It was in one session, and so it was much more measured and complete," muses Hinton, comparing it to *Wheels of Steel*, which was tracked in two distinct chunks. "I think we had a better idea of sounds. We wanted to have a more sophisticated sound on it. But still, we did two albums in six months. Funnily enough, in the '70s, that's exactly what every band would do. They only had their material to sell, so why would you not record? And somebody like Saxon want to get in front of people and play—total opposite to Def Leppard, who were quite happy to spend three years in the studio, do a world tour and then they go back to the studio for three years. Saxon were much more of the in-your-face, 'I'm going to play,' you know? And more like, 'I'm gonna play and you're gonna bloody listen.' But no, I thought they were super-confident and getting more and more constant in their own abilities. I definitely saw an upswing in their own personal techniques. They were much quicker with takes. And after touring the States, I think, they had a better idea of what they wanted."

On August 16th, the very first Monsters of Rock is held at Castle Donington racetrack. The lineup features Touch, Riot, Saxon, April Wine, Scorpions, Judas Priest and as headliner, Rainbow. A commemorative album is issued and as discussed the recordings from Saxon's set are used on the expanded 2009 reissue editions of the first two albums and then also the 2006 reissue of *Strong Arm of the Law*.

"People won't forget it, and obviously the memories are there all the time," reflects Byford, asked about Donington. "It was the first outdoor festival we played. We were like the new kids on the block on that festival. Rainbow, Priest, Scorpions... I suppose for April Wine it was sort of their first big gig as well, and Riot. But there was really only us and Maiden and Def Leppard that hadn't had any real radio or TV success. So when we had walked on stage, I think we had done 200,000 records of *Wheels of Steel*, so it was fantastic. I think a lot of people were quite shocked at how big we were, actually. So it was a great day, and we found this old tape in the manager's attic, and there are bootleg versions of it around, but you can tell the bootleg versions, because they have one extra song, on the cassette. But there's one from the Rolling Stones Mobile that hadn't been heard for 30 years, so when we played it, it took us back definitely."

Biff figures the band had played about 60 gigs in the ramp-up to Donington, already rising from the clubs through the civic halls, and arriving in front of 60,000 fans to what amounts to a hero's welcome.

"Like I say, it was our very first roll of success there, with *Wheels of Steel*, and it was just a snapshot of what was happening in England. People were into us, weren't they? So it's a good snapshot of what the '80s thing was, especially for a lot of the younger fans, and obviously through the recordings, for people abroad who weren't there. But I think they were all surprised as to our popularity. Ritchie was having a great gig; he was in a great mood. But shortly after that we went out with Judas Priest in Europe, which was our first European tour. So yeah, it was a great time, and a milestone for the New Wave of British Heavy Metal, because it was the first time that a band from it, like us, got to play in front of 70,000 people, really, to play our style of music, which was a lot more aggressive, a lot more sort of working class audience-oriented, rather than superstars playing long solos and things."

As September of 1980 rolls around, the band see one last single issue from *Wheels of Steel*, namely "Suzie Hold

On," with Sounds announcing that the band's second album has just gone silver in the UK. November 14th sees the release of *Strong Arm of the Law*, which debuts at No.11 on the UK charts. Sounds helps the heavy metal cause by bestowing upon the record an arguably generous five-star review.

For the *Strong Arm* cover art, the band stuck to their usual level of simplicity, confronting us with a big Saxon logo then showing us a police badge. Says Pete, "Freddie had a policeman friend, who he bumped into and he said to Freddie, 'Oh, you know, you want to see my badge?' And that is literally how it happened. We approached the art work people and said, 'Well, we want a badge,' and they went off and researched what badges there were. I think it's an American badge. I couldn't tell you which police force it is. I haven't got a clue, because they did that."

Which works in conjunction with the album title. "Well, first off," says Pete, "is that it's so difficult to get the running order right, particularly when you had two sides. So there's running order and sequencing, which can reflect the image of the album, as can, of course, the title. The first thing we did was look down the song titles and think, is there anything strong here that we can actually use? I can't remember how *Strong Arm of the Law* was picked but it was a strong song. And we always knew that it might be a hit single, and it's a good thing to name your record after the hit single, you know what I mean?"

Opening the band's third record is "Heavy Metal Thunder," a fast rocker but predictably so in the pole position and vaguely dissatisfying of riff—very few chords, seesawing back and forth, kind of the opposite of hooky. What is commendable is that it adds squarely to the narrative of Saxon writing about its suddenly formed tribe, even if the title is a lift from Steppenwolf's "Born to Be Wild." But yes, Biff hammers the theme until the punters down front can't help but be swept up in headbanging camaraderie of it all.

"We just think about our music and our audience because we love it," defends Biff. "That's what it is. A lot of our ideas aren't concocted. They come straight from a feeling. We don't sit down and think, let's write a song about la la la.

We're playing in a room and suddenly come up with a lyric or something and that's it. We go with it, we fly with it. I don't think we predetermine. Especially then—we just went with a good feeling, Something was coming out and we just rolled with it."

"Saxon are very different from Motörhead in their approach," reflects journalist John Tucker. "Theoretically, Saxon would be, I suppose, a rock band. They'd been doing this for a long time. By the time their first album came out, they're 30; they're not young. But the thing about Saxon, amongst other bands, was they embraced heavy metal, and they not only went along with it, but they promoted it and pushed it, and they had no problem being a heavy metal band when so many other bands hated the term and didn't want to be a part of it."

Velocities are kept up on the record's second track as is this sense of stripped-down simplicity. "To Hell and Back Again" is a curious number, about a man on death row getting a temporary reprieve, beating Maiden to the punch with this narrative, although "Hallowed Be Thy Name" is a much bigger and better classic. Biff's singing is thespian and passionate and his lyric short but meaningful and imagistic as well, the perfect match to the mournful guitar textures that stand as the song's verse riff. Come chorus time the mood changes, into a sort of carnal, biker, proto-thrash speed metal. As Saxon often do, just as the listener is lulled by the minimal parts both qualitatively and quantitatively, there's a surprise, this time a sort of Pete Gill drum solo complete with double bass, topped by guitar solo squalls.

"I remember Pete Gill doing those drums," chuckles Graham, "that drum backing to Paul Quinn's solo guitar, and thinking how exciting it was. Pete Gill was a really exciting drummer, and really easy to write songs with." Asked it Pete was a bit of a Keith Moon, Oliver answers in the affirmative, "He was, yeah, but he had his own style. And if you listen to the *Live at Donington* record that Biff put out (*Live at Donington 1980*, semi official, on Angel Air, 1999), on that 'Bap Shoo Ap' song—which is also a B-side of one of the singles, I believe—the drum beat is just so powerful and intense; bang, bang—it's relentless. But yes, I remember doing 'To Hell and Back Again,' with Quinny and everybody just jamming out and having a great time. I can remember having breaks and going upstairs and listening to tracks and playing on the pinball machine upstairs in the recreation room, which was the original one from the Who film. They had that it in there."

Moving on, the strong title of the record, along with that stark and scrappy album cover is now joined by a catchy, memorable chorus to the title track, on which Biff cautions, "Stop, get out, we are the strong arm of the law." This is set to basic descending chords that are charming and almost southern rocking, appropriate adjunct to the rest of the architecture which both boogies and shuffles, even though the riff in isolation is squarely biker metal. Biff's lyric is almost awkward, like a Scorpions joint, but sorted out, it's a bit of a funny story, where the guys get stopped by the cops who are pretty sure they have for themselves an easy drug bust. Little did they know Saxon were tea-drinkers—according to the press, in a chiding mood, that was their only vice.

Byford says that it's a true story, and that the band was often getting stopped because of their big American car, with this particular detainment taking place November of 1980. In any event, the story was good enough for the track to see issue as a single, backed with "Taking Your Chances."

As Biff told me in 2015, "'Strong Arm of the Law' is one of those extra tracks we throw in at times when we're doing a two-hour set or something. It's a blues song, really, more based in Free, that sort of style with that repetitive riff. Lyrically, I'm telling that story about a police stop in London on Tower Bridge, and they played the game of, 'We just found this tablet in the door pocket.' And, we don't take that stuff. We can't afford it. Can't even afford petrol. So that's the story about that, really. People do relate to it, still, the stop-and-search thing. Musically it's a shuffle, you know, from the '70s, but it's got more of an aggressive '80s touch to it lyrically. It's a bit of an anti-establishment, 'stop hassling us because we've got long hair and we're wearing denim and leather' type song."

In an interesting commentary on Saxon hitting you right between the eyes, Diamond Head guitarist Brian Tatler explains that "some bands were a bit more commercial. I mean, Saxon probably, I don't know if it was their idea, but they might've been encouraged to write singles and get on *Top of the Pops*. Bands like Zeppelin never really did that, did they? Purple had a few singles. Sabbath had a couple singles. I never saw them as single bands—they were album bands. So maybe Saxon were more, 'You've got to get a hit single, you've got to get on the radio, you've got to get on MTV.' I mean, Zeppelin *III* got terribly slated when it came out, and I remember some of the Sabbath albums, you'd get little acoustic guitar bits in-between songs, and I never liked that. I always wanted it to go from 'Children of the Grave' to 'After Forever' or vice versa, rather than have a little filler bit. But when you get to Saxon, they didn't do any of that. They just go from this to this to this and not mess about. Just slabs of hard rock. And not have any airy fairy bits."

Pete Hinto chuckles when he thinks about Biff and his ability to connect so directly, through songs that always feel like they could be singles.

"One of the things I particularly liked about Biff was the subject matter. This is because both him and me, we grew up in a time when we looked at comics when we were young, more than books (laughs). And Biff always wrote lyrics in that comic strip way. It meant that every song, you could actually, like, make a comic strip out of it. And that's what I really liked. Also he wrote lyrics that were extremely down-to-earth and that could be identified by and with the audience. Because one of the things we always used to say, if you're in a band, you've got to understand your audience. And once you understand what your audience is, you could tailor everything to that audience. Especially in the beginning, you need to have a solid fan base, so you need to know what the average fan does. What did they wear? What did they do? And that's always been a Saxon thing. 'Motorcycle Man'—a lot of guys in the band as well as the fans liked motorbikes. 'Denim and Leather'—that describes what the guys wore and what the fans wore. They've always been able to identify with everyman, and that, I think, lyrically, is Biff's huge strength."

And again, planes trains and automobiles... "Yeah, totally (laughs). You're right; they're all about fast cars and not so much fast women. There's a few in there but it's a lot more about driving. It's a later song, but like 'Forever Free' says: 'Forever free, riding with the wind in your hair.' '20,000 Ft' with the flying, so yeah, that is true. But you see, all of that stuff is boyhood stuff. It's what we had when we were young people, as people in Britain. We had the war comics. We had the films about the biker gangs and stuff like that. That's what we had. He was just living his childhood again (laughs)."

Next, "Taking Your Chances" is a sort of hidden gem on the *Strong Arm of the Law* album. The intrigue comes from the fact that it's an uptempo shuffle and yet the verse riff is sort of like Matthias Jabs-era Scorpions, in other words, Scorpions writing for America. It also has two offsetting riffs going at times, one of then a twangy thrash from Paul, with the other featuring Graham stacking chords soulfully. An uncommon sophistication comes from the modulating leap into the verse and then back out again almost jazz-like of melody. Hard to explain, but there's some real New Wave of British Heavy Metal magic to this one, a lean into the likes of Quartz and Holocaust and Witchfynde away from the singles and the ZZ Top.

Side two of *Strong Arm of the Law*'s original vinyl begins with "20,000 Ft," another fast but simple one, rudimentary speed metal before Raven and Anvil take over en route to Metallica. In fact, as a further development toward nascent speed metal and nascent thrash, Pete Gill goes into double bass drums for the chorus. At the lyric end, we get another Saxon song about going fast, this time Biff energized as he looks out the window of a passenger plane, although there are half-hearted gestures toward the idea of flying some sort of fighter jet himself (along with a nod to joining the mile-high club, given the "living my fantasies" line).

Notes Byford, "It's one of those songs that is really thrashing and it's part of our heritage. Against 'Strong Arm of the Law,' the two songs are total opposites in musical style. You've got one song that's rooted in '70s sort of blues, and the other song has an absolutely ridiculous fast riff that only us were writing, and maybe a handful of bands in those days. So yeah, it's a groundbreaking style, '20,000 Ft.'"

The modulated break in this one is driven by Pete's double bass, but the chords instantly remind one of Priest in their new stripped-down guise beginning with *British Steel*, out a few months earlier. In fact, it's not hard to look at *Strong Arm of the Law* as some sort of scrappy demo version of that record, while Maiden evokes comparisons to the more note-dense and fancy pants Priest of the late '70s.

"20,000 Ft" transitions without break into the atmospheric opening of "Hungry Years." Just as it sounds like Saxon is gonna go to battle with a war song, a tough shuffling riff 'n' rhythm arrives, over which Biff tells a historical story of economic struggle. Again, this idea of Saxon writing straight between the eyes is enforced by the lack of too much complication as well as very musical soloing and not too much shredding, more so the suggestion of brief singable melodies. This happens on the fast, heavy ones as well, setting Saxon apart. Arguably, this comes from Paul's and Graham's background in all forms of classic rock.

Recalls Graham, "The middle bit from 'Hungry Years,' pre-solo, that guitar riff, is a thing from an old SOB tune from the early '70s. Paul Quinn did the ascending riff, Paul Quinn did the solo, and the rest of the band helped to make it into a song, to arrange it into a song. And it started from just the guitar riff, my picking intro. That's just something I had kicking around from years before as well. These things came out, you know, manifested themselves in songs. It was only when you get into four or five albums that you start running out of things that you had stockpiled. I think most guitarists are the same. You had these little ditties and riffs, and when you get signed up, first off, you've been a live working band and you've got nearly an hour-and-a-half's worth of songs. It's only later that it starts getting difficult."

"Sixth Form Girls" swings all the way back to the light-hearted, both of lyric and melody. Biff is singing about girls from the dormitory in the sixth form, meaning 16 to 18, although he tells us they are "just 16, teenage dream" at the lyric's close ("I had nothing to do with the 'Sixth Form Girls' lyrics—let's get that straight," laughs Graham). Of course they sneak out and hook up with "boys from the factory," and all this over a backing track that is equal parts punk, early '70s glam and pre-hair metal hard rock, the simplicity of the thing kept from the mundane by Dobby's bobbing bass line and a chorus rich of melody.

Strong Arm of the Law closes strong, in fact, with a Saxon career statement, in the immense "Dallas 1 PM." A reverse fade coalesces into bass and drums. A riff emerges and then some palm-muted chugging. Then there's a counter riff, so three guitar parts are going at once. And yet things stay simple, hypnotic even. What creates more intrigue is the fact that Biff doesn't begin his harrowing tale until the listener is fully put at ease, prepared for the telling. Comforting are the huge melodic chords that stitch the key woven riff together. There's also deft dropping of a beat, keeping the listener on edge.

Of course, "Dallas 1 PM" tells the story of the assassination of President John F. Kennedy, November 22nd, 1963, and it's quite remarkable that few bands have ever gone there. What's more, Biff plainly states what happened, staying away from conspiracy theories, save for one gesture, the use of three gunshots, which the band had no end of complication trying to get right in these days of analog recording. Authentic news reports on that shocking day are sampled, as well as Kennedy himself.

"In those days, Biff and Steve Dawson used to write the lyrics," recalls Pete Hinton. "I couldn't tell you in what percentage they wrote, but Biff as the singer always said, 'I should have the final say on lyrics because I'm the one who sings it.' And I do remember that Steve Dawson was actually reading a book about that, about the assassination. And we had a big discussion in the studio, actually, about how many gunshots we should put on there. Because there was the conspiracy theory that Lee Harvey Oswald did two shots, and that there was a shot done from somebody else on the grassy knoll. And we thought we would put three shots on it to be really controversial. But yeah, there is a conspiracy theory to say that he bloody missed, and that the deadly shot was actually by somebody else. That's a conspiracy theory that will never, ever be proved or disproven."

"And yes, the radio part is actually genuine. And again, I got that from EMI Pathé, which is the EMI thing; I asked them for it and I got it. And the question then is, where do you put it? So I said (laughs), 'It should go somewhere like... here.' And I go, 'Well, so play me the tape,' and they pressed play. And do you know—and we always recorded everything just in case—that was the first time, it was pure luck. I went, 'There' and it fit totally in with everything. And I bet you if I had to do that again, I couldn't have done it (laughs)."

As the three historic gunshots in "Dallas 1 PM" ring out, Saxon perform a sympathetic and respectful musical backtrack to the effect. Here is where we hear the chilling reportage of the shooting but also gorgeous mellow passages as well as mournful, bluesy soloing. A single stroke snare roll takes us into a more uptempo but still rich and moving passage before we're snapped back into the reality of the situation with the arresting verse configuration from earlier.

Says Graham, "'Dallas 1 PM,' I would never have written that without Pete Gill just warming up on drums, playing the beat (sings the beat). I just put me guitar in and put a riff over his... I wanted it the other way around. And then Steve walked in and started playing the bass—boom, boom, boom—and we had the beginnings of the song. And then the others came and then the arrangement was done. And it was very much... that's why it worked so well, because it was a great collective. We all did little bits. All those bits made the song."

"So yes, I remember the moment that Pete Gill laid that beat down and Steve started thumping on the E string, and it inspired me to write a great riff and that's what happened with 'Dallas 1 PM.' And so when we were recording it, we were very fresh with it, and I can remember doing it with the screens around, and Pete Gill was just laughing, with his headphones on, because we were having so much fun and it was sounding great—it was just a great time."

"In fact, as with *Wheels of Steel*, Pete Gill said that on a couple of the sessions on *Strong Arm*, he felt the presence of Keith Moon. Pete is not one to say things—he doesn't suffer fools and he's not a liar and is very straight. In fact, talking straight maybe got him into trouble sometimes. And he felt the presence of what he thought was Keith Moon, when the lights were down and we were recording backing tracks, which is quite awesome. It was an old church, for a start, the Who studio, so it's quite eerie. And it even had the pulpit still in there, and so it was an excellent place to record metal music (laughs). We were recording right where the pulpit was and everything. They left certain architectural features in there."

Another reason the song worked so well was Biff's authentic interest in the subject. He recalls hearing about it when he was 12, seeing the TV coverage and then learning about it subsequently in school. He was reminded of the enormity of the event again when Saxon toured the US for the first time. He then watched some documentaries on it and read a couple books before putting pen to paper, coming up with a lyric that is in synch with the band's overall aesthetic: economic, to the point and hard-hitting. As he told Steve Gett, "Some people may have thought it was a strange subject for a British band to write about, but it was an event that affected people all around the world, not just Americans."

For the US release of the album, the packaging was reduced from its UK gatefold status to a regular sleeve, with the cover additionally going from white to black. As well the track listing was shuffled, with "Dallas 1 PM" serving as first track on side one. With respect to the altering of the cover art, Pete explains that, "We thought, in the UK, that if we had a white background, it would really stand out in the record racks. And that is why, by the way, Saxon is always at the top, because when you flip through the records, that's the only thing you see. Okay, so we thought that would happen. To be honest with you, we felt it was a huge error. We later realized that white had this kind of idea of being nice and pure (laughs). I think we actually suggested to America that they go black. I think we suggested it. I really don't remember the track order being different. I've got an American album upstairs somewhere, but I haven't looked at it for 40 years, actually."

Also, says Graham, "*Strong Arm* was remixed for America. Because what happened is, because *Wheels of Steel* had done so well, and Pete Hinton had been involved, the record company deemed that Pete Hinton should be involved. And I think Pete Hinton got delusions of grandeur, and started sitting behind desks. And we were still a bit naïve and thought, well, he was right on *Wheels of Steel*, he must be right on this."

Expanding on an earlier point, he adds that, "We didn't really understand that—and people don't do that now—if you release a big album like *Wheels of Steel*, like Metallica did on their big album in 1991, they tour for like two or three years on that one album. Def Leppard toured for two or three years on *Pyromania*. What we should've done is tour on *Wheels of Steel* for a couple of years and not rush back into another album. I think that's why it was a bit scrappy. We had the songs, but it was put together six months after the release of *Wheels of Steel*. Hindsight is a wonderful thing, but I think that was a mistake. And we weren't strong enough then as individual band members to say that's a bit wrong; we should take our time. We were guided by people who were doing things, and you don't really think they could be wrong at that stage."

The 2006 reissue of the album includes the live in the studio performance of five of the album tracks, April 25th, 1982, recorded at the BBC. The 2009 reissue includes four of these along with 2009 Abbey Road remixes of "20,000 Ft" and "Heavy Metal Thunder." There's also an alternate version of "To Hell and Back Again" plus an early version of "Sixth Form Girls" called "Mandy."

Wrote Bob Edmands, reviewing the album for Sounds (all important for metal pre-Kerrang!), "Saxon are often confused with Samson, a group whose drummer wears a rapist's mask and sits in a cage on stage. This is quite unfair. Saxon are much more crass. For starters, of course, there's the album title's implicit approval of police strong-arm tactics. Then there's the little matter of a picture inside the gatefold sleeve that has the boys posing in front of Nazi uniforms. Also, there's the name of the band's fan club: the 'Saxon Militia Guard.' Such nastiness carries over to the music. Titles like 'Heavy Metal Thunder' and 'To Hell and Back Again' are familiar enough in the metal morass, but Saxon also offer 'Sixth Form Girls' as a measure of their sexual sophistication and 'Dallas 1 PM' (about John Kennedy's assassination) as a guide to the depths of their political insights. The album's only virtue is that the band play fast throughout and finish their songs more quickly than heavy metal groups used to in the early '70s. However, this is small consolation as you just get more tracks per album."

All told, Edmands' views are a bit unfair given the embrace of metal taking place across England at the time. In other words, he comes off as uncommonly unreceptive, someone who doesn't like metal. Still, on a deeper level, it's possible he cares too much, or understands what's happening all too well: *Strong Arm of the Law* is at best no improvement on *Wheels of Steel*, and at worst, not as good as a half dozen other NWOBHM records that had come across his desk. In other words, he kind of gets it right. With very little impatience needed, it's not hard to dismiss the new Saxon record.

The happier part of the story is that the band didn't miss a beat, leaping from one good tour to another.

As Graham recaps, "Our first tour of America was really fantastic because we landed and went straight on the Rush tour. We did all the east coast with Rush and they were playing stuff from *Moving Pictures* before it came out, so we knew all them songs before the album came out. And then from Rush we went straight on to the *Back in Black* tour and did a bunch of shows with AC/DC. At this point they were still doing theatres like the Boston Orpheum. *Back in Black* hadn't come to be the mega album that it turned out to be although it was catapulting itself up there. And then from that we jumped straight onto the Black and Blue tour which was Black Sabbath and Blue Öyster Cult when Sabbath had Ronnie James Dio, a great lineup playing some great music. I know Ozzy was saying things like 'I don't want to see Sabbath without me' and that, but they were playing great music."

Saxon's self-titled debut. First NWOBHM album ever?

Full page UK music weekly ad for Wheels of Steel.

Biff wants you. Germany, November 11, 1981. © Wolfgang Gürster.

Steve and Biff in Germany, 1981. Biff still wants you. © Wolfgang Gürster.

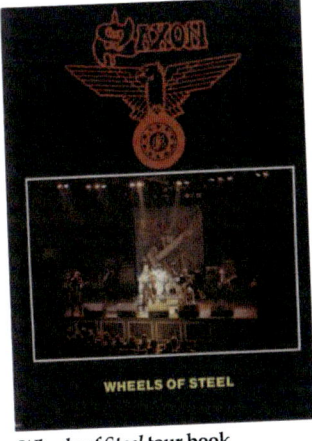

Wheels of Steel *tour book*

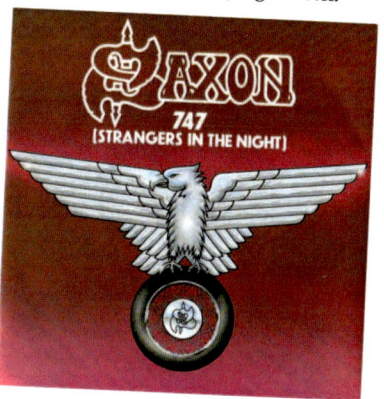

UK picture sleeve for 1980's "747 (Strangers in the Night)." Carrere generally kept the 7" sleeves as simple and straight-forward as the album covers.

Martin Popoff · Denim and Leather: Saxon's First Ten Years | 85

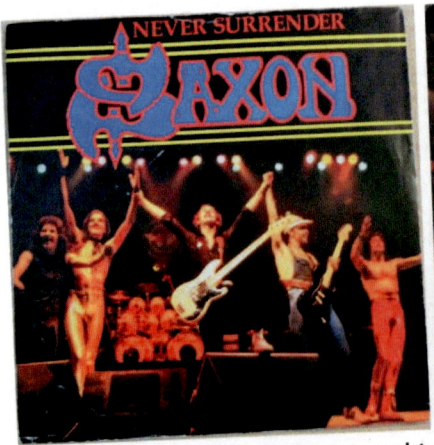

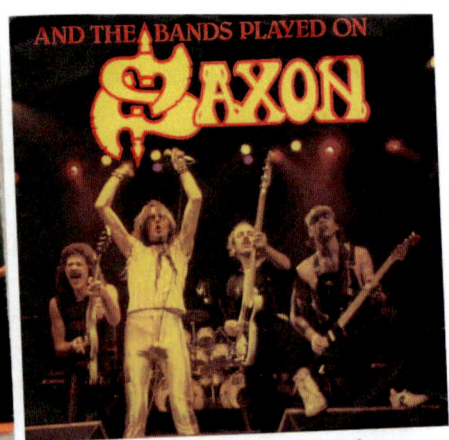

Save a few quid where you can: Carrere use pictures from the same show for these two advance hit singles slated for *Denim and Leather*.

German issue picture sleeve for "Wheels of Steel." Note the use of the iconic band photo from the back cover of the album.

Picture sleeve issue of "Princess of the Night."

Biff and Nigel at Open Air München, May 30, 1982. © Wolfgang Gürster.

First ever Oliver Dawson Saxon concert? Open Air München, May 30, 1982. © Wolfgang Gürster.

More wilderness shots from Munich, Germany. © Wolfgang Gürster.

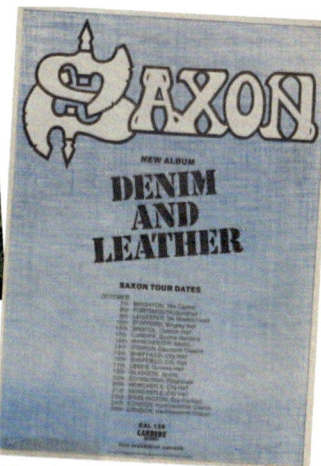

Splurging for a second colour in Sounds.

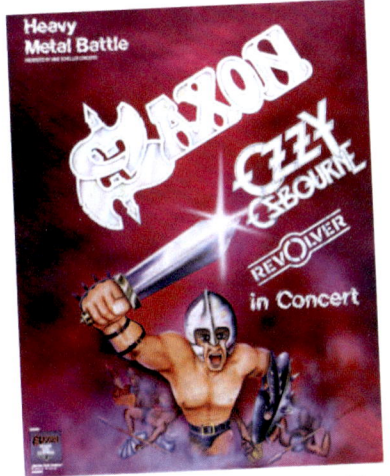

1981 tour poster with Ozzy as support act. Courtesy of Jacques van Gool and Backstage Auctions.

Biff in motion, Toronto. © Martin Popoff.

Notes the Barnsley biker shop shirt. © Wolfgang Gürster.

Monsters of Rock, Zeppelinfeld, Nuremberg, Germany, September 4, 1983 from the *Power & the Glory* tour. © Wolfgang Gürster.

Graham Oliver, circa 1982, sporting what is kind of a good look for him. © Wolfgang Gürster.

Pictures sleeve for "Nightmare" from *Power & the Glory*.

Steve, Biff, Paul, in Toronto. © Martin Popoff.

Biff, bullet belt and Paul, rocking out at Maple Leaf Gardens in Toronto on the *Crusader* tour. © Martin Popoff.

Cassette version of *Power & the Glory*.

Graham, Toronto. © Martin Popoff.

88 | Denim and Leather: Saxon's First Ten Years

Martin Popoff

Chapter 5

Denim and Leather
"A bit more experienced, a bit less poor"

If Saxon thought they could coast a bit after putting out two albums in one year they were frantically mistaken. Shot like a rocket on historic tour after historic tour, they were soon asked to play the UK singles game, common in punk, common in the glam of the early '70s and somewhat common in the NWOBHM, most notably through Motörhead and Maiden.

And so with the band's fourth album not due until late in the year, April of '81, Saxon issue their metal-anthemic "And the Bands Played On"/"Hungry Years"/"Heavy Metal Thunder" extended single.

As Steve Dawson told Rhino, "We got something like a three-day slot where we were going from one tour to another, and the record company said, 'We want another single like "747." Can you write one in three days?' (laughs). So we said, 'We'll give it a go!' So we went into Basing Street Studios and we cut two tracks. One was 'And the Bands Played On' and the other was 'Never Surrender.' We did 'em both in three days. Wrote them and recorded them. When you think about it, the Beatles would write an album and record it in an afternoon, wouldn't they? So, really, if you've got a good unit and everybody's being creative, it's easy to write a tune. It's luck if it's successful. And they both were."

Beginning in the spring and into the summer of '81, Saxon worked at Aquarius Studios in Geneva, Switzerland and Polar Studios, Stockholm, Sweden on tracks to be used on their forthcoming fourth album. The basic tracks were done in Geneva (Biff says the band stayed in a crap hotel while Nigel Thomas, manager and now "producer," stayed at the Hilton), with Abba's Polar Studios utilized for Biff's vocals. Additional "vocal" recording had the band capturing back on tape in England, fan club members doing the gang vocal used on the title track.

With the first new song issued in April, "Never Surrender"/"20,000 Ft" followed in July. And then—not that it would impact Saxon particularly, not right away and not later either—August 1st would see the launch of MTV. The music industry was suddenly propelled into the age of video. Not only were the NWOBHMers not particularly photogenic—Saxon less so than most—in their jeans and patched jackets, but most of the bands never made it to American shores, let alone clear across the country to the powerhouse that was Los Angeles in the golden age of the rock video, commencing in 1981 and riding high for the next 20 years.

"The early MTV days were a bit daft, weren't they?" laughs Biff. "A bit silly. I think it really changed the scene. You either went with it or you went against it. That was the thing. You're either 'Fuck 'em, we're going to make it on our own without them bastards' or you went with it. But I don't think we did either of them, actually. We just carried on as we were and made a few videos. A few daft videos with girls in them, that people tend to like. But it did change things because it was so big, wasn't it? So big, so fast. I think a lot of girls got involved with the whole image of things and then you picked up a different audience, really, from MTV."

But then it was time for the boys to take the stage again, doing it their way, the NWOBHM way. October 5th, 1981, Saxon issues their fourth album *Denim and Leather* and announce that they will be touring the UK with a massive 40,000-watt PA and a 30-foot-long eagle-shaped lighting rig buttressed with 150 aircraft landing lights. The band's October tour dates would be supported by Riot, who found their *Fire Down Under* album issued in the UK due to a petition campaign hungry for anything American and metal.

Noted Paul on the noticeable uptick in the fidelity of this new Saxon record versus its predecessors, "We basically were discovering how to amplify, experimenting with getting a little bit crisper in the sound department. In my case, I grew up with single coil pickups, both Gibson and Fender, and I always struggled trying to get the Humbucker to sound as gritty as that. There was a lot of experimenting with speaker combinations and amp combinations."

Notably absent would be Pete Hinton, who says, "Don't forget, I discovered the band and nurtured them and produced them, but I was very… I've always said that I think producers should only do a couple of albums. I think it becomes wrong to carry on and carry on and carry on. And that they should try something new. *Denim and Leather* was an incredibly successful album. But yeah, don't forget, I was still with the record company. So I'm still working on various things. I was still promoting them, sending them out to journalists, packing them around to radio shows and all that stuff. But no, that was an incredibly successful album. There are some incredible tracks on there. I mean, I wish I could've produced 'Never Surrender' (laughs)."

"That album, we were getting a bit more experienced, a bit less poor," laughs Biff. "We made it in Geneva and we mixed it in Abba's studio in Sweden. So there was a little bit of calming down. Our management was calming down and decided that we weren't one-hit wonders (laughs). They decided to spend a bit more money on us so we spent a bit more time on the album."

"*Denim and Leather* was probably the highest point of those two years, really. I mean, it had a killer track on there. Also it was the first album where we wrote two songs before the album as well. The album was a bit of a mystery, really, because we wrote 'And the Bands Played On' and 'Never Surrender' at least four months before we wrote the album and the record company released them as singles. I remember arguing with the management that we shouldn't put those songs on the album. In those days you had to add the hit singles on the album. But 'Princess of the Night' on that album is classic, a classic metal song."

Says Graham, reversing Biff's sentiment, "I like *Strong Arm* better than *Denim and Leather*, which was done in a bit of a rush. There were things on there that I would've liked to have done again, or to spend more time on. For example, we'd run out of studio time, and I got, I think, half a day to do all my guitar solos. So I felt I was a bit compromised on that, because I like to create something. It takes me time. I like to get in there and create something that means something, not just one you can rattle off."

"Basically, we would get a couple of months to write some songs," reflects Steve, "because you're on a big conveyor belt. You write these songs and you record them and then you go on tour. And then at the end of the tour you might get two weeks holiday, and then it all starts again. Writing-wise, I think basically what really set us apart from the other bands of that time was that we wrote more of what you could call a song, rather than just a riff with lyrics, you know what I mean? If you look at songs like '747' and 'Wheels of Steel,' and maybe 'Bands Played On,' it's more of a tune than just a cliché heavy metal riff, I would think, and with a singer who sings at the top of his voice."

"On the early records, they are credited to Saxon. It was a complete five-man unit that wrote the songs. So how we used to work is it was very rare that we wrote songs with electric guitars. We would go to someone's house and just have the guitars unplugged, and the drummer would just drum on his knees or on the table or something. And when we had the basic thing, we'd go to the rehearsal room and plug in and do it like that."

For an album cover, Saxon smacked the fans square across the face just like their music, offering a band logo that filled up the top third of the cover, the name of the album in white army font commanding a similarly large middle third, and then for what's left, the Saxon eagle from *Wheels of Steel*, as a patch on denim background. Third record in a row with a simple image to go with the band's Motörhead-meets-AC/DC "heads down, meet you at the end" sound.

But once inside, one encounters a new meticulousness, embodied by Paul Quinn's stark, rapid and exacting "Princess of the Night" riff. The music to this new Saxon anthem had in fact been written a year previous, with Biff seeing a snug fit of Quinn's riff with a lyric he had recently conjured. As he told Kerrang! in 1981, "Some time ago we used to park our van at Barry Island in Glamorgan. There's a huge compound there where they keep all the old steam trains that they don't use anymore. They're just left to rot and I suppose that upset us because they really were magnificent machines. Well, you can't beat the days of steam, can you? Anyway, late at night if I couldn't sleep I would look at those ghostly engines and imagine them painted up and back in their glory. It's my romantic side coming out again."

The allure of this song is in its AC/DC "Thunderstruck" structure, as it were. The first verse has Biff singing overtop of Paul's riff and that's it. Second time 'round, it's Paul, Biff and Pete Gill thumping straight fours on the bass drum. After Paul's solo, which is set to an entirely new musical package, sort of speed metal boogie rock, the boys chomp into another verse full band and a full value headbanging payoff is achieved. Just when you think a higher plateau couldn't be hit, we get Graham's solo section, which is executed over the song's verse riff—at first he's atmospheric and textured and then he's peeling off squeals and squalls high up the fretboard. Marbled throughout is the tempering, balancing melody of the chorus, Biff crooning. All told, the band manage the feat of delivering an epic in four minutes, again, through this deft songwriting technique of starting spare and adding tension toward a crescendo of a close.

Speaking of AC/DC, "Never Surrender" is lifted by a chorus that sounds like that band but more uptempo. For a verse riff, the band dig into their traditional rock bag, this one sounding like something that could have fit on the self-titled debut. Biff's lyric adheres to one of Saxon's chief narratives, this idea of coming from nothing but achieving victory through perseverance.

Says Graham on the subtle twin-rhythm harmony of the riff, "I know that Paul has mentioned Wishbone Ash as an influence at times, yeah, and Thin Lizzy. When I listen to 'Don't Believe a Word,' that's where I got 'Never Surrender' from (sings it)—same notes. Yeah. It's not plagiarism; it's just, you hear something, anything that's a great tune, and you want to do something like it, you know?"

Similarities with AC/DC continue with "Out of Control," Paul and Graham playing riffs similar but not exact just like Malcolm and Angus would, or also Keith and Ron, creating that slightly off-kilter guitar weave that almost subconsciously fills spaces. Also like AC/DC, Dobby is playing a one-note bass line over a simple Phil Rudd beat from Pete Gill. There's also a southern rock feel to this one, in both the verse riff and the heroic-sounding chorus. Biff's lyric is deftly written such that it can serve as a tribute to his woman back home or indeed a motorcycle.

"Rough and Ready" is another meat-and-potatoes Saxon track anchored to the band's SOB past. There's boogie and again, southern rock, this one sounding like an uptempo Foghat or Ted Nugent song, albeit with an impressive, busy and non-intuitive bass line from Steve. Lyrically we're back to the theme explored on "Never Surrender," except the extent of the narrator's poverty and street squalor is expressed in more graphic, descriptive and extensive terms. At the end, the message is the same, namely getting through with a British stiff upper lip.

What's becoming apparent across the variety of tracks on the record thus far is that Saxon is not reinventing their wheels of steel. Everything here on the new record is of the same timeless and simple quality found across the previous two albums if not particularly the debut. The big uptick is in the production—the raggedness and dirt and distortion is gone, allowing for concentration on the tight and sober songwriting prowess on display.

Next up is "Play It Loud," arguably one of the record's best—or at least "grandest"—of four epic tracks, in league with "And the Bands Played On," "Princess of the Night" and

"Denim and Leather." Once again, Graham and Paul are into a "tight but loose" guitar weave, point-counterpointing with two simple riffs that combine to create something more interesting, a dialogue. Biff turns in one of his most direct songs of praise on the topic of heavy metal, going so far as to name Deep Purple as the music he was playing whilst catching some rays on the beach, too loud of course, which causes a run-in with the lifeguard. Housed within the concept of playing metal too loud (Byford also upsets the gas-pumper at the truck stop) is the idea of wanting to proselytize to the unwoke, just as any newly minted NWOBHMer worth his salt was always looking to convince nonbelievers that metal is the way. Biff paints that picture nicely here without saying as much.

"And the Bands Played On" is of course Byford's firsthand account of the aforementioned first Monsters of Rock, which took place at Donington Park, August 16th, 1980. Biff talks about the apprehension of what the weather was going to be, that the crowd was 60,000 strong and, apropos of nothing other than a wink to his band, he says we were "strangers in the night." He also mentions a "rainbow shining brightly." Indeed Rainbow were the festival's headliners but they didn't bring their illuminated rainbow, although there were two big rainbows in the scrim graphics to the left and right of the stage, as depicted on the band's first two album covers. One supposes they were shining bright because Saxon played in stark daylight. Intriguingly Biff talks about how originally he had four or five additional verses, about American bands and Judas Priest etc., but he shortened it to make it strictly on topic.

Notes Graham, "I heard a song—you can listen to this and reference it—called 'Whiskey Train,' by Procol Harum. Robin Trower was playing the guitar on that album. And he played this riff called 'Whiskey Train,' in A major. And I heard that song on the radio, at a writing session, having breakfast. And I thought that's a cool riff. Maybe if I sped it up and played it in E major... so I did. Robin Trower's went (sings a riff) and I thought (sings his new riff), so it was a very similar. I know Blackmore has complained that some of his riffs were ripped off. But I didn't steal it; I just heard it and I was inspired to write my own version. And then Paul heard it and thought, 'Yeah, that's great, if I did this guitar over the top (sings it)'... And so all the melody guitar, that's Paul Quinn."

Biff has also indicated that Toto's "Hold the Line," a massive single from that band's 1978 self-titled debut, was an inspiration on the musical structure of "And the Bands Played On." Biff also recalls that the title came from a vintage movie, but he's more than likely thinking of a famous song (and not the title of a movie per se) written in the 1890s called "The Band Played On," which appeared in many films over the decades.

Next, "Midnight Rider" is another ass-kicking metal muncher, yet again, somehow in the spirit of both AC/DC and southern rock, but heavier than both. The rock-solid rhythm bed created by Steve and Pete supports a riff that is almost funky, but sent metal through a distortion level higher than most of the guitars on the rest of the record. At the lyric end, Biff is back to his stories about transportation, only here we've got a "silver eagle" flying the band around on a US tour, augmented by the services of a "midnight rider," in other words, the tour bus. A half dozen US locations are mentioned by name, and Byford fondly recalls Saxon taking America by storm.

Following is Biff's nuclear war tale "Fire in the Sky," which finds Saxon back in speed metal mode, balancing tricky intro riffs against a simple and almost punky verse riff. There's also manic soloing, measured twin leads, double bass drum work from Pete Gill and even a nuclear explosion. Here's where the record's pricey-sounding production pays off in spades. Speed metal, with its note density and tendency toward wall-of-sound drums, requires an elevated level of high fidelity rendering, and "Fire in the Sky" indeed works as one of the band's best technical rockers, taking Saxon further past Motörhead toward Priest, if not the Priest of "Exciter" and "Hell Bent for Leather," at least the Priest of "Steeler" and "Rapid Fire."

Denim and Leather closes with its epic title track, a big and bluesy stripper rock thumper over which Biff describes what it's like to be a New Wave of British Heavy Metal fan.

Explains Byford, "The actual title is from an Alice Cooper song, a song called 'From the Inside,' which is a fabulous album of the same name. And on it there is a lyric that says 'denim and leather.' But obviously there has been denim and leather before (laughs). But it just twinged a chord in my head and when we got a chance to write a song, I was looking to write a song about our audience in the '80s to that point, which is the longest three years anybody has ever spent, basically. From 1980 to 1982, actually two years, we had three albums out in two years. It was crazy really, cramming four years worth of life into that."

"Anyway, that's another story," chuckles Biff. "I wanted to write a song about our fans and 'Denim and Leather' fit the bill, really. We had a big competition in a magazine at the time; I think it was Sounds. That was the forerunner of Kerrang!. Metal got so big in the '80s, they had to have a separate magazine. So we had this competition and 7000 or 8000 people wrote in. I can't remember what the question was, probably something dumb like, 'What was my name?' Anyway, the winners got to come to the studio to record the track with us. So the singing on the end of the original 'Denim and Leather' is actually fans in the studio, about 30 or 40 of them."

Adds Graham, "Again, all the simple riffs are mine, and the musical bits are Paul Quinn's. 'Denim and Leather,' I wrote the riff, which is the easiest riff in the world. And then Paul wrote the arpeggios and the chorus. He came to my house and we did that. But we only did guitar riff and then we took those riffs to the band. Nobody ever did complete songs."

Influential taste-maker for Sounds Geoff Barton wasn't entirely convinced that the new album was a triumph, writing, "'Denim and Leather' is the high point of this slightly erratic, surprisingly melodic and generally rather disappointing latest album from the BTFB (Big Teasers from Barnsley, as if you didn't know by now!). It is a good LP, but the trouble is that the quality of Saxon material will always have to live up to *Wheels of Steel*'s second album standards. And that's not always possible. *Wheels of Steel* was a magical combination of superb songs, devastating production and insatiable hunger for success. It catapulted Saxon to stardom, and it was a one-off, spectacular burst of never-to-be-repeated greatness."

"In their heart of hearts, I reckon Saxon know this for a fact," continues Barton. "And being the band they are, they're unwilling to rest on past glories and just offer the listener a heap of 'Machine Gun' retreads. No, after treading water with *Strong Arm of the Law*, they're now swimming against the tide and using a brand-new stroke, conscious of the necessity to stay fresh, keep options open and above all mature. *Denim and Leather* is the ambitious but sadly not entirely successful end result. This is an entertaining but ultimately unfulfilling album. It's brave of Saxon to try for a subtle shift in style, but the end result just isn't special or satisfying enough. Indeed, I'd feel particularly hard done by if I'd bought both the 'Never Surrender' and the 'And the Bands Played On' singles and had then forked out hard cash for this collection. The new songs are memorable and tuneful, but the adrenaline rush and intensity of old is sadly lacking. 'Don't start to panic; it won't do you no good,' sings Biff. I'm not panicking, but I am, I'll admit, feeling a little bit concerned."

Backing up what the band had been saying about their effusive homeland success, *Denim and Leather* rose to No.9 on the UK charts and went gold in that territory for sales of over 100,000, matching the certification level of *Strong Arm of the Law*, with *Wheels of Steel* now sitting at platinum, which in Britain means that you've moved an impressive 300,000 copies. At the singles end, "And the Bands Played On" hit No.12, "Never Surrender" No.18 and "Princess of the Night," No.57.

Indeed, as Biff alluded to, Saxon had packed a lot of living into two or three years and the cracks were beginning to show, with longtime drummer Pete Gill about to exit stage left. "I injured my finger really badly whilst playing," explains Gill. "I had to have six weeks off for physiotherapy. And when I was fit to come back, the band said they didn't want me to come back. I was devastated. I had joined what was then a local band, gave my full input and co-wrote all the songs. It later transpired that Byford got together with another person and got rid of me and sacked the present management and then later sacked Oliver and Dawson. Absolutely disgraceful."

Chapter 6

The Eagles Has Landed
"I'd bought tickets to see them!"

On June 27th, 1981, Saxon doppel-headbangers Motörhead celebrated a manic, speed-fueled few years at the top of the nascent British metal industry with a live album called *No Sleep 'til Hammersmith*. This followed four studio albums made in quick succession, one dated and unsure, the other three essentially of a suite.

Less than a year later, Saxon issued their own well-received and well-timed single-record live album. *The Eagles Has Landed* also followed four studio albums made in quick succession, one dated and unsure, the others essentially of a suite.

Motörhead's live show was all about the lighting rig shaped like a fighter plane, and Saxon now had a rig shaped like the eagle from their album covers, including the new one. It was said to be 30-foot across, shook by 40,000 watts of power, the biggest PA ever built in the UK for indoor use, all lit by an array of 150 aircraft landing lights. The key UK stand would take place from October 7th through the 25th, 1981, dates that would constitute the homeland leg of the *Denim and Leather* tour, a jaunt that would bleed into the idea of *The Eagle Has Landed*.

"Motörhead's bomber was cool," Biff told me in 2015. "It was just a mangle of bits, really, the bomber. It's not like our eagle, which is actually a fully assembled eagle. I think the bomber is more of a… you know, they bolt it together at the gig. So I think it's a bit more sensible than ours (laughs). The eagle came from *Wheels of Steel*, the album cover, and I suppose those images stay with people because they're such huge live effects. They're legendary and people want to see them. We didn't use ours every tour, so when we brought it out, it was something special. Their live album after that tour was *No Sleep 'til Hammersmith*, and our live album was off of the *Denim and Leather* tour, so there are definitely parallels between Motörhead and Saxon. And the boys in the band, whether it be the old boys in the band or the new boys in the band, they just feel that connection. We're both bands that haven't exactly been the press darlings (laughs). There have been times when we've been ignored or left for dead, written off, and we've come back stronger."

"I'll tell you a secret," confided Biff to Dave Lewis, after the Portsmouth gig on October 8th back in '81 "We aren't actually as loud on this tour as on the last one. The PA is better and clearer, but the loudness thing… it's just a bit of a laugh, isn't it? I think the most we can go up to is 55,000 watts, but if we'd turned it up to that, it would've been unbearable in there tonight. I'm a lot more deaf now than I was when we first started, but it doesn't really worry me. Actually, we put a hold on the volume now. We won't be getting any louder. What's the point? You can get so loud you put people off coming along to see you."

And it had cost a lot to operate. Added Steve, "Nobody has really spent any money apart from fairly humble things like stereos and videos. I think everybody is saving up to buy a nice house, but we've invested that much money in the stage show and things, and it takes that long for money to come through the system that we haven't got that much to spend. I want a Cadillac. That's my first priority: a 1959 pink Cadillac… and a house."

Offered Biff, "I bought the best bike you can get in this country, actually. It's an 1100cc Honda Goldwing. It's like the Rolls-Royce of bikes. I think we will all have quite substantial houses soon. That's what we're working towards. But what you've got to remember is that we're actually doing what we've always wanted to do. So whatever that brings us apart from that is a bonus. I mean, if I were a dustman, which I used to be, and you asked me what I wanted to be, I would say a rock star. And here I am."

Dawson agreed: "When I was a kid of about 12, this mate of mine had this group, but all they had was tennis rackets with elastic bands. But the first time I picked up that racket I wanted to be like the Beatles or Rolling Stones. And now I'm living what I've always wanted to be and it's just great. We get on stage because we love being up there and we want everyone else who comes along from his nine-to-five job or from the dole or from school or whatever, and for that one-and-a-half hours we're on stage, they can like, be with us like in a big gang or like at football, or like anything you do to get away from the mundane side of your life. That's what we all care about. Not how many birds we can pull or how much we can get pissed-up or anything. Obviously, we do get birds and have a drink sometimes and do everything that other rock bands do, but it's not our top priority."

The big change at this juncture however, beyond the firepower and the attainable dreams, is that Saxon had a new drummer, usually not a big deal in terms of band news, but in this case transformative. Nigel Glocker would put an uncommon percussive stamp on the live record but more so on the band's next two studio albums, both career defining in different ways, but both with drumming you remember.

"Well, he did join Motörhead for a while," Biff told MetalRules vaguely, asked about the departure of Pete Gill. "I really don't know what the problem with Pete was. He really had a problem with his hand and Nigel joined the band. It wasn't actually my decision. It was just a general decision to keep Nigel because it went really well with him."

In reality, it seemed as if Gill had come down with something akin to carpal tunnel system. Both hands had been going numb and he had been desperately doing all manner of exercise to minimize the situation. On the verge of tour dates to support the hugely successful *Denim and Leather* album, he announced that he had to bow out and that the band should get a replacement. It was really what happened after, the decision to keep Nigel, that soured relations. Biff says that the guys just never heard from Pete again, joking that maybe he's still officially in the band, which is the way, incidentally, that Judas Priest talk about Les Binks! In truth though there was more: Saxon already had to get in a replacement, Mark Pinder, for the writing sessions that produced the two early singles, after which Gill quickly returned, drumming on all the recordings.

"I knew one half of their management team," explains Glockler, on his joining forces with Saxon. "I'd been in a band with him during the late '70s. He made the first move and rang me up. I think they had heard my playing on a hit single I had with the band I was with, so they were up for me coming along. I had a blast with them one Sunday evening to see if it would work, as I'd offered to stand in for a couple of weeks, as I had recording commitments with Toyah, the band I was in. We got together in Brighton on Monday, and the first gig was on that Wednesday and I'd bought tickets to see them! It's actually two days that I had to learn it all, but I did have a notebook for guidance for a couple of weeks after that. I'd written stuff down, like which guitarist starts what song, etc."

"We got him in for the *Eagle Has Landed* tour, which is what it became to be called later," recalls Paul. "I don't know what we called the tour, but Pete Gill injured his hand, and Nigel was in a band with half of our management team, David Poxon, called Krakatoa. And not only was he a fan, but among some of the other people we had to audition, he was the only one who could handle the gig. Others were like pretending that they could play their instruments (laughs), and he could actually do it, even though he had been in what amounts to a popular punk band at the time, which was Toyah. And he'd got that kind of English shuffle style already by then. The difference between him and Pete Gill was that Pete Gill was more John Bonham, and Nigel was towards Neil Peart and Ian Paice, which fit in great with our style as well, because we were a punky version of most of these bands (laughs)."

The dynamic of Nigel's hiring was that it was understood that he was a stand-in until Pete came back. But halfway through the tour dates it had been decided that Nigel would stay, despite the flak the band was taking in the press for hiring a drummer from a post-punk band, not a true punter, as it were.

Nigel Glocker was born in East Sussex on January 24th, 1953, making him 28 when he joined Saxon, although he'd only been a part of the industry for really a year.

"I started playing drums when I was seven or eight," explained Glockler, in conversation with Dmitry Epstein. "Before that I was always digging out tins, metal plates, anything that made a noise basically, and, sitting on the floor with this stuff around me and a pair of my mother's knitting needles, would proceed to make one hell of a noise! Then a friend of the family noticed how I was always tapping my knees to records and persuaded my dad to get me a snare drum and a cymbal. I guess, it went on from there, and a bass drum, a rack tom and a hi-hat stand followed."

"However I then started messing around on my older brother's guitar but found myself always trying to play the bass guitar lines, so that was something I got into next. I've got slightly small hands for normal guitar—I found it hard to really stretch the fingers to reach some of these ridiculously hard chords. Hence my nickname The Rex, as in T. Rex because of small hands. But the neck on a bass guitar is that much thinner, unless it's a five- or six-string. So I played that for a couple of years, but then, at school, I had a go on a full drum kit and that made my mind up. We got a school band together playing covers and it went on from there, meeting other local musicians, forming bands etc., the usual stuff."

Asked by Epstein about his drum idols, Nigel says, "Bill Ward was one of the first—I'd never seen anyone hit a kit so hard! I was a big Sabbath fan—still am; I thought the stuff he did was amazing. Also, of course, John Bonham, and another fave was Carmine Appice when he was with Vanilla Fudge. Then I got into an Italian band called PFM—their drummer, Franz Di Cioccio, was unbelievable, and he was using a big kit with a full range of toms. I'd never seen this before. I had to have a similar kit. This is where I discovered the melodic side of drumming. I used to sit on my kit in my bedroom at my parents' house, wear headphones and play along for hours to PFM albums, with everything in the kitchen downstairs flying out of cupboards. My mum and dad were great for putting up with it!"

"Phil Ehart from Kansas was another great fave. Then I got into Neil Peart, Simon Phillips, Phil Collins, Terry Bozzio et al, all drummers that combine rhythm and melody. For pure groove in rock music though, I don't think you can beat Phil Rudd of AC/DC—amazing! There are some superb players out there, in all forms of music. I almost forgot Chester Thompson, Alex Van Halen and Bill Bruford. The list goes on and on. Obviously, their main function is rhythm and groove but I also got into drummers that do so much more."

Speaking with Jeb Wright, Glocker also cited "fusion-type players like Billy Cobham and Lenny White. Mel Pritchard from Barclay James Harvest and Barrie Wilson from Procol Harum were two players I loved. I'd love to be the second drummer in Genesis—that would be fun! To play alongside Phil Collins would be special. I've been a huge Kansas fan since their first album. I think every member has been a brilliant musician, and as for Steve Walsh's voice, wow! It's hard to explain about Phil's drumming; I mean, I know what I love about it, but it's hard to put into words. He really has a unique style. Suffice to say there were many hours put into playing along with Kansas tracks."

And then, as Nigel explains, he was as much taken by the NWOBHM as the Saxon guys were. "Yeah, it was like a breath of fresh air in the middle of all the punk/new wave stuff. I remember seeing the first Saxon album in my local record store. I got *Wheels of Steel*, *Strong Arm* and *Denim*. I had the first Angel Witch album plus a couple by the Tygers of Pang Tang. It was all good stuff, but like any new musical event, all the record companies were falling over themselves to get in on the act so inevitably there were a lot of bands signed who didn't break through and got forgotten, gems to be discovered maybe? I was playing in other bands when the NWOBHM exploded onto the scene, originally."

On March 27th, 1982, just a month before *The Eagle Has Landed* hit the shops, Saxon found themselves halfway around the world in Los Angeles, headlining a show at the Whisky a Go Go. Support on the night was Metallica, playing their second show ever. Also at that gig, says Paul, "We met up again with Ozzy Osbourne, who'd just lost Randy and was in a complete state. We tried to cheer him up with champagne, which probably wasn't a good idea. But we wanted to see if we could cheer him up. Mötley Crüe dropped by. We didn't actually meet Metallica at that time. They opened on our show but we were not around when they played. We used to sound check them and then go to eat at the hotel."

Adds Nigel, "I remember Ozzy coming backstage in the dressing room; he was really upset because it was a few weeks after Randy had been killed. And then our tour manager said, 'There's a band at the dressing room door that want to meet you; they're a local LA band and they're starting to do quite well and they call themselves Mötley Crüe.' And so they came in and Ozzy was in and that's how they first met Ozzy and then later went on tour together."

Recalled Lars Ulrich, writing in an internet post, "Supporting Saxon; had great sound this time. Dave (Mustaine) and I played great. Ron (McGovney) and James (Hetfield) so so. Went down pretty good. Had a good time but never met Saxon. For us at the time, this was like winning the lottery. Not only was this our first Hollywood gig, but in the early '80s, Saxon were one of the biggest, most exciting and influential hard rock bands in the UK and Europe. I had actually seen them six months earlier in Brighton on the *Denim and Leather* tour where I even managed to sneak backstage, ha ha. Back then, our set consisted mostly of cover songs and most of those were Diamond Head songs. Funny story: after the first set, this guy on Saxon's crew comes into our dressing room and asks us, in a very matter-of-fact tone, whether we had ever heard of a band from England called Diamond Head."

There were some ruffled feathers for years that Metallica never got to meet the Saxon guys that night, exacerbated by the fact that Metallica had asked if they could use the fan that Biff had on stage to keep him cool, and that the crew said no—of course the band themselves had no knowledge of any of this.

"We did four shows in two days," recollects Biff. "It was a bit of a showcase gig. And I think everybody who was anybody was there, in LA at the time. We had Metallica supporting us on the Friday, two shows, and then we had Ratt supporting us on the Saturday, two shows. But it was a little bit like a Who's Who of... I mean, Ozzy Osbourne and Sharon were there; loads and loads and loads of people were there. We were very well-liked within the younger bands of America. I think us and Maiden and Motörhead were influencing quite a lot of bands from Metallica to Mötley Crüe, to, you know, all of them, really. Lots of the American bands that I see now from that era come up and say, 'Oh yeah, yeah, we loved you guys in the '80s.'"

Graham appreciated Metallica knowing who Saxon were but he felt such accolades were an exception.

"Saxon was always a band like Thin Lizzy in America or Status Quo or Slade—people know our songs but we're always like the underground band bubbling under. We were never at the forefront. Like when I went to see Metallica years later, they dragged me in the dressing room in England at the gig at Sheffield and they're saying, 'Guy, we can't let you leave, you've got to come and play on stage.' I couldn't believe it because we look to California for our inspiration in America. And these guys are thinking we're great. I didn't realize. Lars Ulrich said the photo on the back of *Wheels of Steel* was the most devastating photo he'd ever seen, and to me it's just some photo I clicked backstage at the Marquee. I remember doing it—we sat on the bench having a cigarette or something. So you don't realize these things, People sometimes don't associate songs like 'Princess of the Night' with Saxon. Lots of guys in the audience in America know the song and some of the other songs but they don't put the two together. But in Europe it's a totally different ballgame."

Reflects Biff further on those times, "I mean Maiden were doing the same gigs, you know? Both our record companies were like powering in there and getting a lot of shares. So both bands were doing massive tours supporting bands. Our labels saw a style of music they could work with, a new style, slightly different approach. And both bands were based on great singing, don't forget. Which the American market loves. We spent a lot time there touring, and the legacy still survives; that legacy of the '80s is a powerful, powerful legacy, really. Not just for us, for everybody. But yes, in the States, we toured with Rush, we toured with Molly Hatchet, quite a lot of people actually."

The Eagle Has Landed was issued in May of 1982, serving as an impressive greatest hits package—and indeed on some level, almost all of these songs were hits. Of course that precludes anything from the first album, but the 2006 reissue of the album rectified that situation, offering a rendition of "Frozen Rainbow." What is impressive is that on the reissue the hits kept coming, with the inclusion of "And the Bands Played On" and "Dallas 1 PM," notable omissions from the original vinyl version of the record. The album was supposed to be a double, but in the chaos of editing the two-inch tapes, much of the recorded songs got lost. Biff regrets that the band didn't issue a double, with the press also complaining about the short running time as well as the functional but drab packaging.

All told across the album, the live versions were predictably grittier and more energetic than the studio versions but they were pretty close in execution to the studio works, not half as brutal as *No Sleep 'til Hammersmith*, as it were. Most of the material, in fact, was from the band's stops at the Hammersmith plus Nottingham, with a third show in Sheffield having been recorded as well.

Asked whether the record was a fair representation of the band live, Steve told Rhino, "As far as technical stuff will let you do it, yes. But you're never gonna get a true live sound because if you're in a big room with a giant PA and a massive back line, that can never, ever be reproduced on a record. You can come close, but…when a rock band plays, it's rare, I suppose, that there's never any mistakes. Or Biff might forget words. So it has to be a bit of not-quite-live added after, if you know what I'm trying to say. It's not cheating, it's a live thing, but, you know, if for instance Paul broke his guitar string in the middle of one of his solos, you can't leave it on, so you have to re-do it. But, yeah, it's a good representation of our sound at the time, and it's a good representation of the songs."

Pete Hinton had no doubt in Saxon's live abilities. As we've heard, it was a big part of the reason he had signed the band to Carrere. But he singles Biff out for particular praise.

"Yes, well, the thing about Biff is, when all is said and done, as a stage performer he's second to none. That was what really came on for him when we were in the early days, that we could trust him to connect with the crowds. Now over here, when we were growing up, our parents used to listen to a kind of music that was called music hall. I don't know if America ever had it. This is before Sinatra and before swing and all that. And Biff, I swear, could've been a music hall comedian. He's so funny on stage. He doesn't plan anything—it just comes out of his mouth and he's so funny. Their manager David Poxon said this to me; this is in the early days. He said, 'I can't believe it, Pete. The crowds were actually queuing up at the front of the stage and in an orderly fashion, they took it in turns to go up to the stage and have Biff's hands put on their head.' He said it was like a religious experience for them (laughs)."

Predictably, dependably, Saxon would be back at home touring the new live album, playing about 20 dates between mid-September into the first week of October. But the ultimate celebration of the release of their first live album would take place August 21st with an appearance at the third Donington Monsters of Rock fest, alongside DJ Tommy Vance, Anvil, Uriah Heep, Hawkwind, Gillan and headliner Status Quo.

"That's a great festival to play," muses Nigel. "Monsters of Rock '82 was my first big outdoor show and I was extremely nervous, particularly as our management had decided to leave my tech in the US. I ended up setting my kit up wearing a disguise. We flew to NYC the next day. The audience was amazing, but I was too stressed to really enjoy it (laughs)."

Unfortunately Biff didn't enjoy it either. The band's stage clothes had gone missing so Biff had to wear a black-and-white striped ensemble which he hated. What's more, Status Quo's crew had done everything they could to ruin the band's set and put Biff off his game. They worked on Quo's lighting trusses while Saxon played, with one roadie crashing into the band's guitars and putting them out of tune. The final straw came when Saxon were being pressured to get off the stage, literally through a crew member walking up to Biff and telling him as much. Defiantly Saxon played a couple more numbers, shuffling off in defeat. Byford recalls being backstage in tears over the missed opportunity to really shine at Donington 1982, telling the promoter to fuck off, with the band soon on a plane back to the States to play a gig at the Capitol Theatre the very next night. It's the perfect metaphor to represent the beginning of the band's grand American experiment, an experiment that would find Saxon dying a slow death, living it up to be sure, but squandering the good will they had built up through a string of albums forever to be regarded as heavy metal classics.

Chapter 7

Power & the Glory
"It grabs you by the throat and pulls you in."

No question that as 1982 came to a close, folks had decided that they loved Saxon and they were an exciting proposition within the glory of the New Wave of British Heavy Metal. But after four quick albums of rockscrabble, rudimentary rock somewhere in the vicinity of Whitesnake, Kiss, Motörhead and Vardis stuck in a blender, fans were beginning to grumble that there wasn't much meat on the bones.

The addition of Nigel Glockler to the ranks on drums, and of American Jeff Glixman to the production team, would prove to be the tonic for the troops, Saxon, on March 21st, 1983, unleashing their heaviest and most exciting album to date, a white-hot beacon of heavy metal truth and toothsomeness called *Power & the Glory*.

Years down the line, Biff nonetheless fully understood the magic of the band's position circa the early '80s. "I think when you are younger, and you're writing for your generation, and when you become big, and songs become really popular and you have single hits and you're on TV all the time, there tends to be a certain legend that grows up around those songs. And you know, we think it's brilliant, really (laughs). I mean, to have had songs like that is amazing. You have to think, would 'Wheels of Steel' or '747' be a hit now? You know, probably not. Because the fans aren't there in the millions. But we do love the songs and we do play them all the time. It's a type of music that came out of England, this quite aggressive metal music with melodic structure. And I think it's *that* that people like. Those songs are really sing-along songs, aren't they? And all that '80s period, if you listen to AC/DC or Whitesnake or Iron Maiden or any of those bands, it's a melodic structure."

"I just think it was a movement, really, that four or five bands were involved with," continues Biff, surveying those times. "And those four or five bands are still thought of as the people who brought music back from the '70s really. In the early '70s, it was really big, with Led Zeppelin and stuff, but then it fell off with the punk thing. And we brought it back, really. You know, Van Halen broke it for American music, didn't they? And before Van Halen it was really REO Speedwagon and Journey and things like that. Then there was Mötley Crüe and Metallica. It was a movement really. Judas Priest, Iron Maiden, Motörhead, us, Def Leppard to some extent, and tons and tons and tons of young kids who were too young for the Purple, Led Zeppelin, Sabbath period came back to rock music in the '80s and we were there."

The writing sessions for *Power & the Glory* took place in a portion of a manor house in Battle, on the south coast of England. It had been run as a hotel to help cover the upkeep, but all Biff remembers, besides the medieval décor, was that there were hamsters all over the place.

Saxon needed a rethink by 1983, and nothing helps a rethink for a band more than getting outside of your own country to try fashion together your next move. No question, things were humming along above the surface, but behind the scenes, that band was bleeding money, mostly to their management and label, both of which the guys were starting to realize did not have their best interests at heart.

"It was in Atlanta, Georgia," recalls Biff, asked about the recording of what is thought by many to be Saxon's best record. "It was pretty good actually; we had a great time and it was easy. We had pre-produced the songs here so it wasn't really such a big deal. I don't know what Jeff Glixman had done before. He did Mother's Finest and a few other things. I think he was an engineer actually. And after ours he did the Sabbath album, *Seventh Star*. I think our manager knew him, basically. He was probably cheap (laughs), knowing our management at that time. But we had parties every night. We were well into the scene in Atlanta."

The end result barely sounds like the same band though, against the gritty midrange and compression of the previous records. "I think it's because we sort of got into the sounds," agrees Biff. "We really didn't like the sounds of the first three albums. They weren't really hi-fi, frankly, for us. They were all blood and guts in there. There were no sort of finesse sounds. And don't forget, Jeff Glixman was an American, so you get sort of more of a polished sound. But it does sound good, *Power & the Glory* did."

"And Nigel is a massive part of that album," figures Byford. "When he came into the band it was like we had a fifth member. You see, Pete Gill didn't really have much to do with writing songs. In fact, a lot of the time he didn't even turn up for rehearsals, later on in his career."

And so Nigel was a writer, "straight away," says Biff, even if what one really notices is the tornado of energy he brought to the songs, the fills, even 'the fill,' in a sense, how he helped turn any given Saxon song into a blizzard of shock-socket sound.

"The one big thing for me," muses Nigel, "for that album, it wasn't any particular track. The big thing was, although I had done the live album, it was important to me to put my stamp on things. Because I was aware of how well loved Pete Gill was. So it was a great test for me, sort of a proving ground for me. Not so much for the band, because I was touring with them before we wrote that anyways. But for the fans. I think, well, we don't want it to change in any way because I'm there, because I felt I had to prove myself to the fans."

As for where he was coming from stylistically at this point, Nigel says, "For me, my drumming style, I've never been into heavy rock drummers per se. I was always into the more technical drummers. At the time I was listening to a lot of fusion stuff, like Chick Corea, Phil Collins, and Neil Peart of course—I was a huge Rush fan. People like Cozy Powell didn't influence me at all, so maybe that helped change us a bit. I mean, who knows?"

"As I say, *Power & the Glory* was the first album we did in America," continues Biff. "Our business manager, Nigel Thomas, always wanted us to be spending time in America because he always thought that if you are going to be popular, that was the place to be popular, to be lastingly popular. Because the English music scene was, and still is, very faddy. You can be quite big for a couple of years and then after that you're gone. This goes for pop music as well as rock music. So he wanted to consolidate our success in America. And he basically insisted to the record company that we use an American producer. So we were writing the songs in a place called Battle, which was the site of the Battle of Hastings, 1066. And Jeff Glixman came to see us and we liked what he said and he had some pretty wacky ideas and we went to Atlanta to make it. He was a great guy."

But there's a danger in ascribing too much of the credit for *Power & the Glory* being almost too hot to handle production-wise, to Glixman, who proved himself to be much more behaved when he worked with Kansas and the like. Indeed, all told, *Power & the Glory*, recorded at Axis Sound Studio, is not a very American-sounding album. Oddly, it's almost more NWOBHM than the older stuff, even though there are strange opinions that surface from time to time—from within the band and without—that's it's somehow more "commercial" sounding.

"No, it's funny you should say that," agrees Biff. "I don't think so either. A lot of people in Europe think that is our best-sounding album. And I don't think it sounded too American. I think it sounded a bit Deep Purple-ish. It sounded a bit '70s English, which I suppose can be construed as American. I mean, there are a couple of songs on there that are heavily produced for radio. But generally, 'Power and the Glory' and the other power tracks, they are just quite good solid rock. It was the first album we had where the actual sound was great from a hi-fi quality point of view. All our albums before that were just aggressive, energy, enthusiasm, brilliant hook lines, you know what I mean? (laughs). But *Power & the Glory* was quite special and it was the first time we spent any length of time in America and we had a good time, really."

Asked about the writing of the album, Biff counters, "I'll tell you about how we write albums generally. We still write them today the same. We always start with the guitar riff. Nearly always start with a guitar riff. Or I'll start with the title. It's very rare that I'll write lyrics or melodies before we have a guitar riff. So what we'll do is go write the song without melody or lyrics, just a basic heavy rock song, with nothing on it, again, just guitars, verse, chorus, verse, chorus, middle eight, chorus, solo, key change, out. So we'll work out the entire song musically first, so it has tons of power, yeah?"

"I mean, while we're writing it, I might be singing along, and I might even be playing guitar on it because I write some riffs as well sometimes. But I'll be singing along. And most times the song will speak to me and give me a title. Sometimes I'll write down, say, 'Princess of the Night' in a book. We have a title book with us all the time. But it will say something to me and I'll work the melody out as we're working on it. So that's how songs are created in Saxon and that's how they've always been created. And that's why I write all the melodies myself and all the lyrics myself, and basically the band write the music. In a rock band, the melody is the guitars and the vocal melodies together. So basically, there isn't one thing that sticks out. I'll have a certain idea, like 'Princess of the Night,' and it's an idea I had to write as a song, but the title came first. But most of the time I'll wait 'til the music is done and I'll see what it says to me."

Adds Steve Dawson, "We sound like we sound because that's how we play. We're not brilliant musicians, by any shadow of a doubt, but, in the absence of not being able to be a virtuoso, you invent your own way of writing tunes, and that's what the Saxon sound was."

An impressive exemplar of great songwriting is the opening title track to *Power & The Glory*, although it's not technically the title track, as it subs the "&" for an "and." In any event, it's a barnstormer, a speed metal at comfortable speeds, a gorgeous fast-tracker that recalls the fiery magic of the other blue NWOBHM album of the day, Savage's *Loose n' Lethal*, which similarly benefits from an electricity-drenched production job from the metal gods, as does, come to think of it, but slightly different, a third great blue record from the era, Savatage's debut, *Sirens*. Biff's lyric was written as a protest to Britain's involvement in the Falklands War, a topic that emerged on many a rock song of the day. But he keeps it universal, although there's the twist that the character in the tale is a mercenary, a paid private soldier, a soldier of fortune.

"That's the one that I had the most part in the writing of the song," says Graham. "I even named the song. I took the line from 'The Lord's Prayer.' Because I'd heard somebody say 'power and the glory.' And it just inspired me to write the riff. So I did this riff, and the solo is mine in that, and all the guitar at the end is mine."

As for naming the album after this track? "We nearly always call the album one of the titles of one of the songs," says Biff. "And there really wasn't a title on that album that was as good as 'Power and the Glory.' But I don't particularly like the album cover to tell you the truth. I think it's just a photograph of a guy who did a picture of a head and a bloody glove." Indeed there's a pointlessness to the narrative of the cover image, but at least the record had a narrative, even if what we got was a futuristic version of the first album cover. Dominating this hasty idea however was the electrifying cover text in glowing pinks, yellows and blues—pretty cool.

"Power and the Glory" would be issued as a single in April of '83, a month after the wider album's issuance. Backed with "See the Light Shining" (a reach-back to glory days), it's one of two singles from the album, the second being "Nightmare"/"Midas Touch," launched in July of '83. There'd be a proper video for "Power and the Glory," featuring live footage interspersed with a storyline which had the band storming a castle, weapons drawn. It's not as embarrassing as it sounds, except for the fact that the guys are dressed in jumpsuits of rather cheery colours.

Next up is "Redline," about the heaviest shuffle you'll hear in your life. And here's the rub: even an ordinary riff on this record is elevated through an insane level of chemistry, performance and production fire. And it all sits heavy on a bed of massive drums.

"That's one of my riffs," notes Graham. "I was inspired to do 'Redline' from the old Montrose album, you know, that kind of riffing album. I was a kid when that came out and it was a really influential album for a lot of rock musicians in England, the first Montrose album" (indeed the "Redline" riff is very similar to the central premise of that record's "I Don't Want It").

"I'll tell you what Jeff did," says Biff, specifically on the tones at hand, so blistering on this track. "He built a big box about 15 ft. square and put the guitar cabinets in it and put the microphones in there and that's how he intended to get his guitars sounds. We had great fun actually, because he plays keyboards, Jeff. And he had a Hammond organ in there. Anytime we went into a jam, he'd dash through the door and start playing the Hammond. It was quite good fun actually. He was a nice guy. I think he might be somewhere there in the distance, on 'Nightmare' perhaps."

Adds Quinn, "The producer Glixman was heavily into Purple and he'd fire his Hammond up at any opportunity. A lot of the takes were preceded by that. He and me, we'd have a go at. It's a pity we didn't record them actually. But he'd be busy playing Hammond and I'd be sitting down with a 24-track. There were whispers that people were going to turn us into AOR monsters if they weren't careful, but in the case of Jeff Glixman, he'd done heavy bands before and we weren't too worried about that; he'd done people like Gary Moore, R.I.P. We were experimenting with our sound maybe a little too much around that album and maybe *Crusader*."

At the lyric end of "Redline," Biff is asking some gal for a ride on his fast car. By this point Byford had already splurged on himself, getting a black Porsche 928 with his first royalty check ever, which was £4000. But the ironic thing is that during the making of *Power & the Glory* was when he met his second wife Christine, who used to pick Biff up in her own Porsche 911 and whisk him away, to the point where he feels like he wasn't a big part of the making of the record, showing up to do his vocals and little else.

"Warrior"—riff courtesy of Paul, says Graham—maintains the metal mayhem of the album, this one being another brisk pure metal rocker like the title track. Its chorus is about as heavy as the band had ever furiously played up until this point, and when that chorus collapses back into the groove of the verse, well, it's Nigel and his percussion pocket that is the marvel at hand.

"Nigel Glockler," laughs partner in rhythm section Dawson. "Well, playing with Pete was like playing with... you didn't know what was coming next, like a Keith Moon-type. Just a powerhouse drummer like John Bonham. You've only got to listen to some of the things that Pete did, like say on 'Suzie Hold On,' with the middle drum fill. I had to keep my eye on Pete all the time. Pete drove the band along, if you know what I mean. It was as though he was separate from the band and he drove us along. I think that's what gave us a lot of the sound of the original band. When Nigel Glockler came along, he was a different type of drummer, and brilliant drummer, and a perfect timekeeper. But a part... not really a driver of the band. And when I played with Pete Gill, I had to keep my eye on him all the time; if we were coming to a stop or a stab, I had to watch it. But with Nigel Glockler, I knew what we were going to do all the time, more or less, once we played together for a while.

Just two totally different drummers—both great, and both enjoyable to be in a rhythm section with."

As for his memory of Glixman and his methods, so much a part of the success of the record... "Well, what Jeff did, first of all, he built all these little cabins if you like, like a little garden shed. And he put all the guitar speakers and the bass speakers inside these cabinets, so the whole room was just dedicated to the drum kit. Just for mic'ing it up. You couldn't hear the guitars. You could hear them through the headphones, but you couldn't hear them in the room. Unlike today, it was done on tape, on 24-track tape, so doing overdubs and things was more... editing, should I say, was a lot more difficult than it is now with ProTools. So it meant that the band had to play, and play tight. And he just used a technique of closed mic'ing of the drum kit, and then another set of mics so many feet away, and then another set so many... you know, at the edges of the room. Because Axis Studios is a really massive studio. Mostly probably live recording. And so he had a mixture of three different layers of mics, to get the sound, because obviously then, sampling was in its infancy."

Clarifying further, Steve explains that, "You would have like three sheds (laughs), inside this room, and then just the drum kit in the middle. And we just played around Nigel, egging him on, getting him to put a good performance in, and then we would listen in to our instruments on the headphones. I mean, I think the real secret to it was Jeff Glixman's enthusiasm. He was so enthusiastic about getting the performance out of the band and making it a good time—that's the secret."

"I liked working with Jeff, nice guy, great guy," notes Nigel, providing his recollection of the recording environment. "I liked him because he used to work with Kansas, which at the time was one of my favourite bands. In fact at the studio, Steve Walsh dropped in, which made my day. I think that was after he had actually left Kansas. He was doing that Streets thing, I think. But it was nice to meet him, because he's always been one of my favourite singers. The atmosphere in the studio was great.

We found a great Indian restaurant in Atlanta, which is extremely important to us (laughs). Run by a couple guys from Birmingham, in England. So that was great. No, the atmosphere was great, the band was cooking. And I think the album, when you put it on, I think the sound jumps out at you. It really does—it grabs you by the throat and pulls you in, you know? I think it's great. 'Watching the Sky,' I liked very much, and 'Warrior'—those are probably a couple of my favourite there."

"It was the first album I ever recorded out of the UK," continues Nigel. "And it was an important one for me, as it was my first Saxon studio album. I felt I had something to prove. I was so happy when the album reviews came out, too. We'd all worked so hard on the writing and recording. I loved Jeff's drum sound too and the studio was excellent. Actually, the production as a whole really worked, as the album had some balls."

"But we chose Glixman purely for the people that he had worked with," continues Nigel. "We knew the Kansas stuff, and he had done Gary Moore by then, I think. When choosing a producer, we tried... I'm not going to mention any names, but we had a couple of other people in, big producers, because we were getting producers in while we were on the road. One of them came in and said, 'Well yeah, if you're not using the second bass drum, then we might not put a mic on it.' And I'm like, 'Yeah, well, I might suddenly do a fill that I want to use the other kick drum. So you've got to give me that option.' Another one said, 'Well, if you don't use all the toms on all the songs, then I'll take the mics off that.' But hell, I make this stuff up as I'm going along. You know, give me some spark, please. So that was out, no."

Framing *Power & The Glory* and explaining a bit more about this strange wooden shed situation, Paul Quinn figures, "It was our first American recording which, our management at the time were convinced that we would take off big time in America if we could kind of tailor it slightly sound-wise, rather than writing. So that was the idea behind that. We found Jeff Glixman because he knew a friend of ours, Gary Moore, and did his album, the late

Gary. Jeff and his keyboards... he was Jon Lord for our jams. He's good at making you relax, before you play a take. If you're having that much fun... Jeff took us out in his Porsche and frightened the shit out of us. Because he loves his speed, that boy. You know, those Porsches can corner on like one wheel I think, (laughs)."

"That was the first time we built the big wooden cage for the Marshalls," continues Quinn, "and knocking those together was funny. We started recording in the control room on that album, which was quite a departure for a guitar player, because you've got to monitor really loudly, and make sure the EQ isn't all in the tweeters. Otherwise the guitar just goes nutty. It doesn't sound... It comes back through the pickups and you can't control the sustain. But the speakers in particular were in the wooden cages, with the mics, and the amps were outside them, which was wood. Wood sounds nicer. Not as fair on the environment, but you know. The boxes were acting as an isolation booth for Nigel, and I think the bass rig was in a different room altogether, to stop the vibrations hitting the drum kit. And he had most of the studio itself, the big room, all to himself."

As for other extracurriculars, "We went to see quite a few bands from there," says Paul. "We went to see Priest, and K.K. came down when we had started, when we weren't anywhere near finished. We also went to see Johnny Winter, who apparently, he's cleaned up again. He was saying then that he was lucky to get through his inception days, because everybody else was dropping like flies from the drugs and the booze (Johnny has since died, in 2014)."

Closing side one of the original vinyl was the only type of dialed-back track one could picture on a record this scorched by electricity. "Nightmare" is the album's Magnum-esque pomp rocker as it were, even if it's played with drunken intensity, raw and loud and proud, with little bits of commercial melody struggling to break free, most notably through the triumphant chorus. "Nightmare," like the title track, was also the subject of a proper production video, which saw Biff tormented by bad dreams in a small and very wobbly bedroom. The band join him at various points and again, all told, the clip is not the worst video of the nascent MTV age.

"'Nightmare' was a great song to write because it started off with Biff and me jamming in the rehearsal studio," Nigel explained to Marko from MetalRules. "There's also a promo video made for that song and in my opinion it's horrible! (laughs). What were these directors on about? I just got the Mötley Crüe DVD and they're saying the same thing. They did 'Looks That Kill'—what is *that* all about? They said the same thing: 'What the hell was that all about?!' I think the same, but you just let these directors go with it. I don't know what these guys were thinking. 'Nightmare,' oh God, if that comes on it's fast forward—next! Or if there are other people around, 'Quick, look over there! Gone.' I felt such an idiot on that; I really did. What the hell am I doing sitting on the floor with one drum? It's great for guitarists but what am I supposed to do with one drum? (laughs)."

Indeed, Glockler can be seen, albeit very briefly, sitting on the ground, holding his drum sticks and singing along. Sure, if you are in fact Nigel Glockler, it might stick out to you, but otherwise the image raises no eyebrows.

"I think most of the videos from that period were a bit strange," said Nigel, speaking with Jeb Wright. "It seemed to be a case of video directors trying to out-do each other creatively, and not even bearing in mind what the song was about. Actually I don't think ours were *that* bad compared to a lot of others I've seen."

Over to side two, and Saxon proposes a proto-thrash called "This Town Rocks," which, interestingly houses the album's happiest melody thus far, inside of the chorus, which is almost Van Halen-esque and hair band-ish in disposition. Lyrically, the song celebrates metal, which is, as we've discussed, a play and a ploy that had worked for Saxon all along so far, writing about the punters, the tribe, standing up for them with fists in the air. What's more, Biff name-checks a bunch of places, with the pay-off being that he belts out that *this* town knows how to rock, which made it a fait accompli as a barnstorming live song.

"Everyone was working really hard," says Nigel, also on the subject of songwriting. "We were staying up sometimes until five o'clock in the morning, writing lyrics and stuff. Graham and Paul were coming up with some great riffs. Which, I mean, you have to have that, because the riffs provide the backbone and the spark of every song, really—unless you've got a melody chord sequence. But basically with us, you know, we need riffs. And then you can take it from there. It's either riffs or a chord sequence that is great for Biff to sing to. And we were all having a go at what's up. Everyone was tossing around, because I play a bit of bass. Biff used to play bass, and Dobby was playing guitar as well as his bass—everyone was swapping around all over the place. As we do now, actually. When we get in the studio now, I might just be jamming around on the keyboards, and Quinny will pick up the bass, and Nibbs (Carter) will get on the drums, and Biff'll picks up the guitar and off we go. We all swap around. Whoever's got a spark in their head gets on that instrument, however good they are at it, and we try to hear what everyone's doing and we take a listen—that's how it works."

Then it's over to what is one of the album's best tracks, "Watching the Sky," which finds guitarists Graham Oliver and Paul Quinn driving the track with dead-set confidence, utilizing licks that are rock 'n' rollsy but at the same time, pure NWOBHM magic. An average hair band could have rendered this song unremarkable. Same thing with the old Saxon—in a *Strong Arm* frame of mind, more than a few songs on this record would have wilted. But within this crucible of alchemical magic-making, Saxon lights the charming alien tale on fire and turns it into a neck-break of a headbang.

"Graham's always played a Gibson," notes Dawson, asked to contrast the band's two axe-heavies. "And as soon as he could afford it, he bought one, and he still has the original one he bought now. It's the one with the Jimi Hendrix picture on it, the SG. And in fact, we are now endorsed by Vintage Guitars. They just made—and it will be on sale soon—a signature model of that guitar; they've reproduced it. And Paul was always, basically, in the early days, he always played a Fender Stratocaster. And I mean, he had other guitars, like Gibson Firebirds and Les Paul Juniors and stuff like that, but his main thing was the Stratocaster. But it favoured him to do that spinning (laughs), because you could screw the strap locks into the back of the strap, and put the two together. That's what allowed him to spin it around. And obviously a Stratocaster is a more workman-like guitar; it can take more trouble, if you know what I mean. But he did try with his Firebird, doing that, and caught the headstock on his knee and snapped it straight off. He was spinning it around (laughs). In fact, that's on film somewhere, because he did it when we were filming a video."

"'Watching the Sky,' that's another one of my riffs," explains Graham. "That came about when we were in Bakersfield. I forget which tour it was, but it's about '82, I imagine. We were in America, in Bakersfield, and we saw something like an unidentified flying object, and we didn't know what it was, and we read reports in the paper the day after that other people had seen it. So we just coined that song, 'Watching the Sky,' and added a bit to the riff that I started. Paul Quinn... now that's really interesting, because that was a really off-the-wall run. And Edward Van Halen heard that, and I used to know his girlfriend. He shouldn't have had a girlfriend at the time (laughs), but he did, and much more; I shouldn't have known her, but I did. She told me that Eddie Van Halen heard that and he said it was a fantastic intro to a solo, which I thought was really flattering—for Quinn anyway."

"Watching the Sky" is Biff's best lyric on a record where—surprisingly and perhaps incongruously given the inspired violence of the music—his lyrics are overall substandard. The song presents an impassioned yearning for answers with respect to extraterrestrial life, Byford invoking the Drake equation, with the reflection that with "fifty billion planets, there's gotta be some life."

Second to last—on the original UK vinyl version of *Power & the Glory*, anyway—is "Midas Touch," a genius construct from Graham that starts ragingly heavy of riff before turning into a verse of dark balladry—it's sort of the album's "Fade to Black." The intro riff returns for the chorus, and what falls out of the thing is the pleasure of getting served another dimension to this record of mostly very smart manoeuvres. Biff's lyric is an insane proto-power metal fantasy tale of an old man with a withered hand who in fact is quietly protecting the world from Satan. It's quite the image, this figure, lurking about the bookstore, doomed to shuffle about, all the while guarding the gate of Hades until the Nazarene comes.

One not so smart move was the swapping of this occult classic for the commercial and poppy "Suzie Hold On," for the North American issue of the album. "The record company just wanted to do it," says Biff. "They thought 'Suzie Hold On' was a great track for radio, so they wanted to put it on." Adds Paul, "'Suzie' was off of a previous album, and we decided to re-record with Nigel drumming, for continuity more than anything else."

Power & the Glory closes out with a seven-minute epic in the spirit of "747" called "The Eagle Has Landed," a dark and bluesy and somewhat Sabbatherian track which lends the album a ponderous finish, jammed well, supporting the ultra-live feel of the rest of the record. Again, it's a great addition through the variety it gives the album, all speeds, all levels of emotional brightness represented, smashed in your face by, well, again, in my opinion, Glixman and Glockler.

"'The Eagle Has Landed' is Paul Quinn," notes Oliver. "He is very Hendrix-influenced—that's Paul Quinn, and he's playing the solo in that. So we could mix it up a bit."

"'Eagle Has Landed,' again, it's from my youth, really, the first landing on the moon," muses Biff, addressing the song's epic lyric. "These things that happened during this period stuck in my head obviously. I just thought the riff lent itself to a great song. And 'The Eagle Has Landed' fitted with our eagle (laughs). And just the whole concept of landing on the moon was such a fabulous thing. I like to write what I call picture lyrics. I like each line to paint a picture in your head. It's very important that the songs, when you hear the lyric, that you see a picture in your head. It's quite hard actually. It's quite hard to write a song about landing on the moon in four verses and get the spirit. But I think I did do that. And the music, don't forget that myself and Paul Quinn were very heavily into progressive rock, and maybe there's a lot of that coming out on that song."

All told it's another solid lyric on the record, along with "Midas Touch" and "Watching the Sky." Endearing is the concern that Biff has for the safe return of the astronauts, who Biff clearly views as heroes.

As for the music, says Nigel, "'Eagle Has Landed' started off live with just the basic idea, and then me, Dobby and Paul had a jam in the studio at The Manor, and so that took it a little bit further. But generally it was just all of us together throwing ideas about. Everyone was involved. At that particular point, no one had any sort of home recording gear, so basically we just met, we spent a little while up in Suffolk, where the trucking company that we used to use was, so we started there. Plus we did some on the road, actually, jamming at sound checks. In fact 'This Town Rocks' came out of a jam, at an American sound check."

Notes Paul, "I can remember definitely the beginning of 'Eagle Has Landed.' It was something I played in the sound check, and we tried it in the Stone Room at The Manor. It's sort of 'scary Hendrix'-influenced, slightly towards 'Voodoo Chile.'"

No doubt pushed by the US touring (at the expense of home country dates), *Power & the Glory* got to No.155 on the Billboard charts. European touring had also paid off, with the record pulling in 1.5 million in sales worldwide and getting to No.1 on the metal charts in Norway, France, Sweden and the band's most significant stronghold, Germany. At home, the album climbed to a respectable No.15 in the charts and was well-received by the all-influential local press.

"I rate that as one of the best albums we ever made," muses Steve, summing up. "And working with Jeff was fantastic. But we didn't know what to expect. You know, you get these names put forward and you turn up at the studio, you heard what he's done and then you meet. We did it at Axis Studios, and he just came from the start as really one of the band. And what he used to do, well, the studio was quite large, and Jeff Glixman is a keyboard player, and so what we would do before we would do a take, we would all go into the studio, including Jeff, and jam to some songs, maybe a blues song or Hendrix or something. And then when we were all fired up he would run back up into the control room and say, 'Right, do a take.' And it worked real good. Because there was no 'him and us,' if you know what I mean."

"Because a lot of the producers sort of stifle your performance, because they're trying to make things perfect, and rock 'n' roll music isn't meant to be perfect. It's meant to be a bit dangerous and edgy. So yeah, I agree totally. *Power & the Glory* is one of my favourites, and Graham and I now, we do play 'Power and the Glory' in our set. Can't get enough of that song. But absolutely, I agree totally. I think if we could've kept that up, with that sound… I mean, the guitars just sounded enormous. Yeah, I totally agree. Yet in England it didn't get a lot of good reviews. Not in England it didn't. The English are really strange people."

The 2009 reissue of *Power & the Glory* included a bevy of interesting artefacts. First there was a live rendition of "Denim and Leather," which had been used as the B-side to the "Power and the Glory" single back in '83. This was followed by a "Jeff Glixman version" of "Suzie Hold On," which is different from the new album version and of course different from the old *Wheels of Steel* version—Biff is basically ducking all the high notes, essentially putting on a guide vocal. Next are 1982 Kaley Studio demos of new songs "Turn Out the Lights" and "Stand Up and Rock," both essentially mid-paced commercial metal tracks best left on the cutting room floor. There's also a version of "Stand Up and Rock" called "Make 'em Rock" that can be found on the expanded hardback book edition of the album (BMG Europe 2018); this also includes an added version of "Turn Out the Lights."

A third new song called "Saturday Night," sounds like a single in the making, given its thumping 4/4 beat and vibes back to the band's successful evocations of AC/DC. Closing out are fully four more Kaley Studio demos, covering tracks from the album, namely "Power and the Glory," "Redline," "Midas Touch" and "Nightmare."

Of note, the record's cool reception in the UK could have come from the fact that the fans there were staring at another case of an act more or less abandoning them, pushing off for America. Saxon only did a few one-offs at home in support of the album, notably at the Royal Court Hall in Nottingham to record a live video, and a show in Leeds which also featured Battle Axe, Spider, Anvil, Twisted Sister and Girlschool—at this gig, Biff was lowered from the ceiling straddling a motorcycle.

But they did play Finland, as Nigel recalls in conversation with Marko from MetalRules. "Yeah, on the *Power & the Glory* tour we did several gigs then, Helsinki and some ski resort up in the north. God, I was so drunk there! Tell you what was great though, there was a sauna in the dressing room. I came off stage and went straight in the sauna. I love saunas. But you have a strange thing; you hit each other with twigs, don't you, in Finland? I don't know about that. I think in England we would go, 'Hello?!'"

It was important for Saxon to deliver a record that credibly held up in the face of the competition coming aboard in 1983, but just as crucial was a sincere attempt at breaking America. In that light, the band set out as sandwich act between openers Fastway and headliners Iron Maiden, in one of the legendary packages of the day—as mentioned in the introduction, the author caught the bands on their Spokane, Washington stop, and the enduring vision, still, 30 years later, is of Biff all in white, foot up on the monitors, fan blowing his hair back as the guys tore triumphantly through the title track of the album.

"Well, it looked like we were all going to break, actually," muses Biff, ceding no territory to Maiden as they existed that year. "It was a massive tour. I think we were all in the Billboard charts, weren't we? And they did break off that tour. It would've been nice to finish the tour, but we only did half the tour for some strange reason. But it was a great tour. We really should've broke off that. We didn't get kicked off. Our manager… yeah, it would be nice to say that, but the truth is the manager just had a contract for half of it. He was a greedy bastard; he wanted… I mean, we went out headlining after that, which was probably because it made more money for him. But we are super-competitive with bands. English people are like that (laughs). We're very competitive. We really didn't have any problems with Maiden. I talk to Maiden's manager once a month; we're good mates, from the same town as me. I think they've always been very competitive, Maiden, and always been very secretive. You don't really know anything about the inner workings of Maiden. And I think that's the same with a lot of bands. AC/DC are the same."

"Yeah, it was a management thing, which I was pissed-off about actually," sighs Nigel, about the full-press rampage that should have been. "We were on an equal footing with Maiden, audience reaction-wise, definitely. I think if we had stayed on that, we would've broken America big time. It's very frustrating that they didn't commit us to do that, but you know, I'm not one of these people that feels bitter. It's like well, what's the point in bloody worrying about it, quite frankly. We're still here now, and we're on the up again, and I figure, you know, that's great. I mean, a lot of bands of that era are gone. We're still here and we're still relevant to the fans, because they're still buying our albums and coming to shows. So you know, great. You can look back a bit and be pissed-off. But I'm not going to dwell on it—it's done, it's gone by, what if, so what? We're enjoying ourselves."

"We all got on very well," recalls Dawson. "Nobody got a big ego, so nobody was wanting to put one over on the other, you know, as in not enough room on the stage or the sound or anything like that. We worked with Fast Eddie before, when we toured with Motörhead on the *Bomber* tour, so we were old mates. But Fast Eddie is a really funny guy. He's just got like a really dry sense of humour. And Dave King, the singer at that time, he had just been in local bands in Ireland. It was all new to him, and so he was just having a fantastic time."

"And you know, everybody in Iron Maiden, Bruce, Steve Harris, we were all just sort of… You see, we all worked together before. Iron Maiden and ourselves were on the tour circuit in England for a long time before we got a recording contract. So we knew them, you see; we'd come across each other lots and lots of times. And in fact, on one bill we played in London, when Paul Di'Anno was singing for Iron Maiden, it was Iron Maiden, Saxon and Samson, and Bruce Dickinson was singing for Samson at the time. All three of us on the same bill, and I think we did that lineup for about four or five shows. And so we also knew each other then. I mean, at that time we were all skint and got no money and we shared a common goal."

"For me it was a totally new experience because I had never been to America before," Glockler told MetalRules. "The guys had been there, playing in support of Rush. So when we went there for the first time it was just great. The audience was brilliant, but all audiences are great everywhere. Every country has its own way of supporting a band. In America they have certain chants; in Europe they have different chants. But it was great going there. With Maiden, both bands were on the verge of breaking through. But I had a problem there; I fell off the stage one evening and ended up with a plaster cast on my leg. I still kept playing though. I used to go to the stage on crutches."

"No problem," is how Quinn remembers this historic jaunt. "Fast Eddie, he's got a sardonic sense of humour, so we could relate to that, being British. We were fans as musicians anyway. They'd been through some famous bands themselves. Maiden, we'd known quite a few years. I saw recently on a Facebook page, this ticket from Manchester, of us, Maiden and Nutz playing together, which is when we first met them. I would imagine it was '78 or '79."

"I like that first Fastway album," says Biff in closing, bringing out that competitive fire with a wink. "It's a bit like the Kingdom Come album, a bit Zeppelin-y, wasn't it? Actually, the North American audiences loved them. I mean, I remember that the singer was very new and naïve and when he started the tour, he learned most of his tricks off of me and Bruce, and so by the end of it, he was quite a good front man. But they were a cross between Maiden and Saxon. Eddie at that time was up and down, you know, but I thought the album was good, actually; I really did like the album. But they did sort of fizzle out and didn't follow it through, like a lot of bands. They just implode, don't they? It takes special people to be in a band for a long time."

"But Dave... that's natural if you've got some young guy who doesn't really have any front man elements already. Yeah, he didn't really rip us off, but we could just see that he was turning it on for the girls a bit, the attitude, and getting the audience going in the right bits. When he first started the tour he was useless, but after awhile, he got really good at it. But that's where you learn your craft from, from other people. You have to be an apprentice. I'm not saying it's wrong, I'm just giving you a story from the tour (laughs)."

Commented Nigel about the dynamic between Saxon and Maiden, "Of course there's always rivalry between bands, but generally it's nothing nasty. You just want to be better than anyone else! We had *Power & the Glory* out and they had *Piece of Mind*, incidentally, my favourite album of theirs. It was a great tour; both bands got on really well and Steve and Nicko are good friends to this day."

Maiden would earn a gold album for *Piece of Mind* in America on the back of that tour, for sales of over 500,000 copies. And Fastway's self-titled debut wasn't far off; it certainly outsold Saxon's record, rising to and impressive No.31 on Billboard. But even though they weren't on the campaign that long, Biff is fairly certain that his guys should have received gold certification for *Power & The Glory*, even if only after their headlining run for the record and into the cycle for 1984's *Crusader*. In other words, Biff is suspicious that a gold award should have been forthcoming for *Power & the Glory* sometime around the summer of 1984.

"I remember Spokane very well," muses Graham, hearing that the author was there down in the front, loving the presentation of what I feel far and away is the band's greatest album—and tour. "I had a day off after that, and I drove back to Seattle to visit Al Hendrix and to see Jimi Hendrix's grave."

Biff (the Hoople) doing some more *Shouting & Pointing*. © Martin Popoff.

Nigel Glockler rising above his big kit, Toronto. © Martin Popoff.

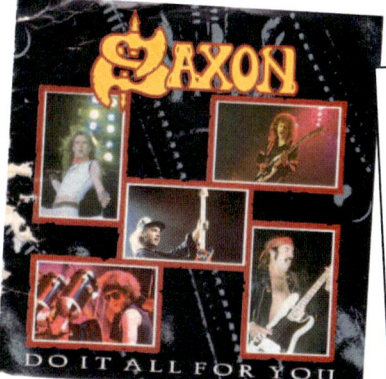

The picture sleeve singles for the *Crusader* ballad and the *Crusader* almost-ballad.

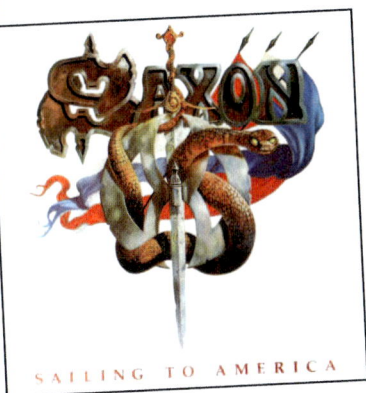

Biff and Nigel, March 4, 1984, Neunkirchen, Germany. © Wolfgang Gürster.

Steve Dawson, same gig as left. © Wolfgang Gürster.

Martin Popoff — Denim and Leather: Saxon's First Ten Years | 133

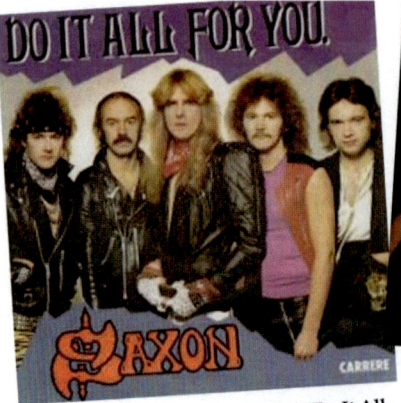

Another picture sleeve version of "Do It All for You," this one from France.

October 6, 1985, Munich, Germany.
© Wolfgang Gürster.

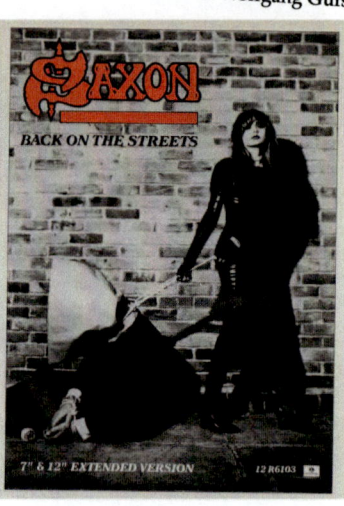

The gal from the front cover of *Innocence Is No Excuse* appears again in these two ads for the first single from the album, "Back on the Streets."

Decent but also vaguely biker-ish design went into this ad for 1985's "Rock 'n' Roll Gypsy," second single from *Innocence Is No Excuse*.

Biff, with a wee bit of eyeliner, 1985, selling the new album.
© Wolfgang Gürster.

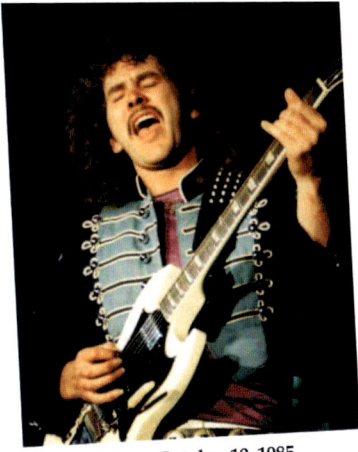

Graham Oliver, October 10, 1985, Böblingen, Germany. © Wolfgang Gürster.

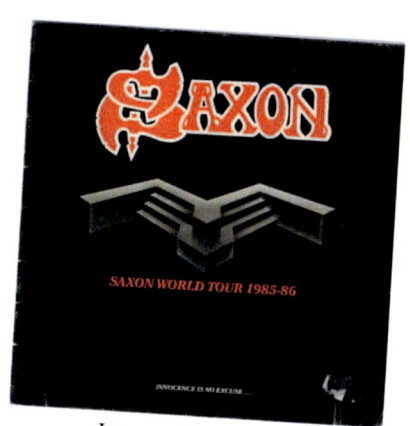

Innocence Is No Excuse tour book.

Biff from same gig as right, with guitar. © Wolfgang Gürster.

Paul Quinn, June 1, 1988, Stuttgart, Germany. © Wolfgang Gürster.

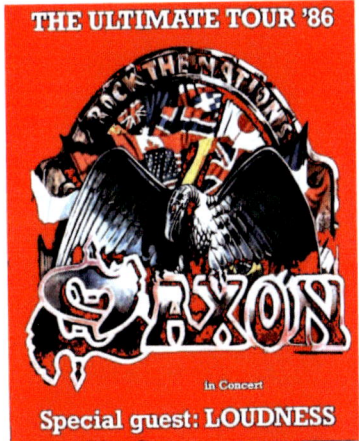

Rock the Nations tour poster with German dates; support by Japan's most famous metal band Loudness.

A very shiny Graham Oliver, October 26, 1986, Sindelfingen, Germany. © Wolfgang Gürster.

Ad for "Rock the Nations" in picture sleeve and 7" shaped picture disc formats.

Graham and Biff backstage, December 22, 1989, in Aalen, Germany. © Wolfgang Gürster.

Swanky full colour ad for 1988's *Destiny* album.

Paul signs his life away. © Wolfgang Gürster.

Biff telling Graham his days are numbered; 1989, Aalen, Germany. © Wolfgang Gürster.

Stylish ad for second *Destiny* single "I Can't Wait Anymore." Note the absence of the Saxon logo.

136 | Denim and Leather: Saxon's First Ten Years   Martin Popoff

Chapter 8

Crusader
"It covered pretty much the four corners of the musical square that they played in."

My, how the metal world changes in the blink of an eye.

Moments ago it was all about the New Wave of British Heavy Metal and, in tandem, a second career act for the likes of Kiss, Ozzy Osbourne, Black Sabbath, Blue Öyster Cult, Scorpions and Judas Priest. By 1984, only Def Leppard and Iron Maiden were thriving outta the NWOBHM, but the old timers were still around, now joined by a raft of boisterous baby bands out of the LA area, namely Mötley Crüe, Quiet Riot, Ratt, Dokken and Great White. There was Twisted Sister too, and also Queensryche and a new thing called thrash.

Over in Saxon's world, there was the type of concern going on that was happening around the lion's share of NWOBHM acts suddenly confronted with hair metal and the MTV age. Indeed, as the heroes of our story transition from *Power & the Glory* in 1983 to *Crusader* in 1984, brethren bands like Accept, Krokus and Raven would be wondering what to do with themselves as well—even Lemmy and whoever was in Motörhead at the time would go into a phase that we might call "fumbling about."

"Again, we were always getting in a new producer," reflects Graham, "and Kevin Beamish, he was used to doing REO Speedwagon. Some of these producers just lighten things up. It was a confusing situation, because American radio said they wouldn't play us because it was too British heavy metal. Yet in Britain, it was seen as a softening up for America. It was a bit strange. And then at that point in time Mötley Crüe and all that kind of glam rock, pretty boy rock, came out. MTV was just starting as well, where imagery was a big thing as well as AOR-oriented tracks. So I think you get pushed down a road with producers. I mean, if we would've done '747' and got three producers, you could have three different versions."

"We ended up writing most of *Crusader* on the tour bus," explained Biff, speaking with Steve Gett from Hit Parader. "We bought a couple of mini-amps and while we were travelling, we'd sit in the back of the bus playing our hearts out. We actually talked with lots of different producers, including all the obvious ones like Mutt Lange, Tom Allom and Martin Birch. But in the end, we felt that Kevin would be the best for us. His appeal was that he's trained in classical music, so he's a good arranger. He plays guitar and he knew what Saxon was about. He heard a few of our albums and it wasn't as though he was going to come in and try to change the band. He knew exactly what we needed to retain and what we needed to give in order to make *Crusader* different and better than the last album. We'd like to work in England every time, because it's nearer home, but it just can't be done. This time we checked out various studios, but since Kevin Beamish lives in LA, and he had worked at the studio with REO, we decided to go there. It turned out to be a great place, and we were all happy with the way things came out."

Indeed Saxon were now two records into this world where the producer that management pushed and prodded them toward was going to make a difference as to what type and tone of record that band would put out—especially if the guys in the band were amenable to the idea, admittedly hungry for success, willing to toy with the formula for a slice of American pie.

Enter Kevin Beamish, who was, yes, as Graham Oliver puts it, "used to doing REO Speedwagon."

"There was an English fellow by the name of Nigel Thomas who was a manager," begins Beamish, "and he started to manage my career in 1983. He had several English bands, and he put them through to me to produce—Lionheart was one and Saxon was another. He managed Saxon and was attempting to increase Saxon's image and fan base by coming to Los Angeles and making what was still a heavy metal record, but adding a little more melodic influence and all that. And coming off the huge success that I had had recently from REO Speedwagon's *High Infidelity* (certified diamond in the US for sales of over ten million copies), the idea was to kind of spread their instruments out a little bit."

"So he contacted me and set me up with the band. Originally, I went to England to do pre-production with the boys, up in Barnsley, which is close to Sherwood Forest, in that area. A little teeny town, but it's funny: in the restaurant in a hotel in London, they had the Barnsley Chop on the menu, and the guys laughed. They didn't know what the hell they were talking about. 'What's a Barnsley Chop?' Anyway, we went up there, and did pre-production for a couple of weeks, before bringing the whole shebang out to Los Angeles to Sound City Studios, where we recorded the album. In the meantime, there was a break while I was in Barnsley, and I went to the crypt where they buried all the kings, in the city of York, where they have the big cathedral and all that; all the kings are buried there. I had a few days to do nothing, so I just took off by myself in a rent-a-car. I also drove in to Scotland and went to Loch Ness; never did see the Loch Ness monster (laughs). But yeah, came back to LA ten weeks later and began to record the record at the now famous/infamous Sound City Studio."

Kevin confirms that the band was on board for trying to sweeten up their sound a bit. "Well, yes, they were. They sort of looked at Nigel Thomas with a squinting eye a little bit. But he was the manager of several artists in the past that had been very successful, so they were kind of going with it. You know, the previous album, *Power & the Glory*, was right down the middle for the European fan. But yeah, they wanted to try some new stuff, and I brought a bit more melody into it with several of the songs."

Rolling into the recording of what was to be *Crusader*, Saxon had metaphorically shifted toward this new solitude. They'd recorded in the UK and then in mainland Europe. Crossing the divide for *Power & the Glory* had them in the States to be sure, but only as far as Atlanta. Now they were in the heart of hair metal, a genre only a year or two old, but soon to dominate the conversation clear through to 1991.

"Graham Oliver always added a lot, but the whole band was there and we'd all work together," continues Beamish, on the sessions. "On things like 'Just Let Me Rock,' we used big old Syndrums and stuff. We were trying to be a bit more modern and have something for everybody."

Kevin then draws an interesting parallel to his experience working with REO. "Yes, well, what happened with REO Speedwagon… that was a band who were big in the Midwest, but no real image on the east or west coast. And similar to Saxon, REO would be on the road nine months of the year, and they would come off and they'd have a couple months and then they'd make a record and go back out on the road. First album that I did with REO was *Nine Lives*, and that was their ninth album on Epic Records. So basically, I had this idea; I said, 'Look, what I see in working with you guys, what I think you need to do is get off the road for a lot longer than just a couple months to write and record a record and go right back out.'"

"Also, I said, 'You have nine albums out there. Why don't we sort of go back through all these tapes, all the way back to 1971 or whatever it was, and put together a compilation of greatest hits?' Being a little bit stretched on the greatest part. So, indeed, we went back and took everything out of the Sony library, Columbia at that point, and put out *A Decade of Rock and Roll*, which I remixed every song on there that had made any level of noise, you know, and found all kinds of interesting things. On one song—can't remember which one—there was a 40-piece orchestra on this ballad that never made it to the original record. That kind of stuff. But what happened was, it gave the guys some time to get off the road in order to write 'Take It on the Run' and all that."

"So it was kind of the same idea as to what we were trying to do with Saxon, get them some more time to really... instead of just slapping a record together, hodgepodge songs, try to put something together that was definitely accessible to not only their hardcore fans, but to some new people as well. And, you know, in a smaller sense than REO, it did work that way."

Saxon in studio mode was all business, says Kevin. "It was about two months, probably, at Sound City and I mean, it was serious business. It was not a lot of partying and whatnot. Biff, he's the king of the band. He keeps a tight rein on things. But we did have a lot of fun. I remember, couple of stories, Dawson, the bass player, we'd get to the studio about noon, and we'd work 'til probably two in the morning, that kind of thing. So we would go out to dinner at a restaurant pretty much all the time, or bring food in. Dawson was particularly funny. 'What do you guys want to eat tonight?' 'Well, we want some seafood or something like that.' So we went to the seafood restaurant, and he's a bass player, right? So he's looking at this menu, scratching his head, and he goes, 'Well, I'd like to have the stripped bass, please.' Striped bass was on the menu. But he wanted to stripped bass, as in bass guitar."

"Another time, 'We want spicy food tonight.' Okay, so I took them to this Thai restaurant and the chef, the owner, had just got back from his yearly trip to Thailand. He takes off a month and goes back to Thailand and he's spicing it up like he did back at home. So Steve, they asked him, 'Do you want it mild or spicy?' 'Oh, spicy!' So he's eating his food and I'm watching him, because I know how spicy it's gonna be—I go to this restaurant all the time. And he's looking at me, and his eyes start watering and he's got sweat on his forehead and the back of his neck, and he wipes off his face, and he looks at me, 'That was brill, mate!—that was brill!" For some reason, I remember that (laughs)"

"Also, I took Biff up to a nice... you would call it a cabin, but it wasn't. It was a nice house up in Lake Arrowhead, which was about an hour-and-a-half drive from LA, up in the mountains. And I believe we got snowed in. I can't remember; we might've got snowed in. And all we did—it was just him and me, no one could get out, nowhere to go—we played some old video game. And the game was kind of like going through this castle and it was a difficult game back then, to get won. Hours and hours and days. And pretty much on the third day, just him and I playing, we're learning all the nooks and crannies, and it was like, we're jumping up and down screaming because we finally figured it out. But as far as partying and all that, there was not a lot of that for this album. It was serious work. And as you can tell, you listen to the whole thing and there's some pretty intricate production there. And that stuff takes focus and time. I'd like to tell you that it was a drinkfest with women, but it really wasn't."

Notes Steve about the place, speaking with Rhino, "I've just seen that Dave Grohl movie, *Sound City* and we recorded *Crusader* at Sound City...on that desk! In fact, in that film, they show the cover of *Crusader*! It doesn't mention us, but the actual producer of that film rang me up when they started to make it, 'cause he wanted to know if I had any photographs of while we were there. Unfortunately, that's probably one of the only places I haven't got a photograph of. There were quite a few other distractions in LA at that time. I might not even have been able to work a camera at that moment! (laughs)."

In anticipation of the release of the record, Carrere issued a couple of advance singles. January 1984, the guys go with the upbeat and hummable "Sailing to America" as the first volley from *Crusader*, backed with "A Little Bit of What You Fancy," also an album track. More on "Sailing to America" later, but there are indeed parallels to Def Leppard's "Hello America" and all the controversy that song created for the Sheffield band, underscored by Def Leppard's conspicuously Americanized sound. Into March and Saxon continue playing Saxon-lite, issuing "Do It All for You" backed with "Just Let Me Rock," again both album tracks.

The cover art for *Crusader*, issued April 16th, 1984, would be the band's best up until that point, certainly. It's a painting by the Derby-based Paul Raymond Gregory, who would go on to create fully 17 images for use on Saxon records moving forward. *Crusader* was his first album cover commission ever, and the job would extend to elements used in the *Crusader* live presentation. Gregory's Frazetta-meets-Ken Kelly style would later grace album covers from the likes of Blind Guardian, Uriah Heep, Molly Hatchet and Dio. Gregory would also venture into concert promotion, co-founding the Bloodstock Open Air festival. A news article from the day speaks of Biff's appreciation for his work—Gregory had been known for his *Lord of the Rings* depictions—with Biff going 'round to Gregory's place to purchase and pick up the painting to take back to his new house near Skegness, on the coast, halfway between where he grew up and London.

As for the title, true to form with Saxon, sometimes that's all it takes to spark a song, a lyric, a concept for the stage. In fact Steve says that the band just liked the word, having heard it used by Ford for one of their European car models, the Cortina Crusader. As well, there was a red ink crusader that augmented the otherwise black ink logo of the Daily Express tabloid newspaper, something the guys saw every day.

"The idea behind *Crusader* is a concept that ties in everything," said Biff at the time, "the album, the cover artwork, the tour, and of course the name Saxon. It's something we've always wanted to do for a while, but it was a question of approaching it from the right angle. Everything's got a medieval feel, and in fact the stage set in Europe and on some of the American shows will be an actual castle courtyard with suits of armour. We're on a heavy metal mission whenever we go to perform."

The album opens in dramatic fashion with an intro of 1:05 called "The Crusader Prelude." It's essentially a bunch of historic battle sounds setting the scene for the epic to come. Says Kevin, "Biff and I spent so much time going through probably 20 videos, old VHS tapes of movies that were

Anglo-Saxons fighting whoever, to get the sounds of the axes and the 'Crusader!' shouting and all that."

Explained Biff to Kerrang!, "'Crusader Prelude' is a short battle scene that we put together from various soundtrack albums. It's only about a minute long and near the end I'm in the battle shouting orders. That leads into the title track, which is an epic song. It has a lot of surprises in it, things that have never been done before."

Then, as Biff directs, we're into gently picked electric guitar as "Crusader" proper builds toward the first verse, which... it's actually not that heavy, more like something you'd call an uptempo power ballad, but of an epic sort of course, not a boy-girl song. Elsewhere, i.e. in the chorus and the various other musical passages like the breaks and the solo music, it's pretty heavy, although the guitars are tamped down somewhat with the drums taking prominence. Notes Kevin, "Biff, in particular, was a history nut. So 'Crusader' was about Anglo-Saxons and warriors and all that, in the Middle Ages. We used the big Syndrums and all that kind of stuff. Sonically, I mean, there's phasing and a lot of production in there that normally, in the past, Saxon and a lot of heavy metal in general... it's just one, two, three, count it off, bust your ass to the end, kind of thing. There's another couple of records I did similarly at that time."

Indeed the Syndrums are loud and clear, maybe even a little jarring. Still, they are used sparingly, while Nigel enthusiastically executes melodramatic tom fills on his acoustic set, most notably the first extended two-fisted slow burn around his monster set. Is it gratuitous? Well, like those memorable licks from Neil Peart, one can debate whether it's tasteful or not, but one cannot deny that it's something you remember.

Explained Biff on the voluminous "Crusader" lyric, speaking with Darren Cowan, "That came from me writing in the third person; it's a young boy watching knights go off to war, and he wants to go with them: 'Crusader, crusader, please take me with you.' That's where that comes from. It's based on that European history of knights going off to the crusades. The crusades were secondary to it, really, but they were called crusaders, which is a great name. So I just put the names together and wrote a song about a guy who wants to go off to war."

As with many Saxon themes, some of this comes from the romance of what Biff heard about in school as a young boy, recalling the escapades of Richard the Lionheart and whatnot. He envisions these Christian knights in the tale being the young boy's uncles and even his father heading off to war, but alas, the subject of the story is too young to participate in the vanquishing of these heathens and pagans from the east, the "Saracen hordes," namely Muslims. One final note, there's a trace of amusement one can ascribe to the way Biff completely ignores any attempt at rhyming within the verses. Somehow the lines peel off in isolated chunks, resulting in a sort of charming clumsiness.

Next up is "A Little Bit of What You Fancy," a speedy rocker over which Biff revisits a tried and true Saxon theme, the outlaw nature of his upbringing, adding the narrative colour of calling himself a seventh son of a seventh son. Here's where we see some of that Americanization of the Saxon sound. The structure of this one is like a fast Van Halen shuffle, touched by the tradition of boogie, and then the chorus goes light and melodic, where the old Saxon might have kept things grim. Indeed even the title of the song itself is proto-hair metal, but then being stuck in that chorus as "A little bit of what you fancy always does you good" seals the deal, especially given the party-hardy gang vocals applied to this frankly chafing refrain.

Then there's a light bulb moment, or more so, a squarely successful actualization of pop success for Saxon. "Sailing to America" is a rare example in which the band's performance chemistry shines in a melodic context. It all wells up from the intrusive but impressive drums, bass as well, with textured guitar parts in conversation with each other, plus a soaring Biff vocal of long notes augmented by an echo effect.

Biff's lyric is a simple and literal telling of the pilgrims' ocean voyage to the new world, with Plymouth and the Mayflower specifically mentioned. "Yes, very similar to

'Crusader,'" says Kevin. "The title says it all. It makes you think not only of the pilgrims but also the Beatles coming over. It had that vibe to it even though it was sort of a historical idea."

And of course there's a metaphorical link there to Saxon themselves coming over. "Oh God, yeah, because they had a small base here, you know, big club, thousand-seater, maybe some theatres, 3000, that they could get into. But they were trying to make the step up to the stadiums or sheds, which didn't happen. But that was the idea: coming to take over America with the *Crusader* album, and the song 'Crusader' as well, plus 'Sailing to America.'"

Beamish recognized also that Nigel was the new secret weapon in the band, as exemplified by this song's strong groove and memorable fills.

"Oh my God, yeah, and I got along great with him. It's funny, because Nigel Glockler was aware of the fact that I worked with Nigel Olsson, the Elton John drummer, as you know, for quite a while in the '70s. And Nigel, frankly, was never happy with his drum sound. You know, on Elton John records they were great and all that, but we did Nigel's solo album, in 1978 or whatever, came into Chrysalis Studios where I was the engineer there. And Nigel Olsson's drums were very difficult to record because he had these Slingerland drums, where all the toms, the rims, the top rims were like an inch-and-a-half thick away from the skins. The way he played them, he almost had to reach down into each drum to hit it. And he had a kick drum that was four-feet long, and, you know, very, very difficult. And as a Young Turk kind of gig, I figured I had to make Nigel Olsson's drums sound way better, and incredible. And for many years, Nigel, thereafter, in LA, wouldn't do a session unless I was recording his drums."

"So anyway, that leads to Glockler, who knew that story and appreciated it. But you're right, he's a great drummer, with great sounding drums. He had the huge array of toms and cymbals, as was the manner. It was not a business-like kit—it was a big-ass heavy rock kit. But we didn't have to spend a lot of time on it because the drums sounded great. So it was just adding the knowledge that I had of how to please the drummer. He was very happy with his drums. Sometimes with bands you don't quite know what you're getting, but everybody in Saxon was a pro in the sense that there was no weakness anywhere."

Which, again, is particularly on display here on "Sailing to America." In the hands of a less experienced band, the thin premise both lyrically and musically might have wilted, but something about this performance, along with Kevin's "airy" production just makes the track work.

As for Biff's place in the narrative, Beamish explains that, "When we were doing his vocals, I remember that we tried a lot of different microphones, including expensive ones, to say the least, and I wasn't happy and he wasn't happy. So I said, 'Okay, let's go back to this little trick I know.' Which had come up before with other artists. I put a Shure SM7, you know, a dynamic mic, on him, which has a huge sound pressure level capability. You can't distort it like a condenser mic. So it's this $300 mic instead of a $10,000 mic and it was perfect for Biff. If you listen to the presence of his voice on *Crusader*, it's right in your face, which was the sound of the microphone. Whereas with other albums, there's screaming and it's distorted."

"Usually you see an SM7 at radio stations, or there's a broadcast mic like an RE20. You don't think of them as like the go-to microphone in a million-dollar studio. But I'd used it on Kevin Cronin's voice occasionally, for REO Speedwagon. I used it on Dave Meniketti's voice, Y&T, on 'Summertime Girls.' Sometimes you just gotta think outside the box. And then I found out from Bruce Swedien, the famous engineer that did so many things, but also Michael Jackson's *Thriller* album. And Bruce Swedien told me he used an SM7 on Michael Jackson's voice. You can't be hoity-toity in the studio. You gotta find out what works. It doesn't matter what it is. If that's what makes it work, that's what you go with."

Next is the band's cover of Sweet's "Set Me Free," a squarely heavy metal classic from 1974. Sweet would get some additional long deserved recognition in this era through Black 'n Blue covering "Action" and Krokus covering "Ballroom Blitz." Krokus in particular was very much grappling with the same predicament as Saxon was, both being old boogie metal bands from Europe trying unsuccessfully to look good in clown costumes. Why they could sort out glam clothes that passed the smell test for Ratt, Mötley, Dokken and even Kiss but not for Saxon, Krokus or Accept remains a mystery to this day.

"That was something that they were playing in their set anyway," relates Kevin. "They'd never recorded a cover song, but they played it in the set and it always seemed to really jack up the audience. So they said, why don't we just record it? It was their idea."

And it's an idea that was another gesture—along with the pop, the ballad and the American producer—that made sense if you were trying to break America. Bands on the Sunset Strip would have all kinds of success covering old classics, with the whole party kicked off by Quiet Riot's 1983 treatment of "Cum On Feel the Noize" by Slade, who happened to be the sister band to Sweet back in the previous glam era.

"It wasn't a single, though," qualifies Steve," so it doesn't seem like it was an effort to score stateside success the way Quiet Riot pulled hits with their versions of Slade songs, as some have theorized. Sweet had been a pop band, like T. Rex and Mud and Gary Glitter, but they always had rockier songs on their B-sides. We used to play that one during sound checks, and then we recorded it for a laugh and they put it out! We didn't really even record it with an intention of it coming out."

As Paul told Marko Syrjala, marbling in a few inaccuracies, "That just came about because of the fact that Sweet were big Deep Purple fans as well. We were Deep Purple fans and Sweet were. They were doing a lot of single B-sides that sounded like Deep Purple and that was one of them. We used to go to the bars in our hometown and try and find their rocky B-sides. I seem to remember the B-side of 'Black Night' was 'Speed King.' We're going, 'We must get this album.' That was a way to find out how good albums were. And Sweet had a fair number of singles on jukeboxes and that one we particularly liked because it was so close to 'Flight of the Rat.'"

As Biff told Paul Roland, offering yet a third version of events, "It was on the *Sweet Fanny Adams* album. We hadn't heard it in years until Nigel dug it out of his record collection a few months back. Even though we had nine songs already recorded, we messed about with it and did it. It sounded so good we decided to use it in place of one of our own songs."

Then we're back to Saxon sort of second-guessing heavy American rock for the '80s. "Just Let Me Rock" thumps like an anthem to metal straight off the strip, although lyrically Biff seems preoccupied with being ripped-off, or more pointedly, turning lemons into lemonade.

"It's another one of those mid-tempo rock songs that we're famous for," Biff told Kerrang! at the time. "It's a cry to be left alone to get on with making music and not be tied down with the hassles of business. The management crisis influenced that. It brought us down to earth. The management team had a personal rift and split up. David Poxon, who handled the tour arrangements, went off to get involved with Manowar and Ron Blechner, who up until then had only dealt with the financial side of the business, and couldn't handle the day-to-day problems of the tour. We were in America at the time with Iron Maiden, and there were a lot of cock-ups that we had to take the brunt of. So we had no option but to leave him and find someone else. Now we're with Nigel Thomas and everything is fine."

Most memorable on this one is the big dumb chorus, hollered tailgate party style with big back-up vocals. "Just let me rock! Rock!" is the pearl of wisdom Biff figures he needed to bestow upon us, and it's debateable that the world is better for it.

"Me and Biff," says Kevin, asked who does the gang shouts. "I sing on every record; from REO Speedwagon to every heavy rock album that I've produced, I'm always singing backgrounds. Sometimes it's the whole band. But I'm figuring out the harmony parts. And we don't sing it as, you know, 'You sing the middle third and you take the fifth.' Usually we'd sing all together in unison. And then we just double it and stack it up. That's something I was developing at the same time that Mutt Lange was doing it. I was in London doing a band called Charlie and Mutt came in. He was a friend of the band. He came in to sing some backgrounds on this Charlie record, and I said that's what I'm doing too. Stacking them up, having five voices sing one part, double it, and the next part, same thing. All of a sudden it sounds like there's 30 people singing this background, but all the notes are perfect and the blend is perfect. So I'm singing on every song in the background on *Crusader* along with Biff and I believe Steve did a little bit. Nigel and Graham and Paul did some where there had to be like yelling or a scream kind of thing. But melodically it's pretty much Biff and myself, and sometimes Steve."

Dated background shouts are part of the hideously titled "Bad Boys (Like to Rock 'n' Roll)" as well. Graham takes credit for the amusing opening line, illustrative of how there was much collaboration involved with Saxon songs. "It was all bits and bats. I remember doing 'This carousel's going straight to hell.' So we would be providing lines on *Crusader*. When we were doing things, we sat around, you'd have an idea, one or two words, and then it's sort of out there and gets included. And I remember writing, 'This carousel's from hell.' The vocals and melodies were left to Biff to do. But then Nigel Glockler was a strong lyricist as well, because he'd been a scribe. Pete Gill and Steve Dawson were the scribes for the early albums. They'd sit with pen and paper and write things down. Because they were very neat writers and we weren't. And then Nigel Glockler, when he came into the band, he became the scribe."

The idea of Saxon having a scribe was important because Biff had a habit of lounging around and orating forth lyrics but not writing them down. He gives Steve credit for capturing his thoughts in the early days, and remembers Pete Hinton getting down the words to "Hungry Years," indeed making a few alterations along the way, which was also something Steve Dawson did as well, in fact, more extensively.

"Bad Boys (Like to Rock 'n' Roll)" is your basic party rocker about rocking—in the NWOBHM, Saxon wrote about metal; now it was just general rocking and rolling, representing another form of watering down for American consumption.

Speaking of olive branches extended, next we have "Do It All for You," a primary-coloured paint-by-numbers ballad with insane '80s drums from Nigel, in collusion with Kevin, who gets a songwriting credit on the track. "That was the one where I got slammed by all the heavy metalheads," chuckles Beamish. "At the time I had a silly nickname; I was called the Power Ballad Poobah (laughs), which came from, obviously, 'Keep on Loving You' from REO Speedwagon. There was an influence from that situation, melodically and song structure-wise, and it definitely worked; it got them a more diverse fan base. But the critics hated it, Saxon doing this overwrought power ballad."

"So this was 'Keep on Loving You' all over again. But it was funnier with REO. Gary Richrath of REO Speedwagon hated 'Keep on Loving You' in rehearsal. Hated the song. He just said, 'A real boys' band would not play that pussy song, blah blah blah.' And finally, we were recording the *High Infidelity* album, and they were going out on tours while we were in the studio; couple days, Tuesday, Wednesday, Thursday, kind of thing. So I said, 'I don't want to hear your shit anymore. Bring me... take this DAT.' Gary: 'I hate this song—just hate it.' I said, 'This weekend, bring me back the board tape from the show.'"

"And when he came back after the show, he threw this cassette at me. Here it is. 'Now what happened when you played this new ballad? Tell me what happened.' 'Well, after we finished the song, there was this weird sound from the audience.' So I said, 'Okay, Richrath;' I put the cassette in, the board tape, and I said, 'Yeah, that's girls. Those are girls screaming. You just doubled your fucking audience!' The story goes longer, but same kind of deal with 'Do It All for You,' although it didn't have the same impact. But that seemed to be the response. You know, for Saxon, you didn't see a lot of reviews from females, but they were there at shows. And it did apparently sell two million albums all over Europe and stuff, so it was successful in that way."

As for why he received a writing credit, Beamish says he contributed, "certainly lyrically and melodically. They had the basic idea but it was a total collaboration in rehearsal between everybody. Still, Biff was the main guy."

Repeat offender, Beamish was. "Yes, because with Y&T, I was brought in to do the same thing: let's get them a single that's going to get radio play, rock radio play. And 'Summertime Girls' is the song that finally got them into a whole new audience. And as poppy as it is, it's Phil Kennemore, and Meniketti's voice is just killer, as is his guitar work. And it still gets played on the radio all the time, after 30 years. So similarly with Saxon, we tried to stretch out and bring in a bigger, wider audience. If you listen to *Power & the Glory* and earlier Saxon albums, it's kick you in the face and run, just heavy, heavy, heavy, heavy. This had a lot more musical depth and aspect to it."

The song is actually performed full band, even if it's the bit with Biff over naked guitar that everyone remembers derisively. Plus both the pre-chorus and the chorus are interesting melodically. As well, one can be amused simply by the dynamo that is Nigel, who turns in what is the epitome of a stadium rock power ballad percussive performance, lighters foisted upon high.

Then it's time for another party rocker, "Rock City" beginning disastrously, like Kiss crossed with Quiet Riot covering Slade. This is the chorus before us, but then the band settle into a verse that is acceptable, even if Biff misses another opportunity to give us a good lyric. The fan in the know can't help but compare this to the "Rock City" by Riot—both are basically barroom boogie rockers that date their respective records back a few years to post-blue collar British blues boom rock. Not a good look in 1977 and certainly not a good look in 1984.

Fortunately *Crusader* ends on a strong note: "Run for Your Life" is arguably the most creative thing on the record, complex of riff, modulating, heroic and triumphant even beyond the title track. Even more frustrating—graphic by contrast to what could have been—it's Nigel's best performance on the album, it's groovy and with finesse come fill time, the brief flashes of guitar soloing are tastefully woven in Priest-like and even the big gang backing vocal is strong and memorable. Indeed, these big "ay-oh" chants are the type of thing that helped propel Saxon competitors Iron Maiden to the top. Elsewhere, all over *Crusader*, it's just cheese, but here, on this blessed track, the backing vocals elevate the proceedings, encouraged by Nigel dropping back into a cool semi-tribal thing reminiscent of Neil Peart in the '80s.

"That was sparked off by an Italian football chant that they sing at gigs over there," noted Steve, in conversation with Kerrang!. "The last time we were in Genoa, the kids set fire to the hall and the army were called in. It ended in a riot. Our driver and one of our roadies were arrested and beaten up. A pretty frightening experience."

One last note on this powerful closing performance, since the day I heard *Turbo* from Judas Priest in 1986, I'd always drawn a comparison between that record's "Reckless" and this record's "Run for Your Life." In both cases, after an album's worth of shenanigans, quietly, way at the back of the yard, hidden behind the shed, there's a gem of a no-nonsense song that suggests how one might conceivably operate in this new American hair metal reality with heads held high.

Paul Roland, in his review of the album for Kerrang! agrees with me on the closing number (although liking the totality of the thing a bit more than me), writing, "*Crusader* is the band's most consistently commercial LP to date. It crackles with energy, delivering a gauntlet-clad bunch of fives to all who said that the lads from Barnsley were finished. Enlisting REO Speedwagon producer Kevin Beamish has proved a wise move, as he's given them a clean American sound while still capturing their essentially English approach. *Crusader* is dominated by a big 'live' drum sound, gutsy but not grating guitar, tight, punchy bass lines and full-throttle vocals. Side two is by far the better half, containing as it does the lurching 'Just Let Me Rock,' the ZZ Top-influenced 'Bad Boys' and the obligatory 'heavy ballad' 'Do It All for

You,' which ranks in the same league as Sabbath's 'Changes' and would be well worth releasing as a single. Carrere take note! 'Rock City' and 'Run for Your Lives' bring things to a close, bolting full-tilt to glory. The latter boasts one of the most rousing and uplifting codas ever committed to vinyl, while the former concludes with the promise, 'You want it—we got it!' Too true!"

In any event, when all is said and done, Kevin Beamish knew what he had with this band, with Biff, with Nigel, and also with Graham and Paul as axe men. "Yes, they're both great rhythm players. Graham, when he lost his finger in the car door, I didn't know them at that point, but for him to come back and be able to play like that… Like Angus in AC/DC, fingers or no fingers, if you don't have that rhythm in your soul, you're not going to be great. Graham always just laid it down, again, very much like Angus Young in that regard. Paul was also a great rhythm guitar player, but he had more melodic sense and could play more melodically solo-wise than Graham. Not that anybody was any better. If you had two Graham Olivers, you wouldn't be anywhere. Or if you had two Paul Quinns you wouldn't be anywhere. The fact that they were different and played off of each other was what made that work."

"The album was very successful," Biff told me in 2015. "There's a ballad on there that seemed to piss people off. It seems they didn't want us to do a ballad, ever. But 'Crusader' is a mighty song. That song pretty much saved our bacon on that album. It was a huge song around the world. But again, a lot of it is down to production—it's not heavy. It's as if the producer, who was a nice guy, Kevin, it's as if he's experimenting and didn't quite get it right. Didn't quite find a cure."

The 2009 reissue of the album includes almost the entire record in demo form, as performed at Kaley Studio in 1983. Nigel's drum sound is comparatively more analogue but ultimately there's not a lot of variation here compared to the final versions, save for "A Little Bit of What You Fancy," which sounds like a different song, more like a Van Halen joke tune, a fast shuffling boogie. Elsewhere "Sailing to

America" has some added guitar textures missing from the final, and overall there's a slight uptick in aggression, in bite, but in the end, there's no reason to romanticize the demos over and above what we got back in 1984.

The highlight of the bonus edition is the inclusion of two non-LP tracks, also from the Kaley sessions. "Helter Skelter" is an impressive, uptempo rocker—tough heavy metal, but still in the wheelhouse of the new American rock in ascendance in 1984—that makes use of a bunch of the lyrics we'd get as the vastly inferior "Bad Boys (Like to Rock 'n' Roll." "Borderline" mines similar no-nonsense meat-and-potatoes mid-metal terrain, like a cross between old Saxon and a smeared mélange of the heavy tracks on the late '80s albums. There's just a trace of Judas Priest's "Running Wild" to the thing, and enough potential there to where the Saxon fan becomes frustrated at what could have been. Apply to these two songs the scorched earth production values of *Power & the Glory* and we'd probably have two Saxon classics for the ages on our hands.

"It's not a science," reflects Beamish, on what he achieved with Saxon, "but if you can identify the talents in a band, and trends in music, and try to stretch out from that, you can sit there with your base of fans and stay in the same spot for a pretty long time—you can keep putting out the same kind of records. But epic songs like 'Crusader' and then the little sweet songs, three-minute songs, plus the big ol' bad power ballad, 'Do It All for You'… it definitely stretched the box that they were in. So to me it was a success, and I think they thought it was too. A lot of the critics hated it, but some saw it as an interesting phase."

What's interesting is that the direction taken was not one dictated from the boardroom of some big American record label. "No, it wasn't, because you have to remember, the label at the time that signed them was this little French label called Carrere Records, and there was really no input whatsoever from the label, which was just this one French guy. The input was from Biff, and sometimes Nigel Thomas, the manager. But at the rehearsals over in Barnsley, no, everybody was on the same page. This was just, you know, we're sailing to America to do this record that's going to make us bigger."

"And like I say, it did work in a sense. They were huge in Germany and other parts of Europe, and it sold there more than most of the other records. So it's a tough position to be in for the fans. But even if Biff was the leader, everybody was on the same page. Everybody loved the songs and the direction and it was almost like a sigh of relief to be doing something different from what they'd done before. I don't recall any problems at all. We were gung ho through the whole thing. Nobody said, 'We shouldn't do this and we should do that.' The idea was to try to be a bit different and see what will happen. And in that sense, *Crusader* was a success. But after *Crusader*, I don't know what they were doing. They put out a couple of records that just sounded like they took a week off from the road and went and did something. But *Crusader* had a lot of different aspects to it. It covered pretty much the four corners of the musical square that they played in."

"I think we'd lost our boyish naïveté by that time," muses Biff. "We lost a bit of that world where it first feels really great. It was a sense of writing songs then, rather than just running on with sheer adrenaline and emotion. I think *Power & the Glory* and *Crusader* were our biggest selling albums around the world, but there was a sense that they were bringing in producers to produce us, whereas before it was more of a team—a team of mates, really—making records."

Adds Nigel, "We were under pressure from the record company and management to crack the US, even to the point where we were pressured into using Kevin Beamish as the producer. Kevin's a really nice guy, and he's done some really big albums; it's just that I don't think he was right for us. Now if Jeff Glixman had produced it, who knows? I can see why some people might say we were selling out, but it's one of our biggest selling albums in Europe and when we play the tracks live, they're heavy and powerful. It just goes to show how important the production is."

"There are some great songs on *Crusader*," continues Glockler. "The title track is one of our most popular songs live. And I mean, *Crusader* was huge on the continent and in South America. I'm talking from a personal point of view, but personally I didn't like the production of *Crusader*. Like I say, I think if Glixman had done it, it would have been a lot better. I don't like drum sound all. People love the album, but in my eyes, I think the drum sounds could've been better. But that's another thing where management wants us to go with this guy. Which went on further as we were touring in America, management making decisions about stuff that we didn't really agree with. But hey, we were naïve and went with it."

"*Crusader* was my lowest point ever in making records," figures Steve, "because the guy that our managers wanted to produce was Kevin Beamish, who was famous for producing REO Speedwagon, like wimpy AOR rock, which, there's nothing wrong with that—it's great—but it didn't work for a raw heavy metal band from England. He was just the wrong person, and I had endless arguments with him about how it should sound. I mean he watered the sound down. If you could hear the original demos of those songs, they were really in-your-face. But he watered them down, and if you listen to the backing vocals, it all sounds like REO Speedwagon."

"I mean, *Crusader* is okay, but it just isn't how it should've been. It should've been tons heavier, and that just shows you how you can make a mistake. But, our manager, Nigel Thomas, wanted us to become big in America, and he wanted to get an American producer, who basically watered it down. That was a big mistake, because the American people have got their own—and probably Canadian people—have got their own bands. They don't want to hear a watered-down version of their favourite band; they want something new. You've only got to look at Iron Maiden for that, because they stuck to their guns and never really changed, even to this day, and possibly AC/DC. They just do what they do and the public went along with it, whereas if you try to see into the future and say, 'Oh, if we do it like this, that continent will like it,' that's not really going on. There are lots of bands who've tried that and failed. And that's what happened with us."

Surveying the record years later, Graham figures, "'Do It All for You' has got a great solo from Paul Quinn and 'Rock City' was a good anthem, good sentiment, but my favourite is 'Crusader,' which we still do live. 'Sailing to America,' I had to relearn the song and the guitar solo to play in Milan as a special guest with a famous Italian guitarist and we played it really heavy and powerful, like it should've been. I don't know, *Power & the Glory* has much more involvement from me, in the writing and the heavier production. *Crusader* was more Quinn involvement and a different producer. So they're different things. But people like both albums, really, for different reasons. It's not a pissing contest; both albums are good in their own right."

"The band was confused about its direction," says Paul. "The track 'Crusader' is pivotal battle metal that we know how to do, but some of them were variants of pop music. We wanted to keep writing music that we were happy with, but the album got away from us, when we should have said, 'This producer's not working' or 'This material's not working.' We should have gone home and tried again six months later for that album. But the *Power & the Glory* album was a happy period. Jeff had got a studio full of gear that we were familiar with anyway, a Neve desk and that kind of thing. It didn't sound American—let's not say American because that's a wimp-out word—but it didn't sound AOR."

On March 2nd, 1984, with little fanfare, the world got to witness a pioneering and very, very funny rock "mockumentary" called *This Is Spinal Tap*. Despite many bands expressing concern that the movie was about them and their ridiculous lives, it is Saxon that can claim a considerable and substantial connection to the now legendary cult film.

As Nigel told Jeb Wright, "*Spinal Tap* was a composite of a lot of bands. We did have Harry Shearer with us for a couple of weeks on tour. He watched Steve Dawson and copied his stage movements a lot. Where he sticks his arm up but keeps playing with the other hand, that was definitely copied from Steve. As far as I can ascertain, some of the incidents in the film have their origins in other bands' mishaps; Yes and Black Sabbath are two that spring to mind."

"As regards to us, a couple of stories spring to mind. We played in New York at the Palladium in '82 and had a bit of fun with a couple of leaking dry ice machines. The stage there was sloping towards the audience—raked is the proper term. I think this happened during 'Dallas 1 PM.' I counted the song in and Steve and I started playing. By that time, the stage was about a foot deep in dry ice. Steve rushed to the front and slipped over onto his back and completely vanished in the mist! Graham came running out to start the first guitar part and promptly did the same! They were both completely hidden. The stage was soaked by all the water from the dry ice machines and had become like a skating rink."

"Another story was at a gig somewhere—I can't remember where exactly—but it was at the beginning of 'Denim and Leather,' which I always start with the drum beat. It was the first encore and I went to climb onto the drum riser, in complete darkness, and my foot hit a large coil of leads and I fell backwards off the back of the riser. I was actually very lucky I didn't break my neck as I fell onto the floor, as the riser was about three feet high. The funny thing was that the entire band was waiting behind the cabs to go on and all they heard instead of the drum beat was this loud yell from me and a thump in the darkness. I think I took a couple of drum mics with me, but we soldiered on and the song got played."

Steve Dawson elaborated on the *Spinal Tap* connection, in conversation with Rhino. "You'd get journalists coming on tour with you all the time. 'Oh, is it okay if so-and-so from Kerrang! or Melody Maker or Sounds come with you for a couple of days? They're gonna do a live review, blah blah blah.' 'Yeah, come on!' So we didn't know Harry Shearer for the fame he's got now. He was just another journalist. 'This guy wants to come and hang out with you for three days. Is it okay if he travels around with you?' We said, 'Yeah, no problem!' So what happened was, after the concert, we'd just be hanging about in the bar, talking, and he just got us to talk about things that happened on the road. We didn't know he was making *Spinal Tap*. We just thought he was a journalist. So he took the funny side of things and turned them into a film."

Pete Hinton corroborates this, explaining that, "From private conversations I had with them, you know, it was quite usual that you had journalists on the tour bus, to get an in-depth article out of the band. And they were asked to take this guy—or two guys—on, and they thought they were journalists. They had no idea that they were script-writers. I do believe that is true, because he told me that at such an early stage. I've got no reason to believe otherwise. And it's funny, you know their manager, Nigel Thomas, he was completely the opposite of Biff. Nigel was a moneyed person. He spoke with this upper class accent, and guess what was in *Spinal Tap*?—that. And I think he was the one who sort of encouraged the American thing. And Biff maybe went along with it and said, 'Yeah, we'll give it a go, blah blah blah.' But I mean, did it work? I don't know. History will tell, really."

"I can remember, we were on tour with Iron Maiden in America," continues Steve, "and we went to see *Spinal Tap* in the theatre! (laughs). I mean, obviously, Harry Shearer had been with us, but then there was a time period between then and when the film came out, so we'd forgotten about us and we didn't relate any of the gags to us, really. Two of the members of Iron Maiden, halfway through, got up and walked out in disgust! But we were all there, laughing our balls off, because we thought it was funny. Because let's face it: it is quite pantomime and funny, heavy metal music. That's not taking anything away from the serious side of songwriting or the fans, but if you analyze it, it is quite odd."

"I can remember a funny story, where we were working in a studio in London, and I decided to nip out to get some air. And I've got me black leather biker jacket on, I've got a big mustache, skin-tight red jeans and boots, and I didn't understand why all these guys kept whistling at me (laughs) and shouting 'Faggot!' and stuff like that. But that's where we bought our clothes: the S&M shops in London, the porno shops. Because that's the only place you could buy studs and leather belts and all that stuff. But it didn't come across to us. We just liked leather jackets. There was no gay sexual stuff in it at all. It was other people who mentioned that later on. And when you look back, you think, 'Oh, yeah.' And pulling gigs because the ham won't fit on the bread… I mean, that happened all the time."

"But yeah, with Harry, we didn't pick up on it right away, because Harry doesn't look like Derek Smalls in real life. He was just a short-haired weedy guy (laughs). We just watched it and looked at it as a funny film. I mean, okay, you could draw the comparisons in the way Derek Smalls played the bass, which is very similar to me. In fact, he said that was one of the key things that he got: the way I played with one hand up in the air all the time. Just because playing rock bass, a lot of the time you're more or less like a drummer—you just keep things going. You're not really up and down the neck all the time; you're like pumping an A or an E or something."

"So just out of the fact that I'm only playing with one hand, I might as well do something with the other one! That's how that pointing thing got going: because I realized if you're pointing at somebody in the audience… I mean, I've been in the audience at the Sheffield City Hall, and for some reason, if the guy in the band is looking into the audience, you always think he's looking at you. He's not, really. He's looking at two or three thousand people. But I found if I picked on one guy and pointed at him, it made his day and he went fucking crazy. So I thought, 'Oh, this is all right.' So I just pointed at everybody and they all went mad; they loved it. So that's a bit of a pantomime moment—or a *Spinal Tap* moment, if you will—but it was totally done out of just enjoying meself."

And then there's the apocryphal fruit and veg in the pants trick… "There is a famous photo," laughs Steve. "A guy from Sounds said, 'We want to do a feature of the band, and we want to take some pictures of you walking about in London.' So we all thought, 'Oh, if they're gonna be taking some pictures of us, we'd better get into our stage gear!' So I had those stripey trousers on, and we were there in full spandex and leather, walking around London. And we just happened to go by a shop that sold vegetables. And I noticed this cucumber, so I picked it up and put it in the, uh, usual pose, sticking out, and that was on part of the feature! We told that story to Harry, and I think he just altered it slightly about being down his trousers."

Back in Saxon land, further proof that *Crusader* was doing decent enough business was the fact that they'd moved up the tour ladder. Wrote World Metal Report at the time, "Saxon has finally conquered America. The band has called it The Crusader Tour in support of their new album. The tour, also featuring Accept and Heavy Pettin', has been sold out at every stop. Saxon has waited many years for this tour, and without a doubt is one of the best on the road this year. The band has brought along a castle and their huge eagle to give headbangers a complete show. The massive staging only accented the power and the glory of the band's hour-and-a-half set. It has taken the band several years, and as many albums, to finally give their fans what they have been waiting so long to see. This is the band's first headlining tour the US. The group was advised not to tour without a hit single. The band took the chance and won. When the tour reached Los Angeles, the show was already sold out. There was no doubting it; the crowd at the Civic show mainly came to see Accept; however Saxon had their following as well. Accept did a short 40-minute show, leaving the rest of the night to the Crusaders, Saxon."

And they were sporting a new look, as Biff explained to MetalRules. "I think that everybody went a bit more sophisticated at that time. Think of Def Leppard and their success with *Pyromania*, and Motley Crüe, Bon Jovi, Cinderella and Aerosmith, they all had the style in the '80s. Record companies wanted bands to be more sophisticated and have bigger production on albums. But now afterwards it didn't really suit Saxon. I mean, I think we're much better when we are more natural, if you know what I mean. Anyway. it was a pretty good time for us. It was a good time everywhere. I mean we got laid a lot (laughs), so it was very cool time."

"We did great down the west coast and into Texas," recalls Steve. "And New York was quite popular for us, as were the Denver and Chicago areas. We could do 10,000 people down the west coast and into San Antonio and all those places. In fact, the biggest place we ever played in the States was in San Antonio: it was 18,000 seats and we sold 'em out. But then we'd go over to the east coast and play a club for like 300 people. You've just got to keep going in America. Compared to England, you know, it's a massive area, a massive country."

"Unless you get some sort of big radio action... I mean, how it all got started was that we did this song called 'This Town Rocks.' It was a throwaway song with just a good gesture, but it went on the album, and a radio station picked it up and put us on what they call heavy rotation, which I think was every 20 minutes (laughs). So we had a breakout, as they call it in America, and that's what set it off on the west coast. But it never transferred over to the east in such a big way. But we had a few political things with our record company, which meant that we swapped distribution from CBS to... I can't remember who we swapped to!"

"But it came at a critical period," continues Dawson. "We sort of lost the momentum. I'm not familiar with how the record world works in America now, but then there were a lot of favours done to get you success. And somebody like CBS, if they wanted to break you big, it was just a matter of money, as in the promotional machine and getting you on the right tours. So instead of being on, like, Scorpions tours and co-headlining with Iron Maiden, we ended up on tours like Cheap Trick and Triumph and Aldo Nova, which really weren't our audience. We went down brilliant every night, but they weren't a rock audience. So we sort of missed the boat, and I think Iron Maiden just grabbed all the energy and promotion and really put us into second place. Of course, back then, Def Leppard come along and they had a lot of success too. But we were just sort of missing the boat. Although we did keep going to America and doing well, we never really went coast to coast."

Recalls Nigel from those days, "I remember doing the big tour on *Crusader* where we had to fetch the eagle and people like Ronnie Montrose came on the road and we were big fans. I remember standing there in awe thinking,

'Ronnie Montrose is in my dressing room.' And Mötley Crüe, they were great and we got on really well with them. Nikki challenged me to an arm-punching contest during that tour, you know, where you have to hit the same spot until one of you gives in. We were both walking around with huge bruises for days but I beat him! I saw him in the hotel restaurant one lunch time and he said 'No more.' Brilliant! 'C'mon Nikki, where is it then?' And he just said, 'No no no.' So I won that one. I haven't seen them since that tour, actually."

Chapter 9

Innocence Is No Excuse
"I think it's one of the greatest heavy metal LPs of all time."

Post *Crusader*, Saxon had to sit and watch every heavy metal band around them from the '70s and '80s—let's not forget Saxon were active in both decades—ascend the ladder with quick and deliberate steps, higher and higher, tossing to their enablers from upon high, framed gold and platinum awards until they reached the roof empty-handed.

What's more, Saxon were going through label hassles, although that was a bit of a happy story, as they soon found themselves on EMI, directly signed, rather than on an indie with a good distribution deal.

"We've really been doing very little except writing and recording this album," Biff told Rob Andrews of Hit Parader, in the fall of '85. "The fact is, we were prohibited from touring or even recording for a while because we were involved in a whole legal mess with our former record company, Carrere. It's a very complicated matter. Let's just say that we didn't think they were supporting us properly.

We also wondered if we were seeing all the money that was owed to us. Somehow, our books and theirs just never seemed to match, and we were always on the short end. After a bit of time that got to be extremely annoying. We really had no recourse except to take them to court. When we did that, they had an injunction made that said we couldn't exist as a band, no recording or anything. It was a very annoying time for us."

"We've always been survivors; that's the key to Saxon's appeal, as far as I'm concerned," continued Biff. "We weren't about to let a little hurdle stand in our way. We're like a family in this band. None of us can see going out and playing with other people. We've been touring for about eight years now, and our feelings run very deep. We knew we'd come through that bad time and emerge stronger than ever. That's exactly what happened."

With unwarranted confidence, Byford pronounced to Andrews that *Innocence Is No Excuse*, "is our greatest album ever. I think it's one of the greatest heavy metal LPs of all time. It's going to be the standard against which all future albums are going to be measured. I'm very serious when I say that. Saxon has never had to take a backseat to anyone when it comes to playing heavy metal, so all I can say is, 'Watch out Maiden. Watch out Priest. Saxon's out to prove we're the best once again.'"

"We recorded the album in Germany with an English producer, and the results we got were much more in line with what people expect from Saxon. There's a lot of great, tuneful metal on this album, and it's got that rough edge that we like. There are songs like 'Back on the Streets' and 'Broken Heroes' that are classics Saxon anthems. Things were going so well for us that we actually recorded 14 songs in the studio. Now we have enough material to put new songs on B-sides of singles. It's a nice feeling to actually have extra material. The only problem was figuring out what should go on the album and what should not."

Biff went on to express regret for the band's last record. "All of our records are Saxon albums. No other band in the world could've made them. But I definitely agree that we had our balls cut off on *Crusader*. The difference between a classic album and one that doesn't work is very small in some cases, and that was one of those. We used an American producer on *Crusader*, and while we love America and American rock, the fact is that American producers really don't know how to handle a British metal band. They tend to smooth out the rough edges too much. They make everyone sound the same. That's what happened with *Crusader*."

"America is still the most important market for us to succeed in, and we want to come over and tour for three or four months later this year. I don't know if I would agree with the statement that *Crusader* was designed for America. As I said before, we did use an American producer and it was recorded in the States. So the influence was there. People tend to regard *Crusader* as a failure. The fact is that it sold more copies in America than *Denim and Leather*. We know what Saxon can do. And when we see other bands who couldn't carry our guitar cases selling out arenas and selling lots of albums, it makes us say, 'Hey, that should be us.' Let's just say that Saxon is a very confident band, and we're confident, because we know we're the best heavy metal band in the world."

"As Biff told Kerrrang!'s Howard Johnson at the time, "We just sat tight and wrote about 25 new songs which we demoed at Bram Tchaikovsky's studio in Lincolnshire. Then we just did the same as we'd done in '79. Once we were out of contract, we sent demos to all the majors. All we ever needed was a company that was 100% behind us. The only difference between, say, Iron Maiden and ourselves is that they've had EMI behind them for six years. They're not a better band or a worse band; they've just had the push."

Saxon's previous album came up in this UK interview as well, with Biff reflecting that, "*Crusader* was probably the wrong move. A lot of people said that it wasn't as good as *Power & the Glory* and they were right. If they like Saxon to be totally blow-yer-brains-out heavy metal, *Crusader*'s not like that. But a lot of kids say that *Crusader*'s their favourite album. We did write the ballad specifically to get airplay in the States, but it was still a great song. If Journey had done it, it would've been a massive hit. I guess you have to play what people want you to play."

"We recorded in Munich for three months and really put all the icing on the cake," continued Biff. "We been used to doing albums in six to eight weeks and it was great to have the budget to do things properly. The album had to be real heavy and with a spot-on sound and we've definitely managed to achieve it with Simon Hanhart producing. Simon's been brilliant. Within the next three years, he'll be the No.1 rock producer. He's such a perfectionist. Things have turned out brilliantly. Our new LP is the business! We were lucky, having seven months to write the numbers so we could come up with great tunes. We had about 25, and of course they weren't *all* good, but 24 were! With EMI behind us, and great songs in the bag like 'Broken Heroes,' 'Everybody Up' and 'Shout It Out,' we don't really feel any pressure. Now we're with a company that is prepared to work as hard as we are. We've got things better organized."

The jury is still out if the pull-away from Carrere was a good idea. In retrospect, Biff realizes that the band were at their most successful during the Carrere years, and that promotion of the albums was more than adequate, whereas communication with EMI over the years was pretty much non-existent. As well, Saxon were soon shunted over to subsidiary Parlophone. At the time however, there were squabbles over a live album proposed by Carrere and the matter of a £30,000 payment to the band if there was one. In the end it didn't happen, however the label did put out a badly received compilation called *Strong Arm of the Law*, much to the chagrin of the band, who had been dead-set against it.

After two records made in America, the band found themselves working at Union Studios in Munich, Germany, which had by now turned out to be one of the territorial strongholds for the band. The mix of the band's seventh album would take place at Wisseloord Studios in Hilversum, Netherlands. With a fatalistic view of the new record deal, the band were given a pile of money and went crazy, staying up all night, tooling around on three rent-a-cars. Biff estimates that the bill for living it up at the Munich Hilton for three months came in at DM60,000. The guys had been on a small stipend of £1500 a month each, but the narrative was more about living it up on label money and passing the bills through.

"That's where, for sort of dyed-in-the-wool heavy metal fans, we went wrong," said Steve Dawson, speaking with Rhino about the direction of the record they were making. "Our manager was jealous of Def Leppard because of the money, so he sort of talked us into going down that road production-wise. Because it's the production that makes the songs sound different on that record. It's got that Def Leppard production, loads of vocal harmonies and keyboards and big snare drums and stuff like that. The producer was a guy called Simon Hanhart, and it was his first really big record. And it was also the first time that, basically, the writing of the songs were split up into individual credits. On all previous records, no matter who wrote the songs, they were always credited to the band, because that was the way we agreed to do it. Obviously, some guys come up with more ideas than others, and then again some guy might not have an idea for two years and then just come up with a world-beater. That's how it works. So we just thought, 'We'll just credit everything to everybody.' And it worked up to a certain period. But then, towards the end of me in that band, there wasn't really that camaraderie, shall we say. It was guys going on holiday all the time, and I'm stuck at home writing all these songs. So I thought, 'Well, I think I deserve to have 'em credited to me!'"

Adds Graham, "I think the production was good on that album, but the way we ended up recording it was like Def Leppard, everything single, and I think the performance was lost a little bit. Whereas you got the performance on earlier albums but not the production. But Ozzy Osbourne's first album, you don't really notice the production because the performance is so good from Randy and the guys. The listening audience doesn't care what a snare drum sounds like as long as it's a snare drum (laughs)."

As for producer Simon Hanhart, Graham says, "It was one of his earlier projects, so he was pretty much on a learning curve as well. I think that's why he tried to do it like a Def Leppard album, everything recorded separately. I mean, a band is good at playing and producers are good at making records, and record companies are good at selling them. There are exceptions, of course, but we went with it. But to me, it would've been better off doing it as a band performance, in the studio, and separating things. I mean, *Wheels of Steel*, nearly all the album was recorded by me, Pete Gill and Steve Dawson, because Paul Quinn the first week was at home with an illness. So we recorded him with a guide vocal. So you got the performance and that was a good way of doing it. I heard that Van Halen do it like that."

Oliver adds that there were never problems with the blanket group writing credit, which now was changing. "No, not until our manager said that Biff should be writing all the lyrics on his own. Which kind of happened. But the team effort was good. I can remember people just sat around the table throwing ideas in. We should do this, maybe we can do that. And there was no rule book. Everything was flying by the seat of its pants and it was such a creative period. It didn't matter if someone had a good influence in one song or another because it would balance itself out in another. When we started writing, people like yourself would be the judge of the writing content. And I mean, after Pete Gill left, sales went down. After losing Steve Dawson, sales went down. You're losing key members of the writing team, you know?"

Innocence Is No Excuse would see release on June 24th, 1985. For an album cover, the band went with a decent enough idea, badly executed. An attractive girl bites into an apple. Fair enough, but the bite mark is a sort of botched mix of photography and illustration, as is the Saxon logo which dumbly is carved onto the apple, which is... green. "It's a fucking crap cover," laughs Steve. "A fucking bimbo with an apple. I mean, do me a favour..." with Biff adding, "We just wanted the cover to be more woman-oriented; as I said, we did get laid a lot so it affected that (laughs)."

As for the title, Biff says that it contained echoes of the band's lawsuit with Carrere. It also felt a bit upscale and fresh that the record wasn't simply named after one of the songs on the album, although Biff wouldn't have minded if the record had been called *Back on the Streets*.

Album opener "Rockin' Again" reinforces all this Def Leppard talk we're hearing, but that's not a negative. The song sounds big and ambitious. Biff sings the hell out of it and even the backing vocals sit better in the mix than the cheeseball shouting on the last album. Nigel maintains his use of acoustic and electric arsenal, but he's a bit more behaved and uptown, like Rick Allen. The song is dynamic and epic, like "Crusader," and also in that respect, a bit odd for a side one/song one track—normally bands put this kind of thing at the end, although there's some similarity to "Foolin'," which Def Leppard situated as side two/track one. Biff was definitely opposed to the idea of opening the album with "a ballad" as the first track folks heard on their inaugural EMI record, but he could also see the idea of presenting a more "sophisticated" front.

"Rockin' Again," credited to Biff, Steve and Graham, was the subject of a plush video that combines a Mexican set and storyline with live footage, much of it slow motion, a cliché of the MTV age. What's unexpected and pleasant about the clip is that the barroom scene with drinks and card-playing isn't darkened by scowls and gunfire, but lots of smiles and laughing. This transitions to people having fun in the streets and watching fireworks, again, more frivolity and celebration.

"Call of the Wild" is another strong track, an example of success at party metal riffing and rhythm and production, whereas last album out these things seemed forced and fumbled. As with *Power & the Glory*, Saxon sound skilled, only down a different pathway, sure, a little keyboardy but stout of riff and sophisticated of arrangement.

"I'm really into bands with keyboards—Genesis, early King Crimson, Camel and the like—says Nigel, who shares writing credit on this one with the rest of the band. In fact, my favourite keyboard sound-wise is the Mellotron. I used to go out looking for albums or new bands that had Mellotrons; if I saw it mentioned in the lineup on the album I'd buy it! I've found keyboards really helpful with writing. When we were getting ideas together in Saxon, it was so frustrating not being able to play guitar—I'm useless! I would have to sing a riff idea, and even though I had different parts going 'round in my head, I couldn't get the guys to hear what I was hearing obviously. With keyboards I can use guitar sounds, bass sounds, drums and pads and so on and sequence them here at home just to put across what I'm thinking. Then I'd put it on tape and play it to the guys when we went to the studio for a writing session."

"I have such a broad taste in music," continues Glockler. "I listen to everything from metal through to Vangelis to Renaissance chorale music. I just love playing, listening to great grooves, whatever the style. Really, I was never your normal heavy metal drummer. I was listening to Simon Phillips, Neil Peart and the like and so I tried to bring a different angle into Saxon's music, rather than be blinkered and just listen to what other metal drummers were doing. I wanted to try things from a different perspective."

"Back on the Streets" is another thumping, strong hair metal number. And why waste a good movie set? We're back to a Mexican desert scene, trucks rolling through the dust, the band's Eagle flying high. We're also back to the bar, only a different one, but with the same level of drinking, laughing and joking around. "Back on the Streets" pushes the melodic element a little further than "Call of the Wild" including greater prominence for the keyboards. An unfortunate by-product of the band's pretty much successful music writing and recording on *Innocence Is No Excuse* is Biff giving up on his topical and otherwise interesting lyrics.

"'Back on the Streets' is a great sort of '80s-style rock song," figures Biff. "The track listing on the album wasn't great. We would've been better starting with 'Back on the Streets,' maybe. But the record company didn't want to do that, so we had to go with it. The band were going through changes, in management and mentality. People were getting a bit fucked-up. So around that time it was strange for the band. But I mean, the *Innocence Is No Excuse* tour was the biggest tour we ever did; it was huge. So I think people like the album. Maybe some of the press didn't like the changes we were going through. Which is fair enough—I understand why."

"Back on the Streets" was issued as the first single from the album (all over Europe, mind you, and not in North America), backed with the non-LP "Live Fast Die Young," a solid quick-paced rocker that rumbles proud like old Saxon, both at the music end and lyrically, where Biff strings together outlaw clichés but convincingly.

"Devil Rides Out" maintains the pumping party vibe of the record, sounding like dark Mötley Crüe, heavy Dokken or even W.A.S.P.. Basically it's another successful stadium rocker, hard hair metal perfectly valid in 1985. And if it's Def Leppard-like at all, it's back to the heft of *On Through the Night* or *High 'n' Dry*, which should be taken as high praise. Again, this is Saxon competing in 1985, whereas on the last record, they wobbled. Comments Graham, "The only time that Steve got involved in guitar is on things like 'Back on the Streets' and 'Devil Rides Out,' which are both on *Innocence*. 'Devil Rides Out'—that's a Steve Dawson guitar riff. So there were some riffs from him, but not in the Pete Gill days."

With "Rock 'n' Roll Gypsy," we're back into a more melodic hair metal, sure, a little Def Leppard but more like Krokus-lite (notes Graham, "Steve co-wrote that with me—it's a real live song"). The chorus ain't so hot, nor is the lyric, in which Biff mixes time-honoured Saxon metaphors of motion with the gypsy groupie-nailing life of the rock 'n' roller—Byford says in his book that at one point he slept with 36 willing maidens on 30 days, partly because he had a competition going with one of the crew. The overall effect of this track is a sturdy maintenance of the album's celebratory and even victorious vibe. "Rock 'n' Roll Gypsy" was issued as a picture sleeve single in the UK, backed with "Krakatoa," also non-LP. The B-side recounts the tale of the massive Indonesian island eruption of the Krakatoa volcano in 1883 that killed an estimated 40,000 people. Biff's historical tale is set to a fast double bass drum rocker structured somewhat like "Power and the Glory."

"Broken Heroes" finds Biff back on more admirable lyric terrain, succinctly making the rounds of various wars through time and the damage it causes on those who live and those who die. He was inspired to the task by Britain's involvement in the Falklands War, and the dubious motivations of Margaret Thatcher, of whom Biff was a vocal critic.

The song became a No.1 hit in Poland, so of course the band subsequently high-tailed it over there, Biff remarking the following year that, "Poland was tremendous. The kids were great and I really think more bands should go there. It's nothing like you'd think it would be. In fact at most gigs there were soldiers in the audience throwing their hats up in the air and everything! We loved it." Saxon also found themselves selling a ton of records in Greece of all places, with *Innocence* moving 18,000 copies, double the count of *Crusader*.

Notes Graham, "'Broken Heroes' is a favourite of mine, because I did the guitar solo on it and it came out very well. It's one of my favourites along with 'Dallas 1 PM' and 'Sailing to America,' which I was pleased with the solo performance. But yeah, the *Innocence* album, I remember doing the video for 'Broken Heroes' down in Brighton, and it turned out pretty well. But I was ill on that album. I got an allergic reaction to something, so I spent a week in hospital. But when I came out I finished the guitar parts, which were all multilayered. Simon made us work a little bit harder—it was a different way of doing things."

Indeed on this song, a darker track befitting its subject matter, one can hear that there's something positive to derive from this more meticulous method of working. *Crusader* and even some of the older stuff off the debut or *Strong Arm of the Law* might betray the fact that just playing together as a band isn't always the best plan. To reiterate, Saxon sounded like professionals on *Innocence Is No Excuse*. And yet, it's not the authoritative sense of world-beating professionalism found on *Power & the Glory*. There the guys just sound like the greatest band of all time, lightning in a bottle, fully capable of slaying any band on the planet live off the floor or not. *Crusader* proved that the Saxon of *Power & the Glory* was magic that was not a permanent thing, fragile, ethereal, an anomaly, but white-hot when it briefly existed. *Innocence Is No Excuse* proved that Saxon could play with the big boys, play the game deftly and make creditable music suitable to the market. Whether it succeeded commercially is of no consequence, and the fact that it didn't is not really their fault.

Then we're back to pointless lyrics, although "Gonna Shout" is a happy enough headbang, saved by its plush production, pointed playing and surprise breaks of thoughtful arrangement. But again, the vibe is pure commercial, accessible hair metal, but, on the positive, hair metal at its early hairy best, more Helix than House of Lords.

Strength to strength, "Everybody Up" sounds like gnarly commercial Judas Priest, but with a better drummer than Dave Holland, Nigel tossing in disciplined, classy fills, with his first few volleys being some of the best of his early days Saxon performances. Once more though, too bad about the lyric, with Biff basically shouting out stage patter... for the second song in a row.

Can we have a third? "Raise Some Hell" begins with "Raise some hell tonight," and then we're into another surprisingly heavy track, maybe even the record's heaviest, a throwback to the most malevolent material on the second, third and fourth records, say, for argument's sake, "Machine Gun." Once more there's a sort of linear, level-headed Judas Priest vibe circa *British Steel* or *Screaming for Vengeance*, and it's welcome, certainly by this old school headbanger.

The record closes with "Give It Everything You Got," which is a full-throttle, double bass drum shuffle, again, topped by right-angled Judas Priest chords simpler than everything else going around them. Biff's lyric is another in a long line of inspirational lectures to all the underdogs of the world, to pay your dues, work hard and take chances.

And that was it for *Innocence Is No Excuse*, with the glaring omission on the album being a semblance of a ballad. Sure, "Rockin' Again." "Rock 'n' Roll Gypsy" and "Broken Heroes" are quiet and/or melodic in their own way, but bottom line is this album was considerably heavier than *Crusader*, and yet arguably stood a better chance of going gold, given the sweat ethic put into the detailing. Unfortunate to say, but with a barnstormer of an album cover, this might have been the hit collection EMI was looking for from their new North England charges. Interestingly, Biff figures the label brass were happy with this direction for Saxon in that it represented a marked stylistic difference from their other big NWOBHM band Iron Maiden, who, as Byford says, never made a record remotely like *Innocence Is No Excuse*.

Dave Dickson from Kerrang! gave the album a generous 4K review, but had some minor complaints: "What still leaves the band as promotion contenders rather than championship winners at this stage is the production, courtesy of Simon Hanhart. The drum sound he gets is great, big, beefy and thunderous—check out the opening track, 'Rockin' Again,' for instance—but the guitars are just too weak throughout. And while there's plenty of fine soloing going on ('Back on the Streets,' 'Rock 'n' Roll Gypsy') and great chugging riffs to raise some hell to, the guitar sound never snakes out of the speakers and nails your balls to the wall. Also, some of the lyrics, (e.g. 'Devil Rides Out') are a trifle cringe-inducing, but let's not quibble too much. Saxon are back, turning out the business, and it feels right and proper that they should be doing so at last. All I can recommend is that you give this album some serious attention and that Saxon find themselves a serious rock 'n' roll producer and climb back up to Division One where they belong."

The 2010 reissue of the album didn't disappoint, offering the two non-LP B-sides "Live Fast Die Young" and "Krakatoa," along with "The Medley" ("Heavy Metal Thunder," "Stand Up and Be Counted," "Taking Your Chances" and "Warrior"). Rounding out were four variants on album tracks, three live and one 12" club mix.

Memorably, the club mix of "Back on the Streets" was subject to a celebrity review in the UK press with Jon Bon Jovi and Ratt's Robbin Crosby politely saying nice song, shame about the production. Oddly, Ronnie James Dio was tapped earlier to review the original version, lauding Byford's performance and the guitar solo.

"*Innocence* is a good album," defends Biff, summing up. "It's just different, with different production than what we'd been used to before. I like those later albums. They're great. People have grown to love them, actually. Those albums have a big following."

"Me and Biff more or less wrote the lion's share of the songs on *Innocence Is No Excuse*, and that really was probably the nail in the coffin for me," continues Steve. "Why, I don't know. But I'm really proud of some of the songs on that album. I mean, 'Broken Heroes' is probably my finest hour as a songwriter. And 'Back on the Streets' and 'Rock 'n' Roll Gypsy' and 'Devil Rides Out' all were songs that me and Biff wrote. It's just one of those things that happens in bands. I mean, I've just watched that film *Beware of Mr. Baker* (documentary about Cream drummer Ginger Baker) and that sort of sums up what happens in bands—it just happens. So I'm extremely proud of *Innocence is No Excuse*, but I think it could've been a lot harder. Because I think the production is just watered down for the US."

"The idea was to crack America, but it seems to me that if you just be yourself, that's what America likes. I mean, look at Iron Maiden: they've never changed their sound one bit from the first to the last and they're a massive band. There's a lot of bands from the UK who tried to crack America by trying to be American and they failed. So in answer to that question, I'm proud of that album, and it's got some great songs, but it just didn't quite do it in the States, which is where it was aimed at."

"We've always had good fans who have followed us," Biff told Marko Syrjala. "Not all of them, but quite a lot fans did support us and we were able to tour and we still had a great time and some people still think that *Innocence Is No Excuse* is our best album ever. So you just can not tell what people like. I mean it is a strange world musically. Actually it's always been pretty good for us. I think the press over-exaggerated some things too much and under-exhausted some other things.

"You can always look back on things," reflected Nigel, also speaking with Marko. "We were under pressure all the time by the record company and the management. And I think because we toured in America so much we were being influenced by MTV. Let's not even go there! Come on, Def Leppard were the same, Maiden were wearing all that stuff, it was what was going on then. Look at what David Lee Roth was wearing and everyone went, 'Fucking cool!' That was the time then. But it was our first album for Parlophone/EMI, and everyone wanted it to be a big success. Personally, I think it sounds a bit too polished for a heavy rock band, but there are some great tracks on there. That's not why Steve was kicked out. That came after the *Innocence* tour, and I'm not going to discuss that—it's private band business."

Indeed, at this point it was time for the band to experience their biggest personnel change since Glockler clocked in for Pete Gill—Saxon was about to lose founding member Steve "Dobby" Dawson.

"There weren't really any disagreements," explained Steve, speaking with MetalRules, "but we had done a long tour of Europe and America. We finished in Greece and there was talk of making a new album. I felt that the band needed a break and we had peaked at that point."

Adds Graham, "Due to our previous success we inevitably received some negative press, because there were a couple of journalists that really hated Saxon. They were especially having a go at Biff over his new image because Biff had always had a brilliant image and they felt that he had changed. It was stupid, but this put pressure on the band and added tension between Steve and certain members of the band. I believed that this would blow over but inevitably it did not and Steve and the band parted company. When we started recording the *Rock the Nations* album in Holland, Biff played bass as he had previously been a singer/bass player and he was more than competent to perform this duty."

"As for myself, I parted from the band in 1995. This was mainly due to external influences which appeared to be ruling every decision. I firmly believe that if Saxon had had the same management as the likes of Iron Maiden and

Def Leppard, the band would have remained intact and had the popularity that both of the former still share to this day. What I can say is that the original lineup had a massive influence on the likes of Metallica and Skid Row, and in fact I remember meeting Dimebag Darrell from Pantera who handed me a tape of some early recordings which he asked me to listen to. These were truly fantastic times for both myself and the band."

Adding some key detail to the circumstances concerning his departure, Steve told Rhino that, "We'd done the world tour, we came home, and we were going out on two weeks' holiday before we started writing some more songs for another album. I'd sort of been in dispute with the band over the producer, Gary Lyons, as he was sort of washed-up. In the business, it was well known that his ears had gone, and I thought, 'There's no way I'm having a fucking deaf producer on our next album!' I thought, 'That's being Spinal Tap for real!' 'Oh, we got this great producer; he's done the Rolling Stones, Deep Purple. There's just one catch, man.' 'What's that?' 'He's fucking deaf!' (laughs). I wanted Dieter Dierks to do it, who'd done the Scorpions' *Love at First Sting*, but it didn't work out."

"Anyway, I'm home for two days, I get a phone call: 'Can you come to London? Royal Garden Hotel in Kensington. Can you be there for one o'clock tomorrow?' I said, 'Yeah, no problem! I'll ring Graham, and we'll come down together.' He says, 'Oh, no, we just want you to come down on your own.' So it was sort of an ego boost; I thought, 'Oh, yeah, they want to talk about the producer! I might be getting somewhere!' So I get in me car, drive to London, I go into the coffee shop at Royal Garden Hotel in Kensington, High Street, and a guy called Dave Poxon, who was one of our managers, and the other manager, Nigel Thomas, sat there. They order me a coffee, we start talking about albums and producers."

"And then Nigel Thomas just said, 'Uh, there's something more important that we should be talking about.' And I said, 'What's that?' And he says, 'Your future in the band.' I said, 'What do you mean?' He said, 'You haven't got one. We're firing you.' And that were it! That was the end of the story. I was just history in that one moment. But I was sort of sad and relieved in one hit, if you can understand that. I went straight into recording with a guitarist who Phil Lynott had been working with just before he died, and we started making music. Everything was going great, I'd really been enjoying myself, and then all of a sudden the money stops and you end up in court."

"It all just sort of fizzled out then. I was just getting back to being a well-known musician, but I was broke! (laughs). Which is sort of a familiar story. So I just sort of bummed around a bit, and then after about two years, I just quit the music business. When it got to the point where the guys were turning up to take the house away and all me furniture, I just thought, 'I've got to do something with real people instead of time-wasters.' So I just gave the music business up, really, and I became a stripper.

Not a stripper as in taking my clothes off (laughs). Removing paint from objects! It's still been a bit like *Spinal Tap*, though, because as I'm kind of a famous person, I used to get people coming asking for advice all the time. 'How do you make it big in the music business? How do you do this? How do you do that?'"

"And there was this guy who got an antique shop near where I lived, and he was from Liverpool, and he was a songwriter. Well, he wanted to be a songwriter. So he came 'round, knocking on my door all the time with songs. 'I've just wrote this song!' But the song would be like a Bible! It'd be about two inches' thick of lyrics! So I was telling him, 'Look, forget all that lyrics stuff. Just get a cigarette packet, and you want a good chorus and not much else. You don't need all these lyrics.' It was like Bob Dylan times a hundred!"

"Anyway, this guy was living in this house, and he came up one day and said, 'Right, I'm going to build a fish and chips shop on the side of my home!' (laughs). 'Cause he lived next door to a factory, and he thought, 'All these guys want something to eat, so I'm going to make this fish and chips shop.' And I just said, 'Oh, yeah, okay.' But then I drove past his house one day, and there were all these guys building this fish and chips shop! So he comes by one day, and he said, 'Do you want my antique shop? 'Cause I'm making that much money with fish and chips that I can't have the antique shop anymore.' I said, 'Okay!' He says, 'Just sell the stuff and pay me when it's sold.' But part of the business was stripping furniture, getting paint off it."

"So I had the shop for a bit, and because I live in a place that's surrounded by fields, I decided to do it at home. I was just making a fortune! Finally, the bank manager got me in one day, 'cause I were paying all this cash into the bank, and he thought I was selling drugs! (laughs). So that went from there to people saying, 'Can you make me a table to go with these chairs that you've just taken the paint off?' It just went from nothing to massive in about 12 months, and I ended up having a massive factory with like 50 men in it, and having a good time! I bought two brand-new Jaguars and just discovered that you can still have a good time even if you're not in a rock band. In fact, I found out that there's more people who take drugs and stuff that are not in the music business. You know, in the successful business world, all that hedonism, cocaine and everything, there's more in that side of the world than in rock music!"

But back to the immediate sticking point with respect to his problems with the band, it initially came down to the choice of Gary Lyons to produce the follow-up to *Innocence Is No Excuse*.

"Yes, I would've objected to working with that producer, because to my mind, producers can ruin bands quite easily by bullying the musicians. Because let's face it: if there's no band, there's no producer. But when the producer comes in, if he's like a big-time Charlie, the band seems to be the least important part of the production. You get producers who are, like, if the guitarist can't get the solo, 'Oh, we'll get somebody who can!' If the drummer can't keep time? 'We'll use a drum machine!'"

"Rock music is not supposed to be perfect. It's supposed to be a bit rough 'round the edges. And my outlook is that you've got to get the performance out of the band. And that's what you're trying to get down on tape or

ProTools or whatever you're using. That's what you're trying for. You're not trying to pick on people and make them go into their shell. Because as soon as somebody starts pulling you off after one or two takes, you start to go into your shell. You're, like, 'Well, rather than play to my best ability and be on the edge and be a bit dangerous…' So you go safe, you just get through it with no mistakes, and what you get is just a flat performance. A machine might as well have played it, because that's how you've played: like a machine."

"To be in perfect time, all the time, is not really possible if you're playing music that's a bit wild," concludes Steve. "Now, maybe if you're playing Christopher Cross or REO Speedwagon! Let's get them in there—they're crap! (laughs). You know, you can play that sort of laid-back kind of thing, but if you're supposed to be a heavy metal rock band your mum's scared of, then you should be going for it! I mean, I take my hat off to Motörhead and Lemmy. Them guys just go for it every time. What I'm saying is that the producer's job is to get the band down. If he has to work a bit harder, then he has to. So in answer to your question, if I hadn't been kicked out after *Innocence*, I'd definitely have been chucked out by the next one! I might be coming across as an awkward guy, but I'm not. I just want what's right. And you've got to stand up for your beliefs, haven't you?"

When asked—this is still Steve talking to Rhino for the reissues promo materials—about the next album and its cover of Christopher Cross' "Ride Like the Wind," Dawson says, "I would've objected to it, for a start, because I wouldn't have thought of doing that song. Christopher Cross just ain't on my radio waves at all. That sort of music is just for being in the lift or being in the supermarket. It's musical spew."

Chapter 10

Rock the Nations
"We had a producer that was going deaf."

Not long—or certainly not long enough—after a record that found Saxon not doing well despite the music they so long championed riding a wave, the band were back in the studio looking for answers. Metal was working just fine for others; why not us? After all, we should be really good at it now after so much practice. A big change had them working without Steve Dawson however, actually, with a bass player at all.

"He didn't leave on good terms, no," Nigel told MetalRules. "It was a bit tense. So on the album, Biff played all the bass. Originally we were thinking about getting a session player in, a friend of mine. But we were going through rehearsals and I said to Biff, 'Hey, you're good enough,' so he played bass."

As for Steve after nearly 20 years, Glocker said, "I've just been in contact with him over the last four months. We have an expression in British, 'trying to mend bridges,' and he's fine. I think life is too short for all this bullshit. If he comes back to us with any bullshit then, you know, but it's okay, I can talk to him now. I don't think there's any bad feelings there. I said to him, 'You gotta get on with what you're doing and we'll get on with what we're doing.' At least we talk, have a laugh on the telephone. I'm not saying that he's my best friend but at least we can talk."

"It just happened, really," figures Biff. "It's a bit like divorce; you get certain things which happened during those years and it was out of control. It just gets really silly. Some people get sacked. That's what happens all the time. Steve really had a lot of problems with our management at that time. You know, during that time we had a really big management and basically they sacked him out. So, it's really that simple. He's a very long time gone now—1986. It's all water under the bridge, really."

Resentment had been brewing for a couple years now. Biff puts it down to the fact that he was increasingly becoming the focus of the band, which manifest in the number of interviews he would do at the expense of the others getting their say. Granted, he was better at it, less awkward with questions, able to convey his ideas, charm the scribes and sell the records. The flipside of that is that he found doing press increasingly exhausting, and was becoming resentful at the guys getting to beg off interviews, which is exactly what happened to Alice Cooper vis-à-vis the rest of the original band. As well, Biff was the most chummy with manager Nigel Thomas, and would frequently swan off to Thomas' English manor house, he says, with various girlfriends.

At the same time, Biff says that Steve was suddenly acting out, even acting out of character, as it were, wearing glammy clothes and hats (accented with a green feather!), and hassling the label directly about getting the band's singles up the charts, which annoyed management. What's more, he'd become prone to smashing equipment on stage, including Biff's mic stands.

As for Dawson's replacement, ex-Statetrooper bassist Paul Johnson, who is credited on the album but doesn't play, Glockler says, "I don't want to say anything about him. The management found him somewhere; I don't know where. I just don't want to go there. He was all right, but it was a big jump from having Steve in the band to having him. It wasn't right—or I didn't think it was right—and once Nibbs Carter was in the band, it felt right again."

"I was a bass player before I was a singer," Biff told Darren Cowan. "I sometimes play bass while recording and writing. It's easy. I wrote the songs on the bass, so we just did the bass. It sounds great. We had a bass player live. I just did the bass for the album."

Back in the summer of 1986, after the writing and the recording of the next album, Biff introduced Johnson, noting that, "We didn't want to get in a situation where we were auditioning a million blond and beautiful guys from LA. We just wanted someone who had got his priorities right and I think Paul has. He's young and very keen, and with a bit of nurturing, I'm sure he'll turn out to be a star; he's certainly a great bass player. It was one of those weird situations where fate lent a hand. We'd not really decided how we were going to replace Steve and I'd taken my car in to get the tires changed. While I was waiting, I could hear some tasty bass lines coming from the tire store. His is everyone's dream. I think it gives younger bands and musicians a spark to their imagination to keep going, keep working and trying. Steve wasn't really happy with what he was doing for some time, and that caused a bit of friction within the band. We had to write this album very quickly—we actually did it in eight days!—and we felt that with that friction there, we wouldn't have been able to do it, so we wrote it without him."

Added the new guy, "Saxon have always been one of my favourite bands, and Biff *is* my favourite front man, so I can't wait to get out there on stage beside them, with all that power behind me and all those people in front of me. These guys are really great to get on with. They've made me feel really welcome and I've settled in quickly. I'm really fired up about the whole thing."

Explains Graham, "Paul Johnson flew in and played a couple of overdubs because he actually flew into that session, and contributed. But I can't remember what we'd finished already and what he contributed to, but he did attend the session. We knew about him from his playing in South Yorkshire. So we flew him over and had a jam session and we knew he could play, because him and his brother, his brother had done Steve Dawson's solo stuff. The Johnson brothers were known as good musicians; Paul was a bass player, singing and vocalist. And his brother was a guitarist/vocalist, and songwriter as well."

Just prior to the release of *Rock the Nations*, Graham told Kerrang!, "I think this album is more us than anything we've done before. We took too long with our last album, and it came out too clinical, too note-perfect. This one has been done very quickly; I mean, I've just walked into the studio and whacked down a backing track like I would do live, and I haven't done that since *Wheels of Steel*. That's how it should be done, and I think *Rock the Nations* will benefit from that." Added Paul Quinn, "This new album continues from where *Power & the Glory* left off. We've experimented in between times with a few different things, and we've accumulated more knowledge and more ideas in doing so. So now we're using the best of everything we've learnt on this album."

The band, as a four-piece, found themselves ensconced at Wisseloord Studios in Hilversum, Netherlands, working with partying maniac Gary Lyons, who had recorded with the likes of Nutz, Lone Star, Foreigner, UFO and Gamma.

"We had great fun with Gary," Biff told me years later. "In fact, I met him in New York the last time we played there. So yeah, he's just the same, a happy guy. Fun to be around, good guy, and we had good fun with him. And *Rock the Nations* is a straight out-and-out rock album, really. Made it fairly quickly."

On the negative, Biff has also rued the fact that although Gary was a good technical producer, he didn't offer much direction, with the result being that the album was confusing and too varied. Still, his lasting impression revolves around how much of a character Lyons was, recalling that he had his wife and kid would sit in on the mix, and that he'd have a row of vodkas lined up on the desk to help him through with the task at hand.

Asked about his memories of what would be Saxon's eighth studio album, issued October 13th, 1986, Graham goes immediately to Gary: "Well, we had a producer that was going deaf, for a start—Gary Lyons. Which was a bit of a *Spinal Tap* moment. He had mellowed a bit by then. But the top end of his hearing was going, and he was complaining he couldn't hear very good, which I found quite frankly hilarious, that we were even doing it with him."

For an album cover, Saxon went back to Paul R. Gregory, painter of the iconic *Crusader* jacket. Here Paul riffs on the Montrose-derived title, "painting" Saxon as a band that's huge around the world. The dramatic image also plays on the band's championing of the metal cause, the overall effect sitting well in the market of the day, when illustration ruled the roost.

If you happened to have been a member of the rock press in the day, you might have received with your free copy of the album a lengthy four-page press bio that opened with the following warning: "Expect the unexpected from Saxon. A founding member of the so-called New Wave of British Heavy Metal, which hit like a thunderous bolt of lightning in the late '70s, Saxon nevertheless has always shown a talent for going beyond that limited genre. Take Saxon's latest album, *Rock the Nations* (Capitol), for example. Sure, there are the rock 'n' roll anthems, such as the title track, that are the backbone of hard rock. Sure, there's the requisite nastiness, such as on 'You Ain't No Angel.' But there is also a romantic rocker, 'Waiting for the Night.'"

Of which Biff remarks, "I find that a lot of people are pleasantly surprised by us. Perhaps because of the name Saxon, they expect to hear bone-crushing metal. But we're not mainline. We're very heavy on the backing, but we're melodic, a good rockin' riff with a melodic vocal." Hopeful for what might come, Paul adds, "We've been around quite a long time now. When the first album broke big, we were earmarked to go right to the top. But while we're known all around the world, not so much in America. But we're close. I think with this album we'll really start to click."

Into the *Rock the Nations* record and we're hit with the title track. With a horrible intro sequence lacking in any semblance of creativity, fortunately the track converts, come verse time, into a decent enough rocker, one almost worthy of its single and video status, even if the video was but a live montage. Indeed, "Rock the Nations" sports a few nice licks, as well as a modulation, even if Biff's lyric is another phoned-in missive about rocking, with Byford musing out loud about just how much touring the band seemed to be doing year after year.

EMI pulled out all the stops for its UK-only single campaign, issuing 7", 12", pictured disc and shaped picture disc versions. The 7" featured "747 (Strangers in the Night)" on the flipside while the 12" added "And the Bands Played On."

"Battlecry" puts us back in a NWOBHM world, with Biff regaling us about historic battles between the Scots and the English over a bed of double bass drummed speed metal. Inspiration, however, is arguably at no more than a low hum, the track reminding the listener of a Judas Priest grasping at straws all over *Ram It Down*. Still, there's a cool solo section and obtuse melodies at the chorus to lend the track some thoughtfulness. As well, there's a sense of building intensity across the thing, which wins the listener over by the end of the noisy Nigel barrage—Biff says that the band were trying to write more so with the stage in mind versus what they had done on the previous record.

"Waiting for the Night" is a commercial hair metal number, but it's charming enough, especially, again, come chorus time, where Biff does some nice harmonies with himself. But one can really hear the contrast in production values versus the plush *Innocence Is No Excuse* project, with the band getting a true Gary Lyons sound, essentially noisy, basic and exciting. There's a perennial pulse of synth bass here, and some spare keyboard washes, but the rest of the tones are down and dirty, as Biff is in familiar terrain, travelling, and actually, quite touchingly pining for home.

Recalls Nigel, "I remember that I was in Wales and me and Biff and our sound guy went to this rehearsal place and set it all up and the other guys got there the next morning.

We set all the stuff up, we started jamming and we wrote 'Waiting for the Night' that evening. I played the drums, Biff played the guitar and I think the sound guy was playing bass. We banged down the basic track, then I put keyboards on it and we quickly laid down a chorus and sang that so when the guys showed up the next day we were like 'Here you go!' Just one verse and one chorus—it was great!"

"I do prefer that album," continues Glockler. "The production is heavier and there was a better vibe within the band. We were told by the management, who were in America, that we had to go into the studio and we wrote it quickly. It's a lot more raw, production-wise. There are a couple of weak tracks on there I think—probably more from an arrangement point of view—but the management only gave us ten days to write it! It was ridiculous, but we did it."

"Waiting for the Night" got issued August 18th as a single in both the UK and mainland Europe, backed with non-LPer "Chase the Fade," which Graham says, "is very much a Paul Quinn composition. I remember playing along to it, but it's a bit jiggly jiggly jiggly, you know, not my style. So I think Paul Quinn did the guitars on that one, but it never made the album. Because some of those songs that are uptempo and more musical, they're not really album tracks. They're not really easily… If they're hard to play, they're not easy to listen to, I always find (laughs). Whereas you know, some of the songs just flow and translate in a live situation."

Indeed, "Chase the Fade" is somewhat of a layered and lathered heavy metal scorcher, albeit short and also instrumental. If the album tracks had this much grey matter put to them, and then Biff wrote something wise up top, maybe the record would have sat in the consciousness of Saxon fans a bit more upright and proud.

"We Came Here to Rock" sticks it to the PMRC with boldly stacked chords like Accept at the chorus, and something even cooler on the verses, sort of passionate, melodic commercial Judas Priest. Biff's lyric is both succinct and smart, all of it much better than the title, which lets the side down a bit. All told, however, this is a successful experiment in rowdy headbanging.

Side two of the original vinyl starts with slow thumper "You Ain't No Angel," which has Biff singing in more of a hair style than usual, which makes sense given the pole-dancing rock beneath him. Says Graham, "I did the intro to 'You Ain't No Angel' on my Fernandez, and that's in F sharp and that's one of my riffs. The writing was more of a collective on that album, than *Innocence is No Excuse*."

Next is "Running Hot," which sounds like commercial Priest circa *British Steel*, although, ahem, not up to those standards. At the lyric end, Biff opines how a motorcycle and a girl are kinda the same, Byford checking his brains at the door once again, hoping the band's attempts at facile hair metal somehow finds multi-platinum acceptance.

Then we arrive at pretty much the main reason anybody remembers this record, and that's the Elton John cameo on poppy boogie number "Party 'til You Puke."

Recalls Graham, "What I remembered most was jamming along with Elton John. He was in the next studio. And while we were playing in our studio, we bumped into him in the breaks, and we said, 'Would you put some piano on the album?' And he said, 'I thought you'd never ask,' so he played piano on 'Party 'til You Puke' and that made the album. And then he played on 'Northern Lady.' To have Elton John in was great, because he's a real rock 'n' roller, I think he did it in two takes, which was fantastic. Absolutely, he's a rock 'n' roller, so it was like he was like a member of the band. Yeah, spent all afternoon with us."

"We recorded the main tracks at Wisseloord studios in Holland, and Elton was there in another studio in the same complex," adds Nigel. "Elton and his band always seemed to be hanging out in our studio instead of theirs. One day he just got his tech to wheel in his electric grand piano so he could jam on a couple of tracks—he asked beforehand of course. That's how it happened. I think it's great, and he was a good laugh too! I don't think our paths have crossed since. But they should have been in their own studio working but they were always in the control room. So we said, 'Come on and work with this—wield the piano!' Why not? Bang!"

Biff recalls that the connection with Elton was through Gary, who had worked on Elton's collaboration with Kiki Dee, and was prone to calling the '70s icon Reg, as in Reginald Dwight. John had a helicopter at the ready in the back garden, as he flew around attending various British royalty events.

The hairfest continues with "Empty Promises," although this one's a bit more heroic of riff, like early Def Leppard. A pumping singe note bass line locks in with Nigel's slow-burning groove. I say groove, but Glockler sounds kind of awkward here with his melodramatic fills—this is no longer the feverish drum master with the "Midas Touch." A late surprise in the track is a solo featuring guitar through talkbox, which soon gives way to another round of the song's moderately rich an' bluesy chorus, which, again, is somewhat marred by clunky drum fills.

"A catchy song with the ol' Scottish fandango at the end" is how Paul Quinn describes album-closer "Northern Lady." Essentially what we get is a power ballad with a little bit of southern rock and a little less Led Zep to it, given the quiet bits with tambourine and then the hard-charging chorus. Notes Graham, "'Northern Lady' should've had a Steve Dawson credit, because we actually wrote part of that when we were writing for *Innocence Is No Excuse*. It was a bit faster but the same chords. But that was an outtake of the writing for *Innocence*."

As alluded to, Elton John is on this one as well, but it sounds a little surreptitious: the guys had the track playing and Elton tinkled along, with Gary being on the ball enough to record his casual jamming to the track. Some deft sampling later and there's Elton John on "Northern Lady."

And there it was, *Rock the Nations* was done and Saxon was almost done, done in by chasing an American sound, although to be fair, it kind of worked with the band maintaining a presence on the Billboard charts, following the last album's No.133 placement with this one's No.149. In fact both of those positions surpassed those of *Power & the Glory* and *Crusader*, even if history has those albums enduring and these latter '80s records not so much. Another bright spot was that despite the fact that the glory years were behind them, the home country still cared about Saxon, rewarding *Innocence* and *Rock the Nations* with No.36 and No.34 chart placements respectively.

Wrote Dave Dickson, however, in his three-and-a-half K review for Kerrang!, "Maybe Saxon's day has passed, but when I hear tracks like the stirring 'We Came Here to Rock' or the rather moving ballad 'Northern Lady,' I'm first to recognize they still have the potential in them, but these highlights are dulled by the rather more mediocre material between. Saxon seem trapped in that 'chest-beating' mentality that still affects the up-and-coming heavy metal bands, and I don't know about you, but I'm bored with it. There's a track on side two, called 'Party 'til You Puke' that sums it up; reinforced by 'You Ain't No Angel' it's macho posturing that may have been fine in a Son of a Bitch set but ten years on sounds dated. The production doesn't help either. Gary Lyons appears to have shorn off all the edge from Saxon's attack, the guitars don't cut through with any conviction and Biff's vocals lack their previous raunch and fire. All that said, this is still a pretty good album. It's not something you need to be ashamed about when buying but when I reviewed *Innocence*, I looked forward to a time when Saxon could retain their position in the premier league of rock, and… I'm still looking."

The 2010 remastered reissue of the record brought into the fold the two previously discussed non-LPers "Chase the Fade" and "Everybody Up." Additionally there were 7" single edits of "Waiting for the Night" and "Northern Lady," plus the live B-sides issued with "Northern Lady." Finally there are live renditions of "Power and the Glory," "Rock the Nations" and "Waiting for the Night." I guess the band's discussed cover of Alice Cooper's "School's Out" never got recorded, because it ain't here. Biff said the band had recorded the song in demo form over the years and this time there was a good chance it was going to be recorded for public consumption. But no, it's not on the album proper nor is it a bonus track. Of note, Krokus' version of "School's Out" had been a featured song on that band's ninth album *Change of Address*, issued four months before Saxon gave us *Rock the Nations*.

As the band hit the tour trail, Steve Dawson wasted no time in announcing his new power trio USI, featuring Steve Johnson, brother of new Saxon bassist Paul Johnson, and Nigel Durham, soon to be Saxon's drummer! Steve, like his brother Paul, was also part of Statetrooper, which featured as lead singer, Gary Barden from the Michael Schenker Group.

Dawson warned Kerrang! that, "This is gonna be complete mayhem! On stage we'll be like a live Maxell tape advertisement—hard, loud, powerful and OTT. The sound's big enough as it is, plus as a trio, there's more room for plenty of running about on stage. Also, you can make more money out of a three-piece. We can tour in motorcycle and sidecar or even on a long tandem with a trailer! Once I got out of the Saxon institution, it felt surprisingly good. It was like someone had injected me with a drug. All the old fire and enthusiasm came surging back again."

Back in Saxon land, recalls Nigel of this era, "Being in the thick of the touring in America and Canada on the changeover from the Molly Hatchet, Cheap Trick bands to the glammy rock metal bands and then the power bands around about '88… that was a real musical curve that was really interesting to be involved in. I enjoyed every minute of it. I remember Sebastian Bach coming to see us, saying he had seen us down in that club in Toronto, Rock 'n' Roll Heaven, which is closed now. I had no idea these guys were in the audience before they were famous."

Adds Graham on the itinerary, "We played with Manowar and we did festivals with lots of bands. Plus we headlined Reading Festival in '87, which was fantastic."

Not fantastic enough to keep the band's ace drummer (and participating songwriter) from leaving the fold.

"There were a few problems with the management and I was getting a bit-pissed off, really," reflected Glockler, in conversation with Jeb Wright. "It was personal, really, and there were a few things at home. Plus I went off to do this other gig with Steve Howe, GTR, to play something different."

This was after the success of the self-titled album from GTR, whose flagship members were guitarists Steve Hackett and Steve Howe. The wiry Yes wizard was still on board, as was Max Bacon in the all-important vocal position, but Hackett had flown the coop.

"We recorded a second album," explains Glockler, "but the whole thing was very political because Steve was the only one signed to the record company. One minute they were going, 'We need it more commercial than the first GTR album' and the next they were, 'We need it more arty, like Yes.' So we did that and they went, 'No, we want it back the way it was!' So it was all political. What I think was happening was that you had the other Yes and Brian Lane, who used to manage the original Yes, was managing GTR with Steve Howe, and he was thinking, 'Maybe if I get the other members of Yes together…' Suddenly Steve was dropped from the record company and we only needed another month to get the album finished. It was better than the first one, but Arista dropped him. I found that very bizarre, because when the Anderson Wakeman Bruford Howe album came out, it was on Arista. Saxon got back in touch the following year, and you know the rest!"

Chapter 11

Destiny
"It's a Marmite album for us."

"He went to GTR but I think they've broken up," relayed Biff, speaking to Chris Welch, offering an explanation for the new reality, namely the making of a new record without utility man with the plan, Nigel Glockler. "I liked Nigel; he was a nice kid. There was no bitterness there. He left on good terms and didn't start making stupid demands for half a million quid when he left. Some people think when they leave the band, they're owed a fantastic amount of money. I'll never understand that. They think they should have more money than the people left in the band, which doesn't ring true to me. We're rolling around the world trying to promote albums and this guy is sitting in a council house making three million quid."

"Nigel was okay, but also was a bit funny," continues Byford. "Steve's bitter because he was sacked. He just got unbearable to be on the road with, and went very strange, smashing things up, making silly demands, generally being rubbish to live with, completely schizoid. Being in a band gets people sometimes. They think they should be bigger and deserve more than they're getting. But people don't owe you anything, do they? This is the void. All bands go through it. I'd be bitter if I didn't have things to do. I like restoring old properties and generally getting really mucky. I pulled a fireplace out the other day, and 300 years of soot came down. I had these goggles on and when I looked at myself in a mirror, I was black! We'll be touring to support the album obviously, and that could well start in Europe. We will wait to see how the single does. England is a bit of an unknown quantity for us. The last album sold about 40,000 here, and what we really need is a hit to put us into the 100,000-seller league!"

And so with Nigel Durham in tow instead of Nigel Glockler, Saxon carted off to Hook End Manor Studio to come up with what would be the band's ninth album. "We had a great time being there," recalls Durham, "around three months in total, I think. The drum tracks took four days to do so the rest of the time was hanging out watching all the different recording processes. When I joined the band they'd already begun demoing some songs for the album. The mansion house with the studio was awesome and of course as most people know, it was the former home of Pink Floyd guitarist David Gilmour. But I never really liked the drum sound on the album; it's too polished and the cymbals are almost non-existent. But everyone seemed to get on fine at that time."

"Durham never got much chance to play his own style," noted Paul Quinn, speaking with MetalRules, "because he was playing what other people had written before him so I can't really say what he'd play like if he was left to his own devices; I have to cop out on that one. It was written simple but it was also decided that the drummer should be simple."

"He'd played with Steve Dawson before," adds Graham, "so we knew he was a great drummer from his recordings. And he lived local. But when Nigel left, it was confusing to get another Nigel. Because on tour, Biff would always say 'Nigel Glockler on drums!' But yeah, he was with us for a couple of years."

Already breaking in a new drummer and bass player—and losing writers in the process—Saxon would also have to deal with a new producer for the fifth record in a row. Stephan Galfas had recently worked with Savatage and Stryper, so here we was staying in the "S" section, hoping he could help Saxon score the hit they so desperately needed to stay in the game.

There was a chance however that the band's longtime classic years producer Pete Hinton would make his return. As Biff told Chris Welch, "He worked with us for a few days but EMI weren't keen. We would've used him, definitely; he did *Wheels of Steel* with us and all that. He had just done a few thrash bands and said we were the best at playing fast. So he helped us get the fast stuff together over a three-day period. You see, we had made a list of producers to suit the songs and Pete was one of them. Then EMI said they didn't really want him, and we got Stephan Galfas, an American, who's a real perfectionist. He was a tyrant, but he got us into a groove."

Comments Hinton, "I actually did all the demos and routining for *Destiny*. And then I... you know, I mean, I've got such a great relationship with the guys. They said, 'EMI don't want you.' All right, fair enough, okay. I can't make them change their minds. In fact, on the back of the album, there's an extra special thanks to Pete Hinton (laughs). And I think that was them saying, look, thank you; thank you for doing for all the routining and stuff."

"The band's manager contacted me," begins Galfas, on how he got involved. "I was living at the time in London and in New York so I was back and forth, doing a lot of work in London. I guess I had a reputation for... you know, I've done very different records. I've done Kool & the Gang, I've done jazz, Electric Light Orchestra, so I've done a lot of things. I wasn't specifically a hard rock producer, and they were looking to get more melodic, more song-driven. That's where Biff wanted to go. So their manager organized a meeting and I met with Graham, Paul and Biff, and we hit it off. I'm a musician, a guitar player and also an engineer and so I was different from what they were used to."

"I wanted to do it in a residential," continues Galfas, on choice of venue, "because they all had very complicated personal lives that I wanted them not involved with. So we went to Hook End Manor. David Gilmour is a friend and so we got to use his studio. It was his estate, so we got to live in a mansion. It's a typical lord of the manor English mansion, about 20 fireplaces and ten bathrooms. And they had the staff there that did the cooking and cleaning. We were very luxurious, something the band wasn't used to. But because Gilmour was a friend, we basically got it for just the cost of the staff and electricity. So it was a magnificent place."

"And then Swanyard I picked, because it had a great mix room. I had worked there, mixing Well Well Well and Cutting Crew and a bunch of other records. But there was a great live recording room at Hook End Manor, although it wasn't called Hook End Manor. It was Gilmour's house, and he'd just moved to a new place, and that was his studio where they recorded. And so they had a great vibe in there from all the amazing stuff they recorded. It was a real treat, because they got away from home and it was about an hour outside of London."

As for the building of the album, Stephan begins by saying that, "They had some different musicians. They had Paul Johnson on bass and Nigel Durham on drums and this is the only record that they played on, as a rhythm section. But the experience was really positive. Biff is a very talented guy, as well as Graham and Paul, very talented. All of them. Biff worked his ass off on this record. And I got to know them. Obviously, you're living with someone for two months, you get to know a lot about them. They're definitely a crazy bunch of guys but crazy in a positive way. No drugs. Didn't drink when we were working but they definitely could drink you under the table."

"But it was difficult for them because I'm pretty meticulous. So getting the tracks was difficult. From an American point of view, we're more rhythm section-driven. English bands tend to be more top-driven, guitar- and vocals-driven. And since we had a great drummer—Nigel really delivered—and Paul was a great bass player, I made them get it right. Then we finished recording there, mixed at Swanyard, and then we brought it back and I mastered at Sterling Sound."

Stephan intimates that his hiring was a move by the record company that was a bit of a last ditch effort. "Their sales had dropped off dramatically, prior to this record. Bands have their sell-by date and this was their ninth studio album. And the two just had not come up to anywhere near sales expectations to make money. So this was the record that basically was going to make or break them—if they didn't do well, they would get dropped. And the record ended up doing well. I've been blessed to have some big success with John Waite and Meat Loaf and Cher but my influence growing up was the British rock scene. I was a Beatles fanatic. Britain is the only place, I think, where you've got white people with soul. I was trying hard to keep my American influence limited and really work on just bringing out the best of their British-ness. Because let's face it, they were one of the founders of British heavy metal, one of the originals."

Asked by Chris Welch at the time if it was fair making comparisons to the likes of Def Leppard, with respect to where Galfas might have wanted to take Saxon, Byford says, "No, not at all. Def Leppard makes synthesized music. It's put together over a long period of time to listen to as a product. We think they have great production ideas, but we're not influenced by them. Our influences come from us. We have never sounded like anybody else, really. We have always been Saxon. We have learnt a lot over the years, and we are putting that to good use now. We have nine albums out on back catalogue, and they all still sell, so we know the fans are still out there and the future is bright. There won't be any more changes. Three more members and that should do it. All we need now is a new drummer and singer. I'll sack meself and we'll be away."

"EMI picked that producer for us," figures Graham, "but I don't think he was right for us. He had his own agenda. And the involvement of the band, it wasn't the band, a five-piece. For example, 'Ride Like the Wind,' Paul Quinn did that solely, the arrangement, the vocal arrangement. Everything's down to Paul Quinn on that song. It's just not the album it could've been if we could've worked as a team again and produced it ourselves—it would've been a better album."

"Steady bass player," continues Graham, on the subject of Paul Johnson. "For example, Stephan Galfas had Nigel Durham record all the drum tracks to a click track, with absolutely no music, just on memory. So there's no groove there. How can you groove with no music? It was just an experiment, to me, and it would've been better off being done how we used to record in my opinion. But Hook End Manor was fantastic. It was a state-of-the-art place, a mansion. Marvelous place to record. He'd sold it to this studio, to Inside Studio, and we were gonna call it Outside Studio. But it had been David Gilmour's personal home and studio."

"They were outsiders, absolutely," adds Stephan, on the two new members of the band. "Yeah, they were younger and they didn't fit into the culture. They had to be kind of groomed for that. Like I said, great players but young guns. They know everything. Which is… we all did when we were young. Whereas Graham and Paul and Biff, they knew who they were; they knew what Saxon was about. I mean, Nigel and Paul did a great job. There were no hassles, there were no fights, there was no anything. But I told Biff, 'Are you sure about these guys?' And he said, 'Well, can you get a record out of them?' 'Absolutely.' It was, 'Well, just think about that right now.'"

Following the recording experience in Berkshire and the mix at Swanyard in London, *Destiny* emerged on June 20th, 1988, wrapped in a classy album cover that put illustration behind the band. Instead we got a crisp, clean Saxon "S" in gleaming steel, parked in some warehouse, next to simple yet upscale typography for band name and album title.

Once past the album cover, all hell breaks loose among the fans as they are confronted with Saxon's cover of "Ride Like the Wind" by notorious easy listening artist Christopher Cross. The song, along with the even poppier "Sailing," helped catapult Cross' self-titled debut from 1979 to an astounding five times platinum in the US. It was hoped that some of that rare metal would rub off on Saxon, who just might be able to sell it as another one of their biker anthems.

"That might've been an idea from Paul Quinn," recalls Graham. "Because the idea when we first started it was to do it like a biker song, and to have people on Harley-Davidsons or powerful motorbikes riding, not a horse, but to translate it to motorbikes. That was the original embryonic idea."

However Nigel Durham says 'Ride Like the Wind' was Biff's idea. "I think the record company wanted the band to do a cover for some reason. I'd never heard of the song before but when we did it everyone seemed to like it so that's how it ended up on the album. Basically it's just a cover version, but a lot of people seemed to like it."

"I like his albums," Biff told Chris Welch at the time. "I think we do a good performance. It's like a cross between 'Addicted to Love' and 'Wheels of Steel.' Everybody seems to like the album, except Kerrang!. There's been a lot of claptrap about it being ultra-commercial. It's only commercial in that I'm singing better, more relaxed with a bigger range. The lyrics are a lot deeper and less rock 'n' roll. It's not a change, just a natural progression. I wrote most of the lyrics, like I used to do in the old days, before we started writing like a committee. Now I can write about subjects I can relate to. I'm proud of the album, but I won't say it's our best, because I've said that about all the others. Let people make their own minds up."

Filling in the gaps years later with Marko Syrjala, Biff added, "I liked the song. Christopher Cross is a quite good songwriter and the original song is great. We just transformed that song into rock music. I think that our version is quite cool actually. In Spain and Latin countries, people always ask for that song. So we played that one for them there. We don't usually play that song in northern European countries."

"It was kind of a mutual thing," recalls Galfas, on picking "Ride Like the Wind." "It was a song that Biff liked, and the manager wanted a cover, so we thought we would do a cover that would be something radically different from what Saxon does—Christopher Cross is about as adult rock as you can get. But Biff had a different approach but it was mutual. I present bands with options. I'm not a real dictator in the studio, but as a producer, you have the last say; that's your job. I try choose options we can agree on. The Christopher Cross version was very metaphysical and spiritual and the Saxon version is basically outlaw-themed. Because I tell you, Saxon were outlaws, no question. And Biff has a very strong ego in the band and confidence about himself, but he's not cocky. And he, bizarrely, wasn't doing it for the money or the fame. All of them—Paul, Graham and Biff—they were doing it for the music. Which was something I found very appealing. Because that was always the criteria I had for bands. You want to make hit records? Go somewhere else. If you want to make a great record, that's what we'll do. And they were like, 'We don't give a shit about the record company, we don't give a shit about hits, what we want is a great record.'"

"All the rhythm stuff on 'Ride Like the Wind' is Graham and the leads are Paul," continues Galfas. "But Graham played that rhythm because it's very different for them. Graham was a very feel player. He could've been an American rhythm guitar player. He can play lead, but mainly Paul played the leads. Paul is more flamboyant. Paul would get dressed up in full makeup and the whole deal just to come into the studio—it made him feel like he was on stage. He had to get there. Some bands are like that. I produced Stryper, and they would come into the studio in those god-awful yellow and black outfits. It was so they felt more like they were performing. Paul technically was faster than Graham but Graham had feel. In 99% of the albums I produced, I played guitar in them somewhere, because there's something that somebody couldn't get. That's the only record I can remember that I played no musical instruments, with Saxon. Because the two guitar players covered anything I wanted. I could give Graham anything, play him a record and say, 'Kind of think about this feeling and make it your own' and he could do it. Whereas, Paul plays what Paul plays."

"On 'Ride Like the Wind' we had motorcycle sounds blended in, and wind sounds and ocean sounds," chuckles Galfas. "That was something they came up with; Biff and Graham said, 'Wouldn't it be great to try this?' And I said, 'I've never put sound effects on a heavy rock record.' But I was like, okay, let's go for it. As for guitar sounds, Paul was very precise about what he wanted. I remember one thing; I used 16 mics on the guitar cabinets. We had four guitar cabinets and 16 mics to get the sounds he wanted. Like, he knew what he wanted; he wasn't floundering. He couldn't express it well, because Paul wasn't academically intelligent. He was guitar intelligent. He wasn't schooled. He didn't communicate so well, but he knew what he wanted and I was very patient with him. I wanted him happy because I had a sense of where he was going. I wanted to get his personality—and it's there."

Back to the undisputed leader of the band, Stephan says, "Biff had a strong personality. Here's the deal: an adult male called Biff has to be good. I would tell him that. 'How did you get to be called Biff? You're an adult male. You have a real name.' He goes, 'It's always been Biff.' Because they were definitely working class and that's not a slight; that's a compliment. You should see Biff sing soul songs. He's got blue-eyed soul for miles. I'd sit around with a guitar and play old covers, like Otis Redding. He sang 'Dock of the Bay' to me once, and he had that same sound that all the great blue-eyed soul singers from England had at that time, coming from working class backgrounds."

Can't say, however, that there's much soul to Saxon's "Ride Like the Wind." And the lifeless and unimaginative arrangement to the song doesn't fare much better in video form. Lacking any riding like the wind, what we get is a series of tight claustrophobic shots of what looks like a prison break on behalf of Biff, executed by a bevy of beauties. EMI believed so much in the song that they issued it as a single months in advance of the album (backed with album track "Red Alert") but no one seemed to care. Again, we must take note that *Destiny* was hitting the streets at the height of hair metal mania and moving a million records seemed like shooting fish in a barrel. And yet Saxon kept misfiring. It's almost like the fact that no one could get them to *look* cool just doomed them to being cast aside as relics from an earlier era.

"Where the Lightning Strikes" is played too slow for its wobbly musical premise. Nor are there many lyrics of much consequence. As well, played at this speed, the wetness of the sloggy drums seeps through as do the pointless and dull backing vocals. Next, and next fast (or at least faster than this).

"I Can't Wait Anymore" is an acceptable pop metal conceit appointed by Mickey Mouse keyboards, but Saxon once again get chopped at the knees by the official video conjured for unlikely airplay. Dressed decently enough for once, the band are displayed rocking out way too hard for the music at hand. This tale of spurned love was issued as a single, backed with a live version of "Broken Heroes."

Graham most definitely has regrets about the way Saxon had come across in the videos, explaining that, "They tended to try and influence us to be a bit like Mötley Crüe, you know, in spandex, and Biff got dressed up all like David Lee Roth and people really hated it. I think we had a great image before, but we got talked into it. There's nobody to blame but ourselves. You trust these people. You think these people know what they're talking about. If you want to do well in America, get on these tours and do this and do that, so you tend to go along. I know Biff sometimes gets a lot of stick for that, but it was management that insisted on steering us down that road. But like I said, we fell for it. So it was only ourselves to blame."

Next is "Calm Before the Storm" which has a little more meat on the bones. Stout yet simple of riff, this one's also nicely arcane of melody and includes a modulating section. As Biff told Chris Welch, "'Calm Before the Storm' is about the pits. We've done quite a few fast songs, but they're not thrash. We have never been a thrash band, although we can play fast. We can only play fast when it suits the song. Most thrash is like punk, fast all the time. A lot of people say we started thrash, but all our early songs were about steam trains so there was a need to play at speed! But 'Calm Before the Storm' is about ecology, using up the coal and fishing the seas dry. It's a protest song."

Indeed Biff's lyric is an impassioned tribute to his hard-labouring and long-gone father, with Byford himself having worked in the coalmines briefly himself. The fishing vignette draws a nice parallel, and the end result is a song that not so much speaks to the environment, but those who work to the bone to give their children a better life.

Back on the subject of coal, the Barnsley Main Colliery closed for good in 1991. In a sense, the decline of coal in the UK over the decades is a third theme of this song, namely the end of a way of life, manual labour, where usually before retirement years, a man is taken down by "the iron wheels."

"S.O.S." is an epic Titanic-themed track with a long intro of stormy sea effects that gives way to a riff that is part Geronimo metal Def Leppard, part proto-power metal, in both cases very European. Again, stabbing keyboards detract from the song's heaviness, as does the fatigue-inducing percussion performance from Nigel and the reverb-drenched tones thereof. "We used to play that one live," says Graham. "That's one I really enjoyed doing."

"It's really about people's belief in things being unsinkable, safe and secure," explained Biff. "The ship went down really quick, and you know, they didn't open the third class decks. They were all trapped. Most of the people who died were Irish immigrants."

Ambitious yet dark power ballad "Song for Emma" is next. Huge Def Leppard snare drums drive the melancholy forward, as do braying keyboards, huge backing vocals and recurrent guitar licks, again evocative of Def Leppard circa *Hysteria*—Nigel says that "both 'Song for Emma' and 'We Are Strong' were written in the studio while we were actually recording the album."

Recounts Galfas, "I'm a songwriter and I write a lot of songs, and Biff and I were talking. We were having a beer and shooting the shit, and he had talked about drugs. They were not a drug band, but drugs were proliferating in music at that time. Music was just inundated with cocaine and heroin. And we were talking about drugs and people that had died. And I told him about this girl that I knew very well, that I'd been in love with, and her real name was Emma, and that she had killed herself. And he was like, 'Man, that is an incredible story.'"

"And right then and there, an idea came to me, and I'd picked up his guitar in the room, and it just came for me, from talking about this. The chords came to me and then all of a sudden, within an hour, 90% of the song was done, because it came out of truth and something real. It was a very real thing. The rest of the record was more universal, but he loved how personal it was, so he did it. Paul and Graham came in and said, 'What's that? What is this called?' And Biff turned around and said, 'It's a song for Emma. A friend of ours.' And I was like, 'What a great title.'"

"Song for Emma," logically, would be credited to Biff and Stephan, who receives just the one credit on the album. Elsewhere, there's the cover, but mostly we see the three original members. Drummer Nigel Durham receives no credits; however bassist Paul Johnson shows up three times.

Continues Galfas, "So yes, 'Song for Emma' was very much written both musically and lyrically together. Biff is usually not credited as a musician, but we wrote both the music and the lyrics together, and it was a piece they were very proud of, because it was very personal and different for them. It became very much a fan favourite. They couldn't play it live—it didn't fit into a live show—but it got this incredible following. And it wasn't like I had to have a song on the record—nothing like that. They had a lot of great songs. It was just something that happened organically, one of those rare moments of real music, just two guys in a room writing something together."

Next comes what is arguably the strongest track on the record, "For Whom the Bell Tolls" rocking hard on a sophisticated pure metal riff, at least until the chorus when mournful melody adds a sense of gravitas to the situation, wholly appropriate to Biff's political lyric, which he says is "about the Berlin wall, and is pretty uptempo with the two guitarists playing in unison. A classic Saxon song!"

The song calls for the Berlin Wall to fall, which of course did happen, but not until a year-and-a-half after Saxon's song. Metallica of course have a song also called this, but the lyric there is about an unspecified war situation. The classic Ernest Hemingway novel *For Whom the Bell Tolls* from 1940 is about the Spanish Civil War.

Next we're back to a pop metal place with "We Are Strong," which is essentially a Triumph song from the horrid closing years of that band's slow death. Biff told Kerrang! that the song is "about the strength of the rock movement— 'Denim and Leather' five years on," adding that the next track, "Jericho Siren," "is about the bombing of Poland in the Second World War. We've been to Poland and it's still strong in people's memories there. The Jericho siren was actually fitted to the Stuka dive bombers to make a terrifying noise. We were thinking of calling the album that, but some people wouldn't like it."

German power metal pioneers Helloween have an album called *Walls of Jericho,* and indeed references to the biblical Jericho are rife in heavy metal, given that the story entails a city being crumbled to rubble by the sheer force of sound, the trumpets of Jericho, as it were.

Destiny closes with the album's heaviest track, "Red Alert" being a near speed metal number nicely obtuse melodically but again diminished by keyboards high in the mix. Comments Graham dismissively on the album's closing two tracks, "I just think 'Red Alert' was a bit ploddy. But no, I haven't got much to say. To me they're just album tracks, and if they would've been more than that, we would've done them live. But we didn't."

"We were on the Russian border the day Chernobyl blew up," relays Biff, "playing tennis at the time. We went on to Hungary and the radiation followed us there, down to Austria, and finally back to Scotland. It was everywhere! I'd rather not know if I'm radioactive."

And then that was it for *Destiny*, until the 2010 reissue, that is, which added a 12" mix of "I Can't Wait Anymore," live versions of "Rock the Nations," "Broken

Heroes" and "Gonna Shout" along with monitor mixes of "Ride Like the Wind" and "For Whom the Bell Tolls."

"I'm not a big fan of the album," summarized Nigel Durham, on his date with *Destiny*. "I feel it's the weakest Saxon album to date, song-wise, and just too commercialized. The demos were way heavier and better in my opinion, but when Stephan Galfas came on board in pre-production everything got toned down and simplified playing-wise. He was just doing what the record company wanted, I guess. There were some conflicts about direction etc. but I just went with the flow. I think EMI were pushing hard to try and get Saxon to be more commercialized, which is not what the band is about. This is why they brought in Stephan to do the album. Like I say, the demos were way heavier than the finished album. I really like the *Innocence* album, actually; it has some great songs on it, a lot stronger than the songs on the *Destiny* album."

As a quick summary of those songs, Nigel remarks that "'Where the Lightning Strikes' always reminded me of an AC/DC-type song. "I Can't Wait Anymore' was EMI's choice for a single, I think, and my favourites for drumming were 'Red Alert,' 'For Whom the Bell Tolls' and 'Jericho Siren,' because they're the heaviest tracks on the album."

"After doing the *Destiny* tour," continues Durham, "we came back from the USA to find out EMI had dropped the band, so there was no money coming in from anywhere. But I never really wanted to leave the band."

Recalls Biff, "We were pretty messed-up around that period, actually, and going through some massive problems. It just sort of culminated in that album, really. I'm not a great fan of the album but I quite like the songs. There's too many keyboards on it for me. You know, too many keyboards were put on there, but that's how it goes sometimes."

"It's a Marmite album for us," Graham told Marko Syrjala. "I just think that the producer was wrong. Because he produced the album different from the way we were used to working. I didn't really have much to do with those albums. Our image had been changing since the *Innocence* album and this was a reflection of the times. The next album was *Solid Ball of Rock*, which was Nibbs Carter's first album, That was actually a very enjoyable time for myself and the band due to moving back to writing and recording as a unit."

"Saxon have been produced to death," wrote Chris Watts in his Kerrang! review of the album in March of '88. "*Destiny* is a vinyl crime. It should be arrested, stripped and rebuilt. Then perhaps the band would have the chance for which they've been fighting since '747' and 'And the Bands Played On.' You read that Pete Hinton was on the list of prospective producers, but was kicked off by EMI in favour of Stephan Galfas for trying to push Saxon back to their Barnsley roots. Biff Byford calls Galfas 'a tyrant.' I'd call him and arsehole! An American synth-boy with a truckload of Heart and Starship CDs, sizing up Saxon as worth cultivating for another notch in his list of production credits. A shame. Beneath layers of harmony vocals and blanket keyboards lies one hell of an album. It's not Saxon. Sure, it's Biff Byford, but no way is *Destiny* a roots record. The songs are formula chart hopefuls that have been sapped by the sheer weight of Galfas' knob-twiddling. Look, Saxon had it all. They could've usurped David Maidavale with just the right haircut and satin dressing gowns. They chose their own course and the result is *Destiny*. A great album, but one that isn't Saxon's. I doubt we'll ever hear another '747' or 'Dallas 1 PM' because Saxon have grown up. *Destiny* is a brilliantly executed adult rock album, and it makes me want to cry. All because one megabuck producer wanted to change the world."

The last throes for the band before the decade was out manifested in a little known live album with a dumb title but also... fresh life, through the return of Nigel Glockler and a new bassist in the presence of Nibbs Carter, who is still with the band now 30 years later.

Explained the exiting Paul Johnson, in conversation with Kerrang! toward the end of 1988, "For me, the problems really started when we set out on the *Destiny* world tour, because it was thrown together very quickly. It soon became apparent that it would be very much a Toy Town affair, with a major rock band like Saxon in lots of the little clubs, a big contrast to our excellent *Rock the Nations* tour. The band, for me, had lost all its fire and wasn't even making any attempt to be great. It was kind of sad, you know? But I decided that I would stick it out until after the live album was recorded. There's no way I'm ever going back. I'd just like to put the whole episode behind me now. Saxon were never really a democratic band. I was never told what was going on. I wasn't involved in anything when EMI refused to pick up the next option. The future, however, looks very bright for me. I've got two projects underway at the moment with two name bands, one involves touring here in the UK and the other involves recording in New York. I'm really optimistic now and I can see just what a state Saxon are in. They've lost all the vitality they once had. They still seem to be resting on the laurels they gained eight or nine years ago."

On the acquisition of Nibbs, Nigel Glocker explained to MetalRules that, "What happened was that where we used to write in a studio in Lincolnshire, Nibbs used to hang around there all the time. He was always there when we were there writing, so we knew him. He'd actually worked on the previous Fastway album that I didn't do. So that's how we met him and it was great again."

In what feels like yet another *Spinal Tap* career move for Saxon, the band would end the decade with a live album (*Rock 'n' Roll Gypsies*, out in November of '89), and then start the next one with... a live album.

"Yeah, the *Greatest Hits* one, "says Nigel, meaning 1990's *Greatest Hits Live!*, out September 24th 1990. "Basically what had happened was that an American company had had Saxon since the *Destiny* album and to finish the contract we had to give them a live album to get off them. After that we were without a deal for a while. So we did this huge tour. I think we did 60 gigs in England, and went to places that no one used to play. Not clubs, but proper concert halls that bands didn't bother with. We would just go to all these places and see what happened. It was great and we just kept going. A TV station wanted to tape it for a video since it was a greatest hits live thing and we just thought 'Why not?' We had been cooking for so long, and for some of the songs it was the end of playing them live for the minute. We thought that if we put that out, it would buy us time to start writing and to get another deal since we needed to get something into the market. *Rock 'n' Roll Gypsies* was the one to get rid of the deal, but they didn't promote that very well, so we needed something else out there. So we thought that a video as well, that would be good, and that's *Greatest Hits Live!*. That gave us time to be away and write, and that's when we started on *Solid Ball of Rock*."

Chapter 12

Epilogue
"We do bring the past back with us when we play live but we don't live there."

After the crisis of identity that marked and marred Saxon in the latter half of the 1980s, the band faced another impediment to success in the marketplace's waning interest in all things heavy metal. To be a sure, a metalhead will always be a metalhead, but a large portion of the music-buying public will follow where the excitement and enthusiasm is, where the ad dollars are spent. And for the entirety of the '90s, that was elsewhere, in grunge, in hard alternative, in Britpop, in industrial and techno, and at the tail end, in pop punk and in nu-metal.

Still, Saxon were quietly putting their house in order, beginning to make some fine records aided and abetted by the arrival into the ranks of Timothy "Nibbs" Carter, who would figure on the songwriting of fully eight tracks on 1991's *Solid Ball of Rock*, five of them being sole credits.

This lineup—Biff, Paul, Graham, Nibbs and Nigel—would remain intact through 1992's *Forever Free* and 1995's

Dogs of War (it is generally thought Graham isn't on it but he indeed is) and now we had three studio albums to kick off this difficult decade, not bad considering the state Judas Priest and Iron Maiden found themselves in at this juncture—folks weren't too happy with Motörhead, AC/DC or Ozzy sort of '88 to '95 either.

On July 14th, 1996, Saxon fans were introduced to guitarist Doug Scarratt on record through the release of a double live album called *The Eagles Has Landed – Part II*, which commendably presents mostly recent material, along with a guest cameo by Yngwie Malmsteen on "Denim and Leather."

"Yeah, I knew Doug from before," Nigel told MetalRules. "He lived just around the corner from me at home, so I knew him anyway. We were thinking about who we were going to get and I asked Doug and he said, 'Okay, I'll try.' A friend of ours who had a house in Sussex let us use it, this huge big house. He let us use his living room and his girlfriend had a drum kit so I could just sit down on it and bash something out and Biff came down and Paul did, so it was just us. We tried Doug out, let him blast through a couple of things, and it was great. 'Okay, you're in, pal!'"

Also in 1996, the first rumblings over use of the Saxon name arrived in the guise of an album called *Victim You* under band name Son of a Bitch, which of course is Saxon's first moniker from the late '70s. This featured Ted Bullet on vocals, Haydn Conway on guitars, along with three original Saxon members: Graham Oliver, Steve Dawson and Pete Gill. Soon Graham and Steve would file for legal ownership of the Saxon name, eventually losing the battle, but taking the name Oliver/Dawson Saxon (or, variously, Oliver Dawson Saxon) instead.

Back at home base, next came 1997's *Unleash the Beast* followed by 1999's *Metalhead*, the latter featuring Fritz Randow on drums on account of Nigel bowing out due to injuries. "The medical thing came about later when we were touring," Nigel told MetalRules. "We went to Brazil. I think we did three shows in Brazil just as a one-off thing. When you go somewhere like that, a drum kit to take abroad costs a fortune. So I rang up a drum company over there: 'Can you supply a kit?'"

"Yeah, that was fine, but my kit can be set up by the millimetre the same every night so it was slightly different. I was stretching for something and I didn't feel it but obviously I pulled a muscle. I didn't feel much, just a little bit of pain and thought I had just done something. Then we came over here to Sweden actually and I was playing and tearing it more and more and more like a piece of raw steak. When I was on my back in the bus I was like, 'God almighty!' but when I was playing, it was fine."

"Then we did some English shows and I went to see a chiropractor who did his crap and then the other one, an osteopath, I'd try anything. Nothing was happening, so in the end I thought I'd just see my normal doctor. So he said, 'Does that hurt?' and I went 'Yes!' So he said, 'You've ripped a muscle, so you've got to stop playing for four or five months.' I wasn't allowed to play at all. The band obviously had to go with other people, but I thought I could at least write and do some keyboards, so I got a little studio together at home. I didn't think it was fair to suddenly come back. Fritz was then in the band and I didn't think it was right to come back and go, 'Bye bye Fritz!' So I just did my thing."

Talking with Michael Henry about *Unleash the Beast*, Biff explained that, "I've tried to keep hooks in the songs. A couple of my favourites from the new CD are 'Circle of Light' and 'Cut Out the Disease.' I like those songs in particular because they are atmospheric and quite dark. I write a lot of the lyrics with Nigel, the drummer, but no matter what the song is, or what the lyrics say, I can't sing them any way but melodically—I can't bark them out. 'Cut Out the Disease'... bands these days are afraid to write things that heavy. They think it's uncool to roll out walls of guitars with killer riffs like that.'

On "Absent Friends." Byford explains that, "We had a good friend and tour manager from long, long ago, way before Saxon even. His name was J.J. He worked and helped us for years. When we were preparing to leave for Switzerland to do a festival, he had a brain haemorrhage and died at his house. So we basically wrote him a song called 'Absent Friends.' It was never intended to be a radio song or anything, just a simple lyric that we raise our glasses and toast to J.J. He was a good man and we think of him probably every day."

Continues Byford, "If you listen to our prior CD, *Dogs of War*, you can tell that we were headed in the same direction as this one. All the guitar riffs on both albums are extremely heavy. The reason no bands are playing our kind of music anymore, the heavier stuff, is because the young kids weren't brought up listening to it. They almost consider heavy metal an old person's type of music. And what metal needs right now is for the new bands to stop playing glam rock again, and get down to some good, basic heavy metal. That would bring the genre back to life. People give bands labels. I like to view a band as individual, and not blanket them all together under one label. We play our brand of music and Iron Maiden plays their brand of music. It just so happens that people have labelled our music heavy metal. We are an English rock band playing our style of music—call it or label it what you will. If, let's say, Saxon and the new Bruce Dickinson and the new Judas Priest albums all sold millions of copies, you can bet there would be a ton of new bands all playing heavy metal. So, basically, the future for our type of music lies in the younger players that are coming up in today's music scene. If they really play from the gut and write some heavy music that counts, then the future is bright. But if they just do it to jump on a bandwagon, it's doomed."

Graham and Steve's claims to the Saxon name weren't going away. Starting in 1999, our magazine Brave Words & Bloody Knuckles here in Canada covered the squabble extensively. I recall talking about it with Graham during this period as well as Biff, but it was "Metal" Tim Henderson who dove into the mire most deeply.

As Byford explained to Henderson, "If you listen to our albums, the last three, they're a mixture of more classic rock and a sort of darker, modern feel, really, and that's where we see ourselves. Believe me, there is no war really from our side; our lawyers deal with these things as they come up. The reason I'm doing this with you now, basically, is because their stories that they tell are based on lies and falsehoods. It actually makes it a lot more serious than it is. It's a thorn in our side—that's it."

"If I could just explain it to you in an English sense—because there's no point explaining this in a Canadian sense or an American sense—what actually has happened... now I'll tell you exactly what's happened and this is exactly the truth: when we sacked Graham Oliver, okay, he started a band called Son of a Bitch and released an album called *Victim You*. Meanwhile he sued the members of the band for an accounting because we sacked him, okay? Because in English law, basically when a partnership dissolves you have to give an accounting. It's debatable whether there is any sort of partnership if five people are in the band but only two people write the songs; it's not much of a partnership. And within that structure that he sued us for is how much the name Saxon is worth."

"So when we sacked him, he's claiming an accounting and he's claiming bits and pieces of equipment. He's claiming a fifth share of the big silver eagle we had and he's also claiming a monetary share of the name. The court case is not about the ownership of the name. The court case is actually about what his share of the name is in monetary terms. On the other side, we've countersued him, and we have an injunction pending to stop him using the name Saxon. We've also sued him on a passing-off case. Because he's passing off that band as our band, basically. So when people go and see that band, they expect to see me singing, and they expect to hear songs right from *Solid Ball of Rock* up 'til today. They don't expect to see a couple of old guys from the band playing their interpretation of a few old songs."

"The only reason that we actually get pissed-off is because it's ripping the fans off. We actually get tons and tons of emails to the website. We've just had some now because they've just done a couple of shows in Italy that we actually couldn't stop, basically because the lawyers in Italy are... Italian, what can I say? So, you know, we couldn't stop them and we've already had at least 50 emails saying how crap they were, and they ripped them off. And they even had our photograph... *this* band's photograph on the poster. So basically it's a passing-off case that we are countersuing them with."

"Now, in 1978, Steve Dawson registered the name with Companies House, and there's two things with that. It's completely invalid because they completely changed the law in 1982. The other thing is, we did put an injunction on them in Belgium and produced this piece of paper and Companies House sent us a letter saying it's worthless. So that piece of paper isn't worth the paper it's printed on."

"The name thing works like... if you found out that Cadbury's hadn't patented the name Snickers, you could actually put in for a trademark, and if nobody objected you'd get it. And then you'd phone up Cadbury's and say, 'Oh. by the way, I own the name Snickers,' and then Cadbury's would take you to court because they own the commercial interest in it. So, basically we own the commercial interest in the name Saxon because we have a recording contract for the next five years to release albums under the name Saxon—and those albums are a direct connection with the album we first released in 1979."

"So, basically Graham Oliver's brought this court case as a nuisance thing and because the English legal system is so long and drawn-out, and their lawyers keep stalling and stalling... basically the court case is in October, and then it will be sorted out once and for all. We may have to pay Graham Oliver some money. Money's not the object. What they're doing is basically trying to make it as difficult as possible for us to play anywhere in the world without it being totally confusing for people, and that's what they are trying to do. Their organization and everybody else, they're just out to make a buck out of the fans, we feel. We don't have a problem with them saying ex-Saxon or 'We used to be in Saxon' or 'We're playing all the best songs of Saxon.' I don't have a problem with that at all—they can do whatever they want—but to us, they're just a pretty good covers band."

"This is the way we see it: these bits of paper that they supply, they're all false. I've seen something on the net from a lawyer, that's apparently from both lawyers, which is an agreement. It's not an agreement; it's a private letter from his lawyer to him in September, setting out his case. The lawyers, at the moment, are just about to start winding up all the websites because it's fraudulent. So basically what happens is people talk to these guys and they went along with it, and then they got into serious trouble, and then these guys just take the phone off the hook and basically they get people into trouble by telling fucking lies basically."

"We've sued loads of promoters already for loss of earnings, so it's a serious thing but we can't... the legal system in England is so slow, because it's at High Court in London you see, and people keep jumping in front of us like bloody Duran Duran or something, or Spandau Ballet. You know, they keep jumping the queue. For some reason they've got more money than we have. George Michael was in with his case. The more famous you are, the quicker you can get your case in. It's silly."

"I mean, the only place they can play, really, is a couple of gigs in Chile and with the few Italian promoters that can con the public. They've done a few shows in England at pubs and things but it's very difficult for us to spend the time to try and stop them all. Fans complain to us saying, 'Why don't you stop them?' But it really is difficult. If some guy in Italy wants to put them on as Saxon and use our photograph, and then people go in and see them…"

"The thing is, we've just played two Monsters of Rock festivals in Italy in front of 43,000 people and people are going to go in there expecting to see us. The problem is because the profile of the band in England and possibly Canada isn't very high, people aren't updated to what's happening with Saxon. Generally they're able to go in there and some of the agents and promoters don't know there's two bands going around—they think they're booking the real Saxon. And obviously when they're told they're not the real Saxon, they have two options: they can either cancel or they can go back to the guys and say, 'What's the problem?' And then they lie their ass off so they keep the gig. And then our lawyers send them a letter and come October some of them will be subpoenaed into court and asked, 'Why did you carry on the gig? We've got these letters here from fans, and why did you put the gig on when the fans thought it was somebody else?'"

"And to tell you the truth, they don't have a leg to stand on, really, so that's it basically. It's not as simple as people make out. On bits of paper, saying that somebody's registered the name doesn't mean anything because somebody could register the name Biff Byford, and unless somebody let me know, I wouldn't know, would I? Until someone turns up and says they own that name and then you'd have to go through the procedure of letting the trademark people know that they did it fraudulently and they didn't tell you that there was this and that and the other, and then it is made invalid. And that's what happened to the earlier one. But they're just bits of old paper; it's all they are, really."

"I just want to explain it to you from a truthful point of view," continued Biff. "I don't think Steve Dawson's got any right to the name 'cause it was 1986 when he went. In England there's a six-year statute of limitations, but I don't know what he's doing. And Graham, Graham Oliver was sacked from the band—he didn't leave. And the thing is, we're not a sort of band that earns millions of pounds. We earn so much every gig and it gets shared out, and that's what we earn. If we earn a lot, everybody gets a lot; if we don't earn a lot, nobody gets anything. It's as simple as that—that's how it is. We're in legal battles with EMI Records over our back catalogue, we're in legal battles with our publishing companies over back catalogue. We are actually owed a considerable amount of money."

"But, you know, when somebody's sacked... I'm not going to tell you why he was sacked, but it was for money reasons basically. We're countersuing for that as well. It's just that when somebody's sacked, they're sacked and that's the end of it. Don't forget, we all get our own publishing paid directly. That goes to each band member. I actually set that up nine years ago. Everybody gets paid direct, so there's no problem with publishing money. The record royalties, whenever we recoup, they'll get that direct as well."

"The stupid thing is, they had a deal with Son of a Bitch. They actually had a record deal for three albums, but Oliver's insistence that it should be called Saxon ruined it for them. The problem is that in Europe it's not really a problem. Everybody knows about it and knows they're wankers basically, to cut a long story short, so they don't bother going to see them. It's only in places out of the way that they try and get their foot in there, and they're basically letting fans think that it's us. And Oliver's answer to that would be, 'We can't stop the promoters billing it as Saxon.' But that's not true; the promoters don't bill the two Whitesnake guys as Whitesnake. They bill them as the sound of Whitesnake. So people don't go in there expecting to see David Coverdale. It's not right to say that. Obviously they want them to think it's Saxon because that's the only way they can pull punters; let's face it."

On money matters pertaining to catalogue, Biff told Tim, "We need to know where we are with the accounting for a start, and then we need to know where we are with our copyright. It can take a long time. These companies are so huge. We're sort of a little dot in the landscape to them. They stall and stall and stall. It's really hard; it's just hard. The thing is, sometimes I feel that talking to these people on Oliver's behalf, really I should not bother. I should just say, 'Sod it.' What I'm saying is it's very hypocritical, isn't it? To hate somebody as much as he hates me—or us—and go through the motions of what he does, and then on the other hand expect the payouts when everything is sorted out. That to me is hypocritical."

Back to a happier topic, namely Saxon and *Unleash the Beast* and *Metalhead*, Biff says, "We love the albums. We think we've got a great mixture. We don't want to be a shadow of what we used to be. We don't want to be a band on the club circuit that's playing a few old songs. The only way for us to continue is if we're writing songs that people like today. Obviously people aren't going to like *Metalhead* as much as they liked *Wheels of Steel*, because at that time then in 1980, the whole world was different. We were just coming out of the punk thing and we were just there at the right time. But a lot of our old fans like the new stuff because it's heavier."

"That's what we always were though," continues Byford. "In the early days you could listen to *Wheels of Steel* and all the others. There were quite heavy tracks in there, and there were a few commercial songs packed in amongst them. That's how it was in the early days: we'd have a couple of quite commercial tracks like '747' off *Wheels of Steel* and the record company picked that as a single obviously. But the other tracks were all killer rock songs."

Biff was enthusiastic about the future for Saxon at this juncture, telling Tim, "Basically we're doing loads of festivals across Europe for the rest of this summer and we're in America in August—two weeks in August. The problem is, we're so busy we actually can't find time to do everything. We have to start the next album and it's just a pain really. The next album will be out sometime early in 2001 and I think we may be recording 15 or 16 of the old tracks and give the CD away with the next album, like a thank you/commemorative thing. It's a good idea. Whether or not the record company will do it is another thing. We're going to do that because we feel we'd like to hear the old songs recorded digitally, so they stand up to the old songs on a production level. They might lose something or they might gain something. We're not going to change them too much, just re-record them so they sound great, really. It should be better—my lungs are bigger."

But Biff wasn't done answering questions about Saxon's tangled business web. Asked about original label Carrere, Biff explains that, "We sued them. We went from them to EMI. Don't forget, our manager, Nigel Thomas, died. He actually took a lot of money from us and put it somewhere but nobody's found it yet. With the Oliver thing, I think in some ways he's pissed-off at us because he can't be pissed-off at him, if you know what I mean. It was actually him that managed us through all those early years, right up 'til 1990. So from 1982 through 1990 he was managing us and we were just employed by an offshore company. But yeah, I think sometimes that Graham is so pissed-off that the money went missing that he's suing us instead of him, basically. We're not bothered though; we've countersued him. I've just brought a new claim in for half a million dollars."

"The good thing is, it doesn't affect our music. In fact if anything, we're actually better because of it. I don't think the Canadians are the same but when people attack us we get stronger. In some ways I think it's a positive thing. I use it as a positive thing. I don't see them as any threat to us at all. We kicked out the negative aspects of the band and that's it. We just feel it's a positive against the negative thing. I don't really sound like a worried man. But I wanted to set the record straight with you because it's really not on, this lying. The thing is, they do it so well you tend to fall into the 'feeling sorry for them' trap—everybody does—and it's just a sad thing, really. The whole idea of 'What have they done to me? Oh my God.' I mean, he's supposed to be a fuckin' rock star for fuck sake, not some whingeing fuckin' gas bag."

Summing up, Biff says that, "The record is how I've told you. We feel if the fans knew which band was on, we'd be happy. We're not interested in having wars and things. We just feel that they're ripping people off and we don't think that's on. We don't do a lot of interviews about it—it's really legal, private business—but we enjoy ourselves now, we have a good system, we write the songs in England, record them in Hamburg, Germany with our friends there and German people are well into heavy metal so we feel as though we can record in a great environment for rock music. It's always better to record where people like you!"

I had interviewed Biff about *Metalhead*, the record that arguably kicked off the proper and true rebirth of the band that continues to this day, with Biff describing it as "a mixture of classic metal and a more modern feel, just like the last four albums have been. Because we're really popular again in Europe now, we have to write some songs for the European fans and they're a little more sort of darker, you know what I'm mean? (laughs). So we mix it up a bit, really. So we play some classic melodic stuff, heavy rock with melodic overtones, for our fans who have been with us for a long time. I think it's the best way. We don't want to be a shadow of what we used to be, trying to copy ourselves all the time. We don't really live in the past. We do bring the past back with us when we play live but we don't live there. We don't hanker after the past."

As an update on the legal situation now a couple years later, Biff told me, "Well, we have trouble with them all the time. Nothing much though. They're doing a small disco in Hanover, Germany, and they tried to call it Saxon. But they're calling it Oliver/Dawson Ex-Saxon now, so that's cool. I don't have a problem with that. I mean, they're pretty desperate really, so they do desperate things. Like all people who are on the wrong, they do tell lies to fit the picture. It's pretty easy when you lie a lot, to get the story to fit. Because when you are telling the truth, it's quite hard actually. To get to a certain point, there are so many different roads you have to go down, you know what I'm saying? And their story is just one road, like. Reality isn't like that, is it? Reality is a little luck, a little this, a little that. They put things on the 'net that are really ridiculous. They set out lawyer letters that their lawyers have sent, all sorts of stuff. I'm not going to stoop that low. It's crazy, really. They are desperate men; what can I say? They've been saying things like, 'This is Saxon and Biff left' (laughs). Crazy stuff. And obviously there are some disreputable promoters around in some of the darker places of the planet that that will put somebody on and call them Saxon regardless of what it is."

Oliver/Dawson Saxon would issue a live album called *Re://Landed* in 2000, followed by the *Rock Has Landed It's Alive* DVD in 2002. There'd be another live album in 2014 called *Blood and Thunder*, but in-between, in 2012, the guys finally pony'ed up with some studio material, issuing *Motorbiker*, comprised of a solid batch of traditional metal anthems that had you wishing the guys just got a fresh new name and none of this ever happened.

Back to the state of Saxon's writing at this point, Biff figures, "On the new albums, I've experimented a little bit with my voice and it's not quite so monotonously up there all the time. But when I'm doing sort of the heavy melodic songs, I'll sing the same as I used to sing them. But we want to experiment. We don't want to be boring. It's important for us not to be boring."

On September 24, 2001, Saxon issued their 15th album. *Killing Ground*, like its predecessor, featured cover art by Paul

R. Gregory, and it was also the second record under their solid deal with SPV/Steamhammer, a great home for Saxon if there ever was one. As well, as Biff had telegraphed earlier, there was a bonus CD of old Saxon chestnuts re-recorded.

"*Killing Ground* is a more melodic *Metalhead*," Biff told me a month prior to issue, and two weeks before the shocking terrorist attacks of 9/11. "It's a lot more melodic in its conception and its finish. It's just an accident, really. The guys came up with a few heavy riffs. It's still quite heavy and dark but I made a bit more of a conscious effort to explore the lighter part of our psyche (laughs). We explored our darker side on *Metalhead* and now we're back to more of a historic, life-generated thing. The lyrics… people in Europe are sort of saying it's more like *Crusader* or *Strong Arm of the Law*, actually. Those are both of the albums that they quoted. They lose me (laughs), but there must be some sense in that. It's a bit back to stronger hooks, which is a simple way of putting it. I think the mixture is just about right on this album, really, the mixture of the more modern and the classic style."

Commenting on drummer Fritz Randow and in particular, the shine put on the drum sound, Biff figures, "The guy who did it is quite a young guy so he would put more of a sampled edge on it. We did record everything live, but I think we added a few samples here and there to give it a bit more bite. But the drum sound does change here and there. Some parts are more live than others. The thing is, we're in a bit of a predicament in Europe. It's a brilliant predicament to be in, but we have to cater to our younger fans who have gotten into us in the last four or five years, and our older fans who like the classic stuff as well. It's a bit difficult for us to come out with an album that is all one way, if you know what I mean. We're not the sort of band that just gets a sound on the guitar and runs the tape. We like every song to be different. We like to feel as though we are entertaining the public. It might be an outdated thing, but that's what we feel like we should do (laughs), entertain our fans, really. It sounds a bit naive these days, but we still believe that. We still believe that live as well. I can't ever, ever remember a time we went on stage for any gig—be it a big brilliant massive gig with the eagle rig or a shitty little club—where we didn't try to entertain the audience."

Asked to drill down a little deeper and define who Saxon fans are at this point in their career, Biff says, "Well, the thing is, we are a European band. We're not American or Canadian, we're European. The thing is, our audience, since 1991, has grown very much different, as all rock audiences have. I don't think there's any such thing now as an '80s audience. I think there's a very mixed thing, people who used to be fans that have come back, people who remain loyal fans, and there's new teenagers who got into the music because they're fed up with all the rest of the crap out there. I think that goes for Maiden, Motörhead and quite a few other bands as well. We do spend a lot of time on our songs. It's like wine; we let them mature a little bit and a little bit more. We write for a couple of weeks and then we leave the songs awhile and then we come back and listen, tweak a bit here, tweak a bit there and maybe throw it in the trash can (laughs)."

Beyond the official self-production credit on the album, Saxon worked with the esteemed Charlie Bauerfeind. "He did *Metalhead*, and he also did the re-recorded classics that we're giving away with the album. A guy called Nicolo and I can't pronounce his second name (Nicolo Kotzev—he and Charlie share engineering credits) did the recording of this album. Charlie did a little bit of work on it and then a guy called Herman the German, we call him, Herman Frank, mixed it, with myself and a couple of other people. So it's a bit of a mixed bag, the album. But you have to remember that when we write the songs in our studio in England, that they're pretty much as they're going to be. It's only the actual sounds and the actual mix that really changes. We don't really change much."

Killing Ground included a cover of King Crimson's "The Court of the Crimson King," of which Biff explains, "We tried it in the studio and pretty much decided to do it then and there, really. It sounded pretty good with the guitars and we're a guitar band so we thought, fuck it, let's do it, maybe surprise a few people (laughs). We added a lot to it and maybe brought it into a modern state. I mean, I love the original, I like the Mellotrons and the spirit and the feeling of the original. It's actually a very dark song, and the lyrics, each line is a poem, really; it's a fabulous piece of music. We wanted to do it proud. We didn't want to do it as a gimmick. We wanted to do it as a proper Saxon song. For the vocals, I mean, I'll sing with candles sometimes. If I'm doing something fairly atmospheric like this or 'Shadows on the Wall,' we'd create quite a nice atmosphere, have a couple glasses of wine and a candle, which gets you to focus."

By this point Saxon were indeed settling into a prolific and creative career representative of a band comfortable in their own skins. The records were warmly received but by a limited audience, except it was not so limited that the legend didn't continue to grow. The live shows were of a consistently high standard, performed by a lineup that had just enough youth in it from Nibbs and Doug and whoever was drumming to ride that generational razor's edge to the point where no one had a problem with it.

Nigel Glockler had not drummed for Saxon since *Unleash the Beast*, after which he went into a long period of shoulder rehab. It was never clear that he would ever play the drums again. Fritz Randow played on 1999's *Metalhead* and 2001's *Killing Ground* but then he was gone, replaced by Jörg Michael (Stratovarius, Running Wild) on *Lionheart*, issued September 20th, 2004. Michael was only there for one record, after which, much to everybody's surprise, back comes Nigel, re-joining the band in time for his skills to be part of double live album *The Eagle Has Landed III*, issued June 6th, 2006.

As Nigel told Marko Syrjala, "Physically I think I'm playing better than ever. I think the break did me good, because if I'm playing for too long I start getting a bit bored. Not with the music, but with my own playing and with the forced break that I had, I went away from drums for a little while. I was doing keyboards for writing and stuff and then coming back to playing the songs, it's refreshing again."

"When we knew Jörg was going, Biff said, 'Come on, come back!' and I said, 'I gotta think about it.' I wanted to make sure it was really what I wanted to do. A couple of months went by and I just told them to leave me alone with all these things going through my brain. Initially I thought that I could at least come back for these '80s gigs. He rang me up from Spain and said, 'Well, are you gonna come back?' and I just said, 'Okay, sure.' No excitement in the voice or anything. So he said, 'Really? For the '80s shows?' 'No, I'm back for good.' 'Brilliant!'"

"Apparently they were doing some gigs with Deep Purple in Spain and he went into the sound check and said, 'Oh, by the way, Nigel's coming back,' just completely deadpan, no emotion, just 'Nigel's back.' Nibbs rang me the next day. Actually, the first people I rang up were Lemmy, Mikkey and Phil because they had always been like, 'Go on back, go on back!' Nibbs rang me the next morning, then I rang Doug in his hotel room and Paul rang me in the evening. It was just great."

As Biff told me, "We did this 25th anniversary tour in Germany, of the New Wave of British Heavy Metal, yeah? Basically Jörg went back to Stratovarius, to play violin or something, I don't know. Sorry, stupid joke. And we asked Nigel if he wanted to do the tour, and that's where that came from. And we really liked it. It got to the point where we asked him if he wanted to rejoin the band. He didn't say yes straightaway, by the way. He thought about it for a while, but yeah, we have worked with a lot of drummers now in the last ten years. Nigel had been writing keyboardy, atmospheric stuff, really. He's got quite a lot of music on TV in England."

"If it wasn't for Jörg we'd have probably died on the *Lionheart* tour," explained Nibbs, also speaking with Marko. "He came up with this idea of making sandwiches. Even if we had really good catering, he would just make sandwiches all the time, toasted sandwiches. He was an official gun. He did the *Lionheart* record, did a really good job, and then we did the *Lionheart* tour. I mean, he was on stage with us all the time. It wasn't a 'hired' situation; he was fully into the band and it was a situation where Stratovarius were unsure what they were gonna do. Whatever the situation was, he was 100% with us. He was pretty straight, and we appreciate that he let us know in plenty of time so that we could do the whole *Lionheart* tour and any festivals that we needed to do during the summer."

On the tenor of the *Lionheart* record, Carter mused that, "I must say I really enjoy what Saxon's doing right now. I can remember when I really first started trying to write with the band, I was a bit confused. I used to try and put different elements into the band that didn't really fit. But then Paul actually started using the kind of angle that I was trying to bring into the band and that's developed since *Dogs of War*, really. I mean it's been there for many years. If you listen to 'To Hell and Back Again' and 'Machine Gun' and things like that, it's always been there; the attitude's always been there. But the place that we're at now, the record *Lionheart* is a really good example; there's quite good variation of styles on *Lionheart*. I'm sure it's confused a few Saxon fans but most of that record I think appeals to every Saxon fan. They have to be quite faithful to us to really like it, but I don't think it hurts anybody. The record has got plenty of what you expect from us and quite a lot of other flavours as well."

Another year, another Saxon album, and time to talk to Biff again about what's up. Perhaps it can be felt in Biff's sort of standard line every time out in this modern era, but every Saxon album was beginning to feel interchangeable with the last and the next. Sort of like Accept in the Mark Tornillo era, even if every damn one of them was a solid 8/10 and up, there was a whiff of "too much, too soon" to the trajectory.

March 5th 2007 brought us *The Inner Sanctum*, the first with Nigel back. "Production-wise, it's following on, improving all the time," Biff told me three days later. "It's a good mixture of the Saxon styles, sort of half heavy metal, half rock 'n' roll, and that's really where we are. We started off as a mixture of the two, and we more or less have moved back to that lately. But I think the album gives a good facet of all sides of Saxon, different influences in the band. I just think it's quite entertaining. A lot of people really dig it, because it's not just one song all the way through. They all have different values. For instance, a lot of younger fans are getting into the band by buying the old catalogue, so they're into the rock 'n' roll element as well. So we're in a bit of a win/win situation for us at the moment. Everything is working in Europe right now for us, and hopefully that will move across the Atlantic."

"There are some quite unique things," continues Biff, asked to point out something a bit experimental. "I think the first track, 'State of Grace' is quite unique. I'm dealing with some difficult subjects there to deal with in the heavy metal genre, cathedrals and things. I like approaching quite odd stories. Plus we've gotten a little bit more prog rocky on this. That one has quite a few prog rock elements in the middle, and 'Atila the Hun' is quite a long progressive song. So we are dealing with more of our musical side, which comes more from me and Paul, because we were into prog rock when we were young. So some of the songs are meant to be more musical and less catchy, melody."

More on "State of Grace," Biff calls it "a song that probably only we could do. It's strange, really, sort of like Doobie Brothers crossed with Slayer crossed with AC/DC and a little bit of something else thrown in there (laughs). I love that song. It really does get inside you, actually; it's quite haunting. It's just a mixture of five guys coming together to write a song that is totally theirs, really. 'I've Got to Rock (to Stay Alive)' is a straight out-and-out rock song in the "Wheels of Steel"/"Strong Arm of the Law"/"Solid Ball of Rock" style. But lyrically I like all the songs. It's just two different sides of the planet, really, lyrically. The strange thing is they all work together as well, the songs. And that was something we were worried about in the beginning, when we started putting the album together and recording, that the different styles wouldn't fit. But actually they do. I've obviously approached them with the same vocal performance, so it tends to tie them all together. But lyrically I think it's pretty good. *Lionheart* had some great moments on as well, lyrically."

Pressed for more on that comment about his vocals, Byford opines that, "I'm singing quite full-on these days. We didn't change the style of the performance aspect of the songs when we did the vocals. I sang them all in maybe five days. We didn't do anything different with 'Red Star Falling' versus 'Let Me Feel Your Power;' I'm just singing it louder and more aggressive. We didn't back off on any of the production elements for those songs, so they are quite live. That's what

I'm trying to get at. Everything on there vocally is quite live and done very quickly. We didn't spend a long time trying to get different sounds. So I think it's tied together better because of that."

On the modern methodology with respect to the songwriting, and specifically Nigel Glockler's role, Byford explains that, "All five of us wrote the music, and we usually write the music first. And I usually take it away and do some melodies and rough vocals to it, and then come back and change it all. Nigel's big songs, his major contribution, would be 'Red Star Falling;' he played all the keyboards on that. I mean, we wrote that song as a five-piece. I play bass and he plays keyboards and Nibbs played drums. But you can hear the more keyboard-oriented style on that song, because that's what he's into—as well as his drumming, he's into keyboards. That brought a new element into the band. He plays keyboard parts in the middle of 'Red Star Falling,' which is quite proggy. So his contribution is good. On the last album, *Lionheart*, Nigel didn't contribute anything to the writing, although he contributed to the performance."

"We had a few titles," continues Biff, on calling the record *The Inner Sanctum*. "*State of Grace* was one and *Bloodbrothers* was another one, but that song didn't happen. The thing is, we were doing this huge TV documentary in England, a bit of a fly on the wall thing about us, and I'm writing my new book, an autobiography, at the same time, so I just thought *The Inner Sanctum* was a great title, because I like that religious stuff anyway. *The Inner Sanctum*, the secret place where you're invited, was just a cool thing for the album at this point in our careers."

As pertains the cover art (Saxon has comfortably—maybe too comfortably—settled into a world of illustrations), Biff says, "We had our original artist, who did the album before us, and then actually, a friend of mine, the singer from Blind Guardian (Hansi Kürsch), I was looking at some art work with him, and they got some stuff from a Russian guy that I really liked. So we commissioned the Russian guy to do one, which is the actual album cover. And the back of the cover is a mixture between him and Paul Gregory and another guy we know. So, we're getting more into different styles, trying to connect things. We're always trying to connect things these days, the music with the cover, with the fans and the audience, so it's all a matter of getting the right connection, really."

As for the songwriting, Biff figures, "It's 50/50 between Doug and Paul. Obviously Nibbs is contributing as well in this. He plays guitar, as do I. We're all musicians; this is the thing. But yeah, Doug and Paul are 50/50 on this, really. Doug came up with a lot of *Lionheart*, but I think Paul came up with quite a bit of this album. Their solo work is actually stunning on this album."

Like many members of longstanding heavy metal bands, when it comes to living arrangements, the Saxon guys have scattered. "Nibbs is in Germany; he's got a German wife. I'm living in France at the moment, because it's quiet. Paul's between England and France, as his girlfriend in France. Nigel is down on the south coast, in Brighton."

Pressed for a contrast between the three most recent Saxon albums leading up to *The Inner Sanctum*, Biff says that, "*Metalhead* was the first time we went into the darker side of music and lyrics. We really enjoyed that album. For a band like us to experiment with the darker side is really fun. Not funny, but really fun. And we really went to the astral planes (laughs) and things like that there. In fact, that album is our biggest selling from the back catalogue on SPV. So people are really getting into that album."

"*Killing Ground* happened I think because we got a little bit of misunderstanding with *Metalhead*. We went a little more melodic with *Killing Ground*. But that was a great album as well, actually. And I think *Lionheart* was a mixture of those two. Because we really liked the sounds of *Metalhead* and we liked the melodic elements of *Killing Ground*. And with *Lionheart*, we got to the point where we were happy. And with the new album, we got to the point where we can mix both our influences, which is full-on heavy metal and rock 'n' roll, quite nicely. It's quite difficult to mix two styles, but people accept it. There's more *Strong Arm of the Law/Wheels of Steel*, good-time rock 'n' roll in it."

When I ask if good-time rock "'n' roll might also mean more boogie-based, Biff says, "Yeah, but boogie-based isn't quite in at the moment. When it comes back in, we'll be the first ones to do it (laughs). Believe me."

Saxon was good for an astounding 18th record two years later. *Into the Labyrinth* was issued January 9th, 2009, the band working at Twilight Hall in Krefeld, Germany, Charlie Bauerfeind producing, Paul Gregory back on cover art duties. And then like clockwork, June 3rd 2011, it was time for *Call to Arms*. The big difference this time was that the band was recording in England, and with a new producer, namely Toby Jepson of Little Angels, Gun and late period Fastway fame.

"Toby was really in charge of the performance of the band," Biff told me at the time. "He really concentrated on Nigel's drum-playing and the bass and he spent a lot of time with Nibbs, adding that great live one-take feel on the basic rhythm tracks. Nigel was more arrangements and making sure what people played was good. So it was a good partnership, really. And he worked more with the initial recordings, probably, rather than the overdubbing part of it. In fact, we came to America with that (utilizing Mike Plotnikoff, at Bay7). It was a good partnership, really. We weren't treading on each other's toes."

"The last three records, I think, from *Lionheart*, we've sort of progressed through those three," continued Byford. "The songwriting chemistry was great on those albums but I thought we reached a peak with that production team, so I wanted to use another team. I wanted to get back to the roots a little bit, particularly with the lyrics. The guitarists wrote some riffs that were just really great without all the production techniques that people sometimes used to make them sound better. So we wanted it more within the spirit of the '80s, but obviously with a modern edge to it. So I think we hit the bullet on the head, actually, because it seems that people are really psyched up about the album, just the way it sounds and the way it comes across on first listening. We also sent it away to be mixed. We hadn't done that for quite a while. Usually Charlie, the co-producer, mixes it, and so this time we wanted somebody away, who wasn't as connected with the project. And we wanted it to sound British. That's one of the things we wanted to do and I think that worked as well."

On the military theme, Biff says, "Yeah, I write a lot of songs about soldiers. Maybe I was a soldier in another life before, I don't know. But it keeps coming to me. I'd read a book called *Letters from the Front*, and it's just letters that were found on bodies, or guys sent home to their wives, or wives sent to them—French and English soldiers, quite moving—which is what inspired the lyrics for 'Call to Arms.' So the song is set in the First World War, but it could be set in Afghanistan or anywhere, really. It seems we keep returning to that theme a lot. Yeah, I like it. I used to collect stuff, but not anymore. But I'm quite a historian when it comes to all things war. Lemmy used to collect, and when I collected, I gave him a few things that German fans gave me. Daggers and crosses and such."

As Nigel told Jeb Wright, "We were starting to sound a bit Euro-metal, and we decided to get back to basics a bit more. We changed producers too, and stayed in England to record. I think all these factors helped to make *Call to Arms* the album it is, but better was to come!"

"It just becomes a big thorn in your side," continued Glocker on the various disputes with Graham and Steve. "But it's water under the bridge now. I was away from the band during most of this, but was still involved. Biff took the brunt of it, I think. We don't discuss it anymore; it's just not worth it. Just move on!"

One nice development in the family was that on February 27th, 2012, Angel Air came to the table with a fine and full-on Oliver Dawson Saxon studio album called *Motorbiker*. "Basically it's what me and Graham do best," Steve told me at the time. "We only know one sort of way to write songs and perform them. And I would say it's more in the era of *Wheels of Steel/Strong Arm of the Law*, but obviously we've gotten older and wiser, and modern technology allows you to do certain things with the sound. But basically it's just a hard rock album, maybe metal, in the spirit of that era, in that classic Saxon tradition."

March 26th 2013, Saxon was back with *Sacrifice* and getting a little closer to Accept's turf by recording with producer extraordinaire and soon to be Judas Priest guitarist Andy Sneap. Although according to Biff, "I produced this album myself. I went back to the old days; it has a bit of the spirit of the '80's on it. There's a modern edge to it as well."

Speaking with Jeb Wright about the title track to the record, Byford explained that, "I went to Mexico and went to the Mayan ruins. We were on tour there and we got a private tour of the ruins. This gal was telling me about all of the human sacrifices that went on there and I thought that was a cool idea for a song. I kept it in my head and then it popped up. There were stories of ripping peoples' hearts out while they were still beating. There's a bit of *Raiders of the Lost Ark* going on there. I just thought it would make a great song."

Another highlight is "Made in Belfast," of which Biff relates that, "Originally it wasn't like it is on the album. I wanted to put a Celtic style on it. We brought in a mandolin and we came up with this Celtic riff at the beginning and then it went straight into this bone-crushing metal riff. It's a very unique song. We went back to the bygone age of the shipbuilding times in Belfast. I was in Belfast, as our agent is from there. We were hanging out in the pub there and one day we went to the new Titanic museum there. It's in the place where the old shipyards used to be. It got me to thinking that hundreds and thousands of people used to work there making battleships and cruisers. And then 'Guardians of the Tombs,' coming up with that was like finding something in your garden; imagine you are digging in your garden and you dig up a pyramid underneath your house. It's a cool story, a fantasy song, really. I am just fantasizing about going through life. "

Further on his role in producing *Sacrifice*, Biff explains that, "I have co-produced a lot of albums and I had an idea how this album should sound. I wanted the guys to be natural and just do what they do: play a Les Paul through a Marshall amp and make it sound great. That is really what my philosophy was. I wanted to bring back some twin guitar parts because we've not been doing that for a while. I enjoy the creative process of producing. I get involved a little bit in the songwriting and the arrangements. You just need a good engineer to lay out the sound for you. You have to be careful with the digital recording not to put too much on there. If you have a good engineer, then you can steer it where you want it to go."

Asked by Jeb about "Stand Up and Fight," Biff says, "I wrote that song for a lot of the younger bands out there. They ask me all the time how we survived as long as we have. We just stand up and fight and we believe in what we are doing. That is what my message is, so this song is for them. *Sacrifice* fits right up there with the landmark albums that we've made. With *Call to Arms* we got close to this album. With this one, we really nailed it, because it has that aggression that we used to have in the '80s. There is no ballad on this album. I didn't want a ballad, so we left that behind. Songs like 'Stand Up and Fight' and 'Warriors of the Road' are very aggressive. It has some sophisticated songs on there as well. I think it encapsulates everything we've learned and everything we've stood for. This album is a great marker that says, 'This is it; this is where we are 20 albums later.' You have to ask yourself, 'What made us great? Why did people like us in the '80s?' We are still asking that question now. We want to get that spirit of how we felt when we were 19 or 20 and were doing this and we want to do it a bit more."

Jeb then asked Biff about *Saxon: Heavy Metal Thunder – The Movie*, a professional documentary of the band from 2010 and then recently issued on DVD. "We didn't do it," qualifies Biff. "Some of the people who used to work with the BBC did that. They are big fans of the band now, and big fans of the band from the past. They wanted to tell the story and fill in the gaps. We had editorial control but we didn't stop anything. We suggested they use the old members and get their side of things. I think the whole package is great. It's funny, it's sad and there's some great footage. We have a lot of new fans that may have never heard of Graham Oliver and Steve Dawson. It is good for the younger fans to know the band and to see what all of the fuss was about. Steve was a bit of a stand-up comedian and Graham was living in the past a bit but they still get their point across. You look at it and you see yourself talking about these things and you see the others talking about things and it really takes you back. I think the 'warts and all' style is the way to do a documentary. If, at the end of the day, you look cool and you keep things from being stupid, then I think you should do it."

Added Nigel Glockler on Saxon's 20th album, "The only time you might realize you have something good is when it's totally finished, mixed and mastered. Sure, one can jump around in the control room to a track, but until it's finally completed, you never really know how it's going to turn out. I have to say it's my fave Saxon album. It was hard work but a lot of fun composing and recording it. The band mood/vibe was great from start to finish. I think my favourite track off *Sacrifice* is 'Guardians of the Tomb.'"

Surveying the long life of the band at this juncture, Nigel figures, "In hindsight there are a few things we might have done differently, not so much musically, but mainly business-wise. It's not something I'm going to go into here. I don't like looking back as you can't change what has passed. You have to look to the future. I think we've been extremely fortunate to survive all these years as a lot of bands have fallen by the wayside. Our fans are amazing, so thank you to each and every one of you for giving us a fantastic career."

Andy Sneap is elevated to role as producer, solely credited, for the next Saxon album, *Battering Ram*, issued October 16th, 2015. "The first five tracks of the album are quite heavy," Biff told me three weeks later, "and then it starts to get a bit more melodic later on. But yeah, we wanted to make a statement, 21st album, wanted it to be a rocking album for older fans or newer fans, really, and I think it does the trick."

Byford takes his predilection for military history to the extreme with closing track "Kingdom of the Cross." "I had written a poem about the First World War and put it online last year, and then I was just toying with the idea of putting it to music. Getting an actor to talk the verse, really. So it's just a wacky idea of mine, I suppose, that seems to have worked. Everybody seems to like it. It's a nice theme for the end of the record."

"I've worked with him quite a bit now—he mixed *Sacrifice* for us," says Biff, asked about Andy Sneap. "I did some vocals with him. He did The Scintilla Project, side-project, and I was on that, so I do have a bit of a relationship with him as far as recording."

This was actually a progressive metal concept album, called *The Hybrid*, under the band banner, The Scintilla Project Featuring Biff Byford. Driven by Balance of Power bassist Anthony Ritchie, the band also featured Balance of Power drummer Lionel Hicks. Andy is lone guitarist and Biff does all the vocals.

"So I trusted him enough to give him the producer job on this album," continues Biff. "But yeah, he's a great fan of the '80s, Andy. But he's also a great fan of the modern as well. So he's the perfect guy for Saxon, actually, to stitch the two together. It's like a mashing together of sounds. He didn't really write any songs, but as far as getting the performance from the band, and delivering the goods as far as a great album… you know, we went through the track listing together and we really chose the songs that fit and we broke them in very early. We had like 17 ideas, and between me and him we picked the songs for the album, basically, that we carried forward to work on. A couple of the rehearsal sessions, Paul wasn't available, so he stood in and played guitar. So he was quite involved in all aspects of recording and producing the album."

Asked about the writing dynamic at this point, 2015, Biff explains that, "Me and Nibbs started writing the album. We did about four weeks of writing where Nibbs came up with quite a lot of guitar riff ideas. The other guys were busy or still resting, you know, doing other things. So I started writing with Nibbs, basically, and the majority of the guitar riffs are actually Nibbs' guitar riffs; a couple are Paul's and I think one is Doug's. I don't think there's any jealousy or rivalry—that's the way it happened. Nibbs had got loads of ideas, I'd got some free time, so he flew over from Germany, spent some time with me and we came up with around 15 songs, really."

Which underscores how important Nibbs—the bassist—has been to the band reaching all the way back to record No.10, on which he enters the band contributing to the writing extensively.

Running down a few of the tracks, Biff chuckles that, "'Battering Ram' is really '80s. It just goes around and around; there's no end point to it, lyrically. It's just about a gig, with ambiguous lines about storming the castle. 'The Devil's Footprint' is quite cool; I researched the legend of that. 'Queen of Hearts' is a bit psychedelic and prog rocking and out there melodically. I'm quite proud of some of the lyrics; I managed to get in a song about a Marvel villain, so I was quite happy (laughs). The words came together really well with the riffs, because to me, part of the enjoyment is putting my titles or lyric ideas to the right riff. When it works, then it's a lot easier to come up with the melodies."

2018 was marked by yet another Saxon album, *Thunderbolt*, but the following year delivered some bad news, although it could have been much worse. In September, feeling fatigued after one of his usual bike rides to keep fit, Biff figured he'd get looked at and quickly found himself on the operating room table getting triple bypass surgery. Weeks later he was still in pain and quite tired, but he spoke to the author, ever willing to do press duties, this time for his very first solo album, *School of Hard Knocks*.

"Well, I wrote the song a couple of years ago, 'School of Hard Knocks,' and it's a great title and I like the sort of sentiment behind the title," reflects Biff. "It's definitely autobiographical. And I saw that painting we used on the album cover, which sort of sums up where I came from, really, the industrial North. So yeah, as far as that track and the album cover, both are autobiographical."

With heavy metal at the core—literally at the middle of the album—the front third of the record features the gloriously old school hard rock title track as well as panoramic opener "Welcome to the Show," and then the end of the record presents a lighter side.

"Yeah, well, I'm only a Saxon guy when I'm in Saxon," chuckles Biff. "When I'm not in Saxon, I like all types of music. And it's only to be expected on a solo album that I'm going to do something a bit unusual as far as Saxon's concerned. So yeah, there's 'Scarborough Fair' and of the two songs on the end, one is a song about my 25th anniversary to my wife, and the other one is just about, you know, things running you down but you try to stay up (laughs). Which is what quite a lot of my lyrics about."

Touching tracks, rich of experience, but it is the stadium rock kick-off to the record that really shines. "Yes, sure, the first two tracks, 'Welcome to the Show' and 'School of Hard Knocks' are classic sort of rock songs. I love all that AC/DC stuff, so I like that style. But then it goes into a more proggy and metal style. They've all got something special, I think, but it's definitely different to what Saxon do."

Ultimately *School of Hard Knocks* brings Biff full circle, back to his bleak—but as he told us way back in the beginning of the book, not unhappy—upbringing. "Yes it does, and again, I think the album cover sums up my early childhood. You know, it's a street, it's a British street, probably in Yorkshire. It's got the steam train in there. It's got a factory. So it really says something about where I came from."

And in a sense, about where he is going. It's more than inspiring to see Biff bouncing back from his brush with death, even if his health scare reminds us just how old some of our favourite rock stars are. But strength to strength, at press time, Byford was planning something entirely new albeit poignant and nostalgic for the Saxon legend, and that's UK and European tour dates in support of the solo album, with part of the evening dedicated to reflections about his long life including his tough-as-nails upbringing.

To be sure, there are already scheduled fresh Saxon tour dates and recording plans after that, duly impressive given that Biff is soon entering the hall of the septuagenarian front legends. But the activity around the solo album, not to mention the fact that we were very close to losing Biff and therefore undoubtedly Saxon, should give us all pause to reflect how long a journey it's been for Saxon and their fans together, through numerous eras and movements all the way back to… well, 1977 if you are from Barnsley, and 1979 or 1980 for many of the rest of us. Let's hope there's more heavy metal life in the band—both reflection through the old songs and optimism for the future through new Saxon anthems—and that the guys can continue to bring us fresh music and more live shows for a few more precious years to come.

Discography

Pretty straight forward, the Saxon discography, as it pertains to this book. The only wrinkle is the presence of a couple of live albums, which I've left in the sequence, given no other weirdness with EPs or anything like that.

I've maintained the Side 1/Side 2 demarcation for the entire thing, given that the records covered by this book all came out during the vinyl era. I've gone with UK issues as the cited "first editions," given that this is a British act.

I've allowed myself a "Notes" section to mention in footnote form any fruity li'l foibles I found important or odd enough to mention (this section is not an exact science). I've not bothered with quote marks around songs—too messy: this section's virtually all songs. Also in my "Notes" section, I've made known any alterations in band personnel from one album to the next. The mission: it's a discography constructed more to provide a roadmap as to where, crucially, the songs come from. It's also an index of sorts to the book, a plot map, hopefully a reference tool useful in a number of ways.

I've added individual songwriting credits beginning with *Crusader*, given that every song on every album previous to that gets a blanket full band credit.

Saxon

(Carrere CAL 110, May 21, 1979)

Produced by: John V (Verity)

Side 1: 1. Rainbow Theme 3:07; 2. Frozen Rainbow 2:30; 3. Big Teaser 3:55; 4. Judgement Day 5:31

Side 2: 1. Stallions of the Highway 2:52; 2. Backs to the Wall 3:10; 3. Still Fit to Boogie 2:54; 4. Militia Guard 4:50

Notes: Initial Saxon lineup: Peter "Biff" Byford – vocals, Paul "Blute" Quinn – guitars, Graham "Oly" Oliver – guitars, Steve "Dobby" Dawson – bass, Pete "Frank" Gill – drums.

Wheels of Steel

(Carrere CAL 115, April 3, 1980)

Produced by: Saxon, Pete Hinton

Side 1: 1. Motorcycle Man 3:55; 2. Stand Up and Be Counted 3:06; 3. 747 (Strangers in the Night) 4:56; 4. Wheels of Steel 5:55

Side 2: 1. Freeway Mad 2:37; 2. See the Light Shining 4:52; 3. Street Fighting Gang 3:09; 4. Suzie Hold On 4:31; 5. Machine Gun 5:28

Strong Arm of the Law

(Carrere CAL 120, November 14, 1980)

Produced by: Saxon, Pete Hinton

Side 1: 1. Heavy Metal Thunder 4:20; 2. To Hell and Back Again 4:44; 3. Strong Arm of the Law 4:39; Taking Your Chances 4:19

Side 2: 1. 20,000 Ft. 3:16; 2. Hungry Years 5:18; 3. Sixth Form Girls 4:19; 4. Dallas 1 PM 6:29

Notes: UK cover is white with gatefold; North American issue is black cover, non-gatefold and with same songs but altered sequencing.

Denim and Leather

(Carrere CAL 128, September 25, 1981)

Produced by: Nigel Thomas except for "Never Surrender" and "And the Bands Played On," produced by Saxon and Nigel Thomas

Side 1: 1. Princess of the Night 3:58; 2. Never Surrender 3:11; 3. Out of Control 4:01; 4. Rough and Ready 4:44

Side 2: 1. And the Bands Played On 2:43; 2. Midnight Rider 5:37; 3. Fire in the Sky 3:22; 4. Denim and Leather 5:25

The Eagle Has Landed (Live)

(Carrere CAL 137, May 1982)

Produced by: Saxon

Side 1: 1. Motorcycle Man 4:25; 2. 747 (Strangers in the Night) 4:33; 3. Princess of the Night 4:08; 4. Strong Arm of the Law 4:23; 5. Heavy Metal Thunder 4:10

Side 2: 1. 20,000 Ft. 3:20; 2. Wheels of Steel 8:55; 3. Never Surrender 3:48; 4. Fire in the Sky 2:39; 5. Machine Gun 3:48

Notes: Live album. Nigel Glockler replaces Pete Gill on drums.

Power & the Glory

(Carrere CAL 147, March 21, 1983)

Produced by: Jeff Glixman

Side 1: 1. Power and the Glory 5:53; 2. Redline 3:37; 3. Warrior 3:46; 4. Nightmare 4:25

Side 2: 1. This Town Rocks 3:56; 2. Watching the Sky 3:42; 3. Midas Touch 4:11; 4. The Eagle Has Landed 6:54

Notes: North American issue deletes "Midas Touch" and adds "Suzie Hold On."

Crusader

(Carrere CAL 200, April 16, 1984)

Produced by: Kevin Beamish

Side 1: 1. The Crusader Prelude (Saxon) 1:06; 2. Crusader (Saxon) 6:37; 3. A Little Bit of What You Fancy (Saxon) 3:52; 4. Sailing to America (Saxon) 5:06; 5. Set Me Free (Andy Scott) 3:19

Side 2: 1. Just Let Me Rock (Saxon) 4:12; 2. Bad Boys (Like to Rock 'n' Roll) (Saxon) 3:26; Do It All for You (Byford, Quinn, Oliver, Dawson, Beamish) 4:45; 4. Rock City (Byford, Quinn, Dawson) 3:17; 5. Run for Your Lives (Saxon) 3:53

Innocence Is No Excuse

(Parlophone/EMI EJ 2404001, June 24, 1985)

Produced by Simon Hanhart

Side 1: 1. Rockin' Again (Byford, Oliver, Dawson) 5:22; 2. Call of the Wild (Saxon) 3:57; 3. Back on the Streets (Saxon) 3:56; 4. Devil Rides Out (Byford, Dawson) 4:20; 5. Rock 'n' Roll Gypsy (Byford, Dawson) 4:10

Side 2: 1. Broken Heroes (Byford, Dawson) 5:24; 2. Gonna Shout (Saxon) 3:59; 3. Everybody Up (Byford, Dawson) 4. Raise Some Hell (Byford, Dawson) 3:42; 5. Give It Everything You've Got (Saxon) 3:25

Rock the Nations

(EMI EMC 3515, October 13, 1986)

Produced by: Gary Lyons

Side 1: 1. Rock the Nations (Byford, Glockler, Oliver, Quinn) 4:40; 2. Battle Cry (Byford, Glockler, Oliver, Quinn) 5:26; 3. Waiting for the Night (Byford, Glockler) 4:51; 4. We Came Here to Rock (Byford, Glockler, Oliver, Quinn) 4:18

Side 2: 1. You Ain't No Angel (Byford, Glockler, Oliver, Quinn) 5:28; 2. Running Hot (Byford, Glockler, Oliver, Quinn, Dawson) 3:35; 3. Party 'til You Puke (Byford, Glockler, Oliver, Quinn) 3:25; 4. Empty Promises (Byford, Glockler, Oliver, Quinn) 4:09; 5. Northern Lady (Byford, Glockler, Oliver, Quinn) 4:42

Notes: Bassist credited on the album is Paul Johnson, replacing Steve Dawson. However, the bass parts on the record were played by Biff Byford.

Destiny

(EMI EMC 3543, June 20, 1988)

Produced by: Stephan Galfas

Side 1: 1. Ride Like the Wind (Christopher Cross) 4:29; 2. Where the Lightning Strikes (Byford, Quinn, Oliver) 4:19; 3. I Can't Wait Anymore (Byford, Quinn, Oliver) 4:22; 4.

Calm Before the Storm (Byford, Quinn, Oliver) 3:46; 5. S.O.S. (Byford, Quinn, Oliver) 5:54

Side 2: 1. Song for Emma (Byford, Galfas) 4:46; 2. For Whom the Bell Tolls (Byford, Quinn, Johnson) 3:53; 3. We Are Strong (Byford, Quinn) 3:57; 4. Jericho Siren (Byford, Quinn, Johnson) 3:36; 5. Red Alert (Byford, Quinn, Johnson) 5:05

Notes: Nigel Durham replaces Nigel Glockler on drums. Bassist in both name and deed this time is Paul Johnson.

Rock 'n' Roll Gypsies

(Roadrunner RR 9416 1, November 1989)

Produced by: Biff Byford.

Side 1: 1. Power and the Glory 6:27; 2. And the Bands Played On 2:55; 3. Rock the Nations 4:31; 4. Dallas 1 PM 6:38; 5. Broken Heroes 7:04

Side 2: 1. Battle Cry 5:49; 2. Rock 'n' Roll Gypsy 5:17; 3. Northern Lady 5:07; 4. I Can't Wait Anymore 4:30; 5. This Town Rocks 4:12

Notes: Live album. Nigel Glockler returns, replacing Nigel Durham on drums. Nibbs Carter replaces Paul Johnson on bass. Song credits as per the studio albums. New spelling of "Rock 'n' Roll Gypsy" renders the spelling on *Innocence is No Excuse* as an error, hence in all places, I've gone with the correct "gypsy." However there are new errors, namely "Power and Glory," "Rock the Nation," "Bands Played On" and "I Can't Wait."

Interviews with the Author

Beamish, Kevin. December 30, 2019.

Bushell, Garry. 2009.

Byford, Biff. October 23, 2000.

Byford, Biff. August 25, 2001.

Byford, Biff. March 8, 2007.

Byford, Biff. 2009.

Byford, Biff. October 11, 2011.

Byford, Biff. November 29, 2015.

Byford, Biff. December 4, 2019.

Cox, Jess. 2009.

Dawson, Steve. January 6, 2012.

Durham, Nigel. January 7, 2020.

Galfas, Stephan. January 1, 2020.

Glockler, Nigel. 2001.

Glockler, Nigel. September 15, 2013.

Hinton, Pete. January 23, 2020.

Johnson, Paul. January 15, 2020.

Oliver, Graham. May 1, 2003.

Oliver, Graham. December 19, 2019.

Quinn, Paul. 2009.

Quinn, Paul. September 15, 2013.

Tatler, Brian. 2009.

Tsangarides, Chris. 2009.

Tucker, John. 2009.

Verity, John. December 20, 2019.

Additional Citations

Broadcast Barnsley. From Son of a Bitch to *Wheels of Steel*: the Origins of Saxon by John Kruse. May 4, 2017.

Classic Rock Revisited. Saxon's Biff Byford: Sacrificing Nothing by Jeb Wright. 2013.

Classic Rock Revisited. Nigel Glockler of Saxon: Back on Track! by Jeb Wright. 2015.

Dmme.net. Interview with Nigel Glockler by Dmitry Epstein. January 2002.

Heavy Music Headquarters. Saxon Interview by Darren Cowan. February 25, 2019.

Hit Parader. Saxon: Fast and Furious by Steve Gett. No.238. July 1984.

Hit Parader. Saxon: Denim 'n Leather Forever by Rob Andrews. No.254. November 1985.

Kerrang!. Saxon: The 1984 Crusade by Paul Roland. No.60. January 26 – February 8, 1984.

Kerrang!. *Crusader* review by Paul Roland. No.60. January 26 – February 8, 1984.

Kerrang!. Streets of Fire by Howard Johnson. No.100. August 8 – 21, 1985.

Kerrang!. *Innocence is No Excuse* review by Dave Dickson. No.102. September 5 – 18, 1985.

Kerrang!. Sax Appeal by Mark Putterford. No.126. August 7 – 20, 1986.

Kerrang!. *Rock the Nations* review by Dave Dickson. No.130. October 2 – 15, 1986.

Kerrang!. Dawson Declares USI. No.134. November 27 – December 10, 1986.

Kerrang!. Where There's Muck, There's Biff by Chris Welch. No.175. February 20, 1988.

Kerrang! *Destiny* record review by Chris Watts. No.177. March 5, 1988.

Kerrang! Saxon Facing Destiny by Dave Shack. No.219. December 24/31, 1988.

Kerrang. *Wheels of Steel* review by Steffan Chirazi. No.220. January 7, 1989.

Kerrang!. *Power & the Glory – The Video Anthology* review by Phil Wilding. No.228. March 4, 1989.

Kerrang!. Saxon/Slammer/Iron Heart live review by Paul Miller. No.232. April 1, 1989.

MetalRules. Saxon, Nosturi, Helsinki, Finland by MetalRules Finland Team. November 29, 2001.

MetalRules. Interview with Nigel Glockler by Marko Syrjala. February 6, 2006.

New Musical Express. *Saxon* record review by Paul Du Noyer. July 28, 1979.

Perun.hr. Pete Gill (Motörhead): "It was guitarist Phil Campbell who got me into Motörhead." August 31, 2019.

Record Mirror. *Wheels of Steel* record review by Malcolm Dome. April 19, 1980.

Record Mirror. Saxon live review by Jack Bower. May 10, 1980.

Rhino.com. An Interview with Steve Dawson of Saxon. March 20, 2014.

Shockwaves. Interview with Biff Byford by Michael Henry. 1998.

Sounds. *Wheels of Steel* record review by Geoff Barton. March 29, 1980.

Sounds. *Strong Arm of the Law* record review by Bob Edmands. 1980.

Sounds. *Denim and Leather* record review by Geoff Barton. September 19, 1981.

Sounds. Where Eagles Blare by Dave Lewis. November 21, 1981.

World Metal Report. Saxon/Accept/Heavy Pettin'. No. 3. 1984.

Personal Credits

The graphic design and layout of this book is by Eduardo Rodriguez, who can be reached at eduardobwbk@gmail.com. Pleasure working with the guy—he's done about 35 for me now.

As well, a special thanks goes out to Agustin Garcia de Paredes who served as copy editor/second set of eyes on this book. Like anybody, I hate typos, and hopefully between me an' my partner in crime, we've caught most of them. So cool… Agustin might be the only guy besides me with a copy of every single one of my books. Or if not every one, he's got the biggest collection I'm aware of.

About the Author

At approximately 7900 (with over 7000 appearing in his books), Martin has unofficially written more record reviews than anybody in the history of music writing across all genres. Additionally, Martin has penned approximately 85 books on hard rock, heavy metal, classic rock and record collecting. He was Editor-In-Chief of the now retired Brave Words & Bloody Knuckles, Canada's foremost metal publication for 14 years, and has also contributed to Revolver, Guitar World, Goldmine, Record Collector, bravewords.com, lollipop.com and hardradio.com, with many record label band bios and liner notes to his credit as well. Additionally, Martin has been a regular contractor to Banger Films, having worked for two years as researcher on the award-winning documentary *Rush: Beyond the Lighted Stage*, on the writing and research team for the 11-episode Metal Evolution and on the ten-episode Rock Icons, both for VH1 Classic. Additionally, Martin is the writer of the original metal genre chart used in *Metal: A Headbanger's Journey* and throughout the Metal Evolution episodes. Martin currently resides in Toronto and can be reached through martinp@inforamp.net or www.martinpopoff.com.

Martin Popoff – A Complete Bibliography

Denim and Leather: Saxon's First Ten Years (2020)

Black Funeral: Into the Coven with Mercyful Fate (2020)

Satisfaction: 10 Albums That Changed My Life (2019)

Holy Smoke: Iron Maiden in the '90s (2019)

Sensitive to Light: The Rainbow Story (2019)

Where Eagles Dare: Iron Maiden in the '80s (2019)

Aces High: The Top 250 Heavy Metal Songs of the '80s (2019)

Judas Priest: Turbo 'til Now (2019)

Born Again! Black Sabbath in the Eighties and Nineties (2019)

Riff Raff: The Top 250 Heavy Metal Songs of the '70s (2018)

Lettin' Go: UFO in the '80s and '90s (2018)

Queen: Album by Album (2018)

Unchained: A Van Halen User Manual (2018)

Iron Maiden: Album by Album (2018)

Sabotage! Black Sabbath in the Seventies (2018)

Welcome to My Nightmare: 50 Years of Alice Cooper (2018)

Judas Priest: Decade of Domination (2018)

Popoff Archive – 6: American Power Metal (2018)

Popoff Archive – 5: European Power Metal (2018)

The Clash: All the Albums, All the Songs (2018)

Led Zeppelin: All the Albums, All the Songs (2017)

AC/DC: Album by Album (2017)

Lights Out: Surviving the '70s with UFO (2017)

Tornado of Souls: Thrash's Titanic Clash (2017)

Caught in a Mosh: The Golden Era of Thrash (2017)

Rush: Album by Album (2017)

Beer Drinkers and Hell Raisers: The Rise of Motörhead (2017)

Metal Collector: Gathered Tales from Headbangers (2017)

Hit the Lights: The Birth of Thrash (2017)

Popoff Archive – 4: Classic Rock (2017)

Popoff Archive – 3: Hair Metal (2017)

Popoff Archive – 2: Progressive Rock (2016)

Popoff Archive – 1: Doom Metal (2016)

Rock the Nation: Montrose, Gamma and Ronnie Redefined (2016)

Punk Tees: The Punk Revolution in 125 T-Shirts (2016)

Metal Heart: Aiming High with Accept (2016)

Ramones at 40 (2016)

Time and a Word: The Yes Story (2016)

Kickstart My Heart: A Mötley Crüe Day-by-Day (2015)

This Means War: The Sunset Years of the NWOBHM (2015)

Wheels of Steel: The Explosive Early Years of the NWOBHM (2015)

Swords and Tequila: Riot's Classic First Decade (2015)

Who Invented Heavy Metal? (2015)

Sail Away: Whitesnake's Fantastic Voyage (2015)

Live Magnetic Air: The Unlikely Saga of the Superlative Max Webster (2014)

Steal Away the Night: An Ozzy Osbourne Day-by-Day (2014)

The Big Book of Hair Metal (2014)

Sweating Bullets: The Deth and Rebirth of Megadeth (2014)

Smokin' Valves: A Headbanger's Guide to 900 NWOBHM Records (2014)

The Art of Metal (co-edit with Malcolm Dome; 2013)

2 Minutes to Midnight: An Iron Maiden Day-by-Day (2013)

Metallica: The Complete Illustrated History (2013); update and reissue (2016)

Rush: The Illustrated History (2013); update and reissue (2016)

Ye Olde Metal: 1979 (2013)

Scorpions: Top of the Bill (2013); updated and reissued as Wind of Change: The Scorpions Story (2016)

Epic Ted Nugent (2012)

Fade To Black: Hard Rock Cover Art of the Vinyl Age (2012)

It's Getting Dangerous: Thin Lizzy 81-12 (2012)

We Will Be Strong: Thin Lizzy 76-81 (2012)

Fighting My Way Back: Thin Lizzy 69-76 (2011)

The Deep Purple Royal Family: Chain of Events '80 – '11 (2011)

The Deep Purple Royal Family: Chain of Events Through '79 (2011); reissued as The Deep Purple Family Year by Year (to 1979) (2016)

Black Sabbath FAQ (2011)

The Collector's Guide to Heavy Metal: Volume 4: The '00s (2011; co-authored with David Perri)

Goldmine Standard Catalog of American Records 1948 – 1991, 7th Edition (2010)

Goldmine Record Album Price Guide, 6th Edition (2009)

Goldmine 45 RPM Price Guide, 7th Edition (2009)

A Castle Full of Rascals: Deep Purple '83 – '09 (2009)

Worlds Away: Voivod and the Art of Michel Langevin (2009)

Ye Olde Metal: 1978 (2009)

Gettin' Tighter: Deep Purple '68 – '76 (2008)

All Access: The Art of the Backstage Pass (2008)

Ye Olde Metal: 1977 (2008)

Ye Olde Metal: 1976 (2008)

Judas Priest: Heavy Metal Painkillers (2007)

Ye Olde Metal: 1973 to 1975 (2007)

The Collector's Guide to Heavy Metal: Volume 3: The Nineties (2007)

Ye Olde Metal: 1968 to 1972 (2007)

Run For Cover: The Art of Derek Riggs (2006)

Black Sabbath: Doom Let Loose (2006)

Dio: Light Beyond the Black (2006)

The Collector's Guide to Heavy Metal: Volume 2: The Eighties (2005)

Rainbow: English Castle Magic (2005)

UFO: Shoot Out the Lights (2005)

The New Wave of British Heavy Metal Singles (2005)

Blue Öyster Cult: Secrets Revealed! (2004); update and reissue (2009); updated and reissued as Agents of Fortune: The Blue Oyster Cult Story (2016)

Contents Under Pressure: 30 Years of Rush at Home & Away (2004)

The Top 500 Heavy Metal Albums of All Time (2004)

The Collector's Guide to Heavy Metal: Volume 1: The Seventies (2003)

The Top 500 Heavy Metal Songs of All Time (2003)

Southern Rock Review (2001)

Heavy Metal: 20th Century Rock and Roll (2000)

The Goldmine Price Guide to Heavy Metal Records (2000)

The Collector's Guide to Heavy Metal (1997)

Riff Kills Man! 25 Years of Recorded Hard Rock & Heavy Metal (1993)

See martinpopoff.com for complete details and ordering information.